Polygraphies

Francophone Women Writing Algeria

ALISON RICE

UNIVERSITY OF VIRGINIA PRESS

Charlottesville & London

University of Virginia Press
© 2012 by the Rector and Visitors of the University of Virginia
All rights reserved
Printed in the United States of America on acid-free paper

First published 2012

9 8 7 6 5 4 3 2 1

Library of Congress Cataloging-in-Publication Data
Rice, Alison, 1973–
Polygraphies : Francophone women writing Algeria / Alison Rice.
p.   cm.
Includes bibliographical references and index.
ISBN 978-0-8139-3291-0 (cloth : alk. paper) — ISBN 978-0-8139-3292-7 (pbk. : alk. paper) — ISBN 978-0-8139-3293-4 (e-book)
1. Algerian literature (French)—Women authors—History and criticism. 2. Women in literature. 3. Postcolonialism in literature. 4. Women authors, Algerian—Political and social views. 5. Women authors, Arab—Algeria—Political and social views. 6. Women and literature—Algeria—History—20th century. 7. Feminism and literature—Algeria—History—20th century. 8. Algeria—In literature. I. Title. II. Title: Francophone women writing Algeria.
PQ3988.5.A5R53 2012
840.9′92870965—dc23

2012002036

For

FRANÇOISE LIONNET,

mentor and muse

CONTENTS

Acknowledgments / *ix*

Introduction.
   The Witness Stand: Where the Truth Lies / *1*

PART I. THE AUTOBIOGRAPHICAL SPRINGBOARD

1 Le moi à plusieurs reprises:
   From Confession to Testimony in the Autobiographical Writings
   of Hélène Cixous and Assia Djebar / *27*

2 La singularité de l'altérité:
   Self-Portraiture and the Other in Maïssa Bey / *46*

PART II. TAKEOFF POINTS

3 La terre maternelle:
   Algeria and the Mother in the Work of Marie Cardinal,
   Hélène Cixous, and Assia Djebar / *61*

4 "La célébration d'une terre-mère":
   Albert Camus and Algeria according to Maïssa Bey and
   Assia Djebar / *86*

PART III. EMBODIMENTS

5 Écrire les maux:
   Hélène Cixous and Writing the Body over Time / *99*

6 Sexualités et sensualités:
   Corporeal Configurations in the Work of Maïssa Bey, Assia Djebar,
   Malika Mokeddem, and Leïla Sebbar / *109*

PART IV. REVERBERATIONS

7 Ruptures intimes:
   Sentimental Splitting in the Work of Assia Djebar / *129*

8 Lourds retours:
   Coming Back to Algeria in Malika Mokeddem's *L'Interdite* / *140*

9 Fille de harki:
   Relating to the Father, Country, and Religion in the
   Writing of Zahia Rahmani / *151*

10 Fabulation et imagination:
   Women, Nation, and Identification in Maïssa Bey's *Cette fille-là* / *164*

Conclusion.
   Mass in A Minor: Putting Algeria on the Map / *186*

Notes / *197*

Bibliography / *215*

Index / *227*

ACKNOWLEDGMENTS

With gratitude I wish to acknowledge the many people who provided inspiration and encouragement as I wrote this book. As my dedication indicates, I would like to express special appreciation to Françoise Lionnet, my professor and advisor during my doctoral studies at the University of California, Los Angeles. I continue to seek her counsel, and hope to emulate her openness, generosity, and dedication to the profession.

It has been a great pleasure to interact in person and on paper with the women whose work is represented in this book, and I am indebted to Maïssa Bey, Hélène Cixous, Assia Djebar, Malika Mokeddem, Zahia Rahmani, and Leïla Sebbar for verbal and written exchanges that have touched me personally and enabled me to engage more directly with their creative work.

It would be difficult to name all of the scholars and professors who have had an impact on *Polygraphies*, but I would like to mention a few whose influence is of particular pertinence to my work. Emily Apter, Réda Bensmaïa, Mireille Calle-Gruber, Odile Cazenave, Christiane Chaulet-Achour, Anne Donadey, Hafid Gafaïti, Mary Jean Green, Alec Hargreaves, Mireille Rosello, and Dominic Thomas have all provided valuable insights into Francophone literatures, and they have set examples from which I have had the good fortune to learn.

Since my arrival at the University of Notre Dame in 2005, I have benefited from countless conversations with Theodore J. Cachey Jr., Chair of the Department of Romance Languages and Literatures. His support and advice have been invaluable, and I am deeply grateful. The Dean of the College of Arts and Letters, John McGreevy, has also encouraged me with his belief in the importance of languages and cultures and his efforts on behalf of internationalism and diversity. In addition, I value the administrative wisdom and theoretical perspectives of Joseph Buttigieg, Director of the Ph.D. in Literature Program; speaking with him is always enlightening and enjoyable. My wonderful colleagues at Notre Dame have inspired me in a variety of ways. I am closest to those in the French section, with whom I have met and discussed many topics, and whose feedback I appreciate: Maureen Boulton, JoAnn Della Neva, Julia Douthwaite, Louis MacKenzie, Catherine Perry, and Alain Toumayan. The competence and expertise of Linda Rule, Senior Administrative Assistant in Romance Languages and

Literatures, have facilitated many of the technical aspects of this book, and I wish to thank her wholeheartedly. I would also like to extend a special thanks to Agustín Fuentes, Director, and Patricia Base, Senior Administrative Assistant of the Institute for Scholarship in the Liberal Arts in the College of Arts and Letters at the University of Notre Dame. The research and publication of this book were made possible in part by support from the Institute for Scholarship in the Liberal Arts, and I am especially grateful.

Earlier versions of several chapters appeared in the journal *Women's Studies International Forum* and the collective volumes *Diversité littéraire en Algérie*, *Marie Cardinal: New Perspectives* and *Reading and Writing La Rupture: Essays in French Studies*. I am thankful for the opportunity to include these essays, which have been extensively revised and expanded since their initial publication, in *Polygraphies*.

It has been a delight to become acquainted with Cathie Brettschneider, the Humanities Editor at the University of Virginia Press, as well as Raennah Mitchell, Morgan Myers, and Ellen Satrom. They are models of warmth and professionalism, and I feel lucky to have the chance to work with them.

I am also fortunate to have as familial models a long line of strong, motivated women, and one of them was instrumental in making this book a reality. My ninety-five-year-old grandmother, Kathryn Taylor, helped care for my two young daughters, Rosa and Alexa Morel, giving me precious pockets of time. My mother and father, Gail and Richard Rice, have been a source of constant support; I could never thank them enough. My deepest gratitude goes to Olivier Morel, a fantastic father, an incomparable interlocutor, the love of my life.

Polygraphies

Introduction | The Witness Stand | Where the Truth Lies

> *A text of several layers of color that cancel each other out, writing is therefore not simply testifying.*—Assia Djebar, Ces voix qui m'assiègent *(These voices that besiege me)*

> *Hélène Cixous isn't me but those who are sung in my text, because their lives, their pains, their force, demand that it resound.*—Hélène Cixous, "La venue à l'écriture" *("Coming to Writing")*

Much of contemporary writing in French by women from Algeria is arguably, and uniquely, autobiographical, but not in a traditional sense. *Polygraphies* examines the ways in which seven writers subtly insert the self into the text in order to speak of the lives of others. Allowing the personal to punctuate the literary work is not meant to call attention to the individual in an egotistical move but is instead a measure that enables the writer to express the experiences of *many:* the polyphonous nature of the text is striking, even when the solitary subject seems to be the focus. Each person is inextricably connected to others, and the text cannot help but sing of those others and allow them to sing through the literary work as sources of inspiration.

None of these writers has composed a strict autobiography labeled as such, and yet each has inserted significant elements of the autobiographical into her work, and these writings are strengthened by these revealing, often emotional insertions. By rendering themselves vulnerable in their written work, these writers open themselves up in risky but highly effective ways. They touch their readers profoundly through their unveiling of secrets, through their admission of guilt, through their willingness to admit fault. And yet, paradoxically, they are not confessing their sins. Nor are they seeking exoneration. They are enacting a shifting of terms, calling for a new sort of reading, in accord with their inventive writing. As they seek a language and a style—in French—that recall the history of their own lives as they intermingle with those of others, they ask us not to subject their work to a polygraph machine, to a lie detector that would sift through the true and the false of each line. Rather, they compel us to open ourselves to the multiple truths that are present in the text, even those that surpass the intention of the author, that slip into the text when she lets her guard down, in the watches of the night, in the rhythm of creation.

It is a desire to depict true experiences—their own and those of others—that often leads to the textual representation of the self projected onto a fictional other, or the collection of other voices and their life stories within the personal narrative, in creative works that effectively circumvent conventional autobiographical writings. Rather than putting forth "truth claims" and employing confessional forms, these writers have opted to testify on a different level, in a variety of genres, to current events, to postcolonial politics, to individual evolutions that affect men and women, but especially women, between Algeria and France. This book begins with the premise that the truths conveyed through the creative texts of these daring and innovative writers are not always communicated in straightforward fashion. Writers such as Assia Djebar or Maïssa Bey have often composed literary texts while aware of the danger such writing has brought to others in their homeland. The fact that they publish not under their legal names but have instead taken on pseudonyms points to the risks inherent in free expression in Algeria in recent times.

Some of these writers are pioneers, composers of an earlier generation who received an education when Algeria was officially considered a department of France, a virtual colony but not bearing this label and therefore possessing an unpleasant, ambiguous status. Two stand out for having composed noteworthy texts relatively early in life: Assia Djebar (b. 1936) completed her first novel, published in 1957, before she reached the age of twenty; Hélène Cixous (b. 1937) received the prestigious Prix Médicis for her first novel in 1969, following the completion of her erudite doctoral dissertation. Another important voice among the first Algerian-born women to publish works of fiction is Marie Cardinal (b. 1928): She was the recipient of the Prix International du Premier Roman when her first novel appeared, in 1962. Other women writers composed in these authors' wake, aware of those who had traversed the waters before them and grateful for the examples they had set: Maïssa Bey (b. 1950) began her productive writing career much later with a first novel published in 1996; Malika Mokeddem (b. 1949) saw her first work of fiction awarded the Prix Littré in 1991. Leïla Sebbar (b. 1941) occupies an interesting in-between status as both a follower and a forerunner; born shortly after Djebar and Cixous, her first novel was published in 1981. The youngest writer examined in these pages, Zahia Rahmani (b. 1962), published her first novel in 2003.

These women writers are not only of various generations, they are also of differing ethnic and religious backgrounds, and their texts attest to *otherness*—to their own otherness and to their desire to know the other. They tell of multiple belongings, and they speak of losses, of estrangement from their family, from their native land, as well as from the language in which they have become successful writers. They testify of difference, and the pain it has brought to them and to so many in a colonial and postcolonial setting. This sense of difference has given each an intense awareness that has spurred a variety of innovative writings in different genres, relating scenes and stories in new ways that make a veritable impression and leave an indelible imprint on those who come into contact with them.

PAGE AGAINST THE MACHINE:
THE INTERWEAVING OF TESTIMONY AND FICTION

The Algerian-born philosopher and critic Jacques Derrida eloquently examines a brief prose piece by the French writer Maurice Blanchot, *L'instant de ma mort* (*The Instant of My Death*), in these terms: "Literature serves as real testimony. Literature pretends, through an excess of fiction—others would say lie—to pass itself off as a real and responsible testimony about a historical reality—without, however, signing this testimony because it is literature and the narrator is not the author of an autobiography" (*Demeure* 71). Elsewhere in his analysis, Derrida refers to Blanchot's provocative text as "a fiction," "obviously testimonial and autobiographical in appearance" and argues that these noticeable characteristics might make the author susceptible to suspicion: "[Blanchot] could be suspected of the abuse of a fiction, that is, of a type of text whose author is not responsible, not responsible for what happens to the narrator or the characters of the narrative, not answerable before the law for the truthfulness of what he says" (*Demeure* 55). The question of responsibility when it comes to composing a work of literature is one that Derrida has addressed elsewhere: "I believe that in literature there is the risk of irresponsibility, or the risk of the non-signature (I speak nonsense because it is not I) . . . all of these risks are integral to the possibility of literature" (*Sur parole* 25). Indeed, he insists that literature calls for the greatest responsibility but also provides the possibility for the worst betrayal, for the writer may not be held accountable for what she writes, even if the reader assumes she has written truthfully. Derrida asserts that the simple fact that a writer has not signed an obviously personal testimony as an autobiography does not mean the publication is not truthful. What his many reflections on the topic seem to indicate is that truth is much more complicated that it might initially seem, particularly when it comes to literature.

Literature, in Derrida's understanding, is a space where authors can open up, where they can deign to reveal what they might be hesitant to disclose in another place. It is a location that allows for immense exposure, for communicating confidential information, for divulging secrets. As he explains, "The concept of literature is based on the principle of 'telling all'" (*Sur parole* 25; "tout dire"). "Telling all" is of course an expression that echoes a juridical principle; it recalls an oft-quoted oath that witnesses are compelled to repeat when they take the stand in a courtroom: to tell the truth, the whole truth, and nothing but the truth. When witnesses are called to give testimony before others in this setting, the weight on their shoulders is heavy; a decision of guilt or innocence often hangs in the balance, and they must faithfully recall the exact details of an event or a situation in order for a decision, and a judgment, to take place. A personal testimony, one made on one's own behalf, can occur in a court of law, but it is more common for witnesses to speak from another viewpoint, with words that may incriminate or acquit an accused party. Derrida addresses the phenomenon of testimony, with its judicial implications, and brings it into the realm of the literary, by calling attention to the pervasive prospect of untruth: "There is no testimony that does not structurally imply in itself the possibility of fiction, simulacra, dissimulation, lie, and perjury—that is to say, the possibility of literature, of the innocent or perverse literature that innocently plays at perverting all of these distinctions" (*Demeure* 29).

The omnipresent threat of the irruption of something "untrue" in a testimony presumed to be "true" is what enables Derrida to examine literature in terms of testimony (and vice versa) in various texts, in various contexts. In his analysis, not knowing whether something is true or false is not entirely negative. In fact, this vacillation, this indecision can ultimately impassion literary composition: "The possibility of literary fiction haunts so-called truthful, responsible, serious, real testimony as its proper possibility. This haunting is perhaps the passion itself, the passionate place of literary writing, as the project to say everything—and wherever it is autobiographical, that is to say, everywhere" (*Demeure* 72). Derrida's own writing waxes passionate about the interactions between fiction and testimony, two entities that cannot easily be separated, as the philosopher indicates when he highlights "the meshes of the net formed by the limits *between* fiction and testimony, which are also *interior* each to the other" (*Demeure* 56; my emphasis).

There might appear to be some slippage in these comments between the terms *literature* and *fiction,* two concepts Derrida often takes up in an attempt to specify their varying functions and workings, sometimes in an effort to distinguish between them. While usually the two terms can be used somewhat interchangeably, it is important to keep in mind the critic's distinction that "not all literature is of the genre or the type of 'fiction,' but there is fictionality in all literature. We should find a word other than 'fiction.' And it is through this fictionality that we try to thematize the 'essence' or the 'truth' of 'language'" (*Acts* 49). Whether we employ the word *literature* or *fiction* to refer to a novel, for instance, it is clear that this form of composition allows for the communication of truth, all while protecting the writer from culpability: "What we call literature (not belles-lettres or poetry) implies that license is given to the writer to say everything he wants to or everything he can, while remaining shielded, safe from all censorship, be it religious or political" (*Acts* 37). Such a place of safety is unfortunately not available to writers in Algeria following its independence from France; Djebar has paid particular attention in *Le blanc de l'Algérie* (*Algerian White*) to the plight of beloved fellow intellectuals in her homeland who lost their lives because they stood up for the uncensored expression of their opinions and beliefs. Derrida is aware that he is speaking in utopian terms when he speaks of "this institution of fiction which gives in principle the power to say everything, to break free of the rules, to displace them, and thereby to institute, to invent and even to suspect the traditional difference between nature and institution, nature and conventional law, nature and history" (*Acts* 37). It is important for the philosopher to underscore the potential of literary fiction to disrupt traditional distinctions, to break the rules, to fly in the face of convention—and perhaps even to evade the law.

What is especially powerful about both testimony and literary fiction is that they may not belong entirely to the category of "true" or "false" but participate instead in a process of interweaving: "The author of the two, always the sole witness to that of which he speaks, may speak truly or falsely, speak truly here and falsely there, interweave a series of interpretations, implications, reflections, unverifiable effects around a woof or a warp objectively recognized and beyond suspicion" (*Demeure* 56). The mingling evoked here defies binary oppositions (such as "true" and "false"), moving in multiple directions and thereby eluding detection. As Derrida puts it, the author of either a testimony or a literary fiction subtly introduces many possibilities into a speech organized by an irrefutable point that remains "objectively recognized and beyond suspicion." It is through this mechanism, through this machination, that the testimonial text manages to avoid detection by any machine. It is this strategy that ultimately enables the writer to trump the *polygraph* with *polygraphies*.

In Derrida's definition, evading detection, tricking the machines, getting away with simulation, with feint, *this* is the very definition of literature: "For literature can say anything, accept anything, receive anything, suffer anything, and simulate everything; it can even feign a trap, the way modern armies know how to set false traps; these traps pass themselves off as real traps and trick the machines designed to detect simulations under even the most sophisticated camouflage" (*Demeure* 29). What literature does, and especially autobiographical literary works, is move us beyond the opposition between the truthful and the duplicitous, as a recent rereading of Jean-Jacques Rousseau's *Confessions* argues: "According to Rousseau, the act of confession is situated outside of the traditional opposition between truth and lie" (Margel 23). Rousseau himself therefore shifted the terms, changed the emphasis, so to speak, in order to render obsolete the question of whether or not he was telling the truth in his autobiographical tome: "It is not a question of saying the truth, and therefore of facing the unavoidable risk of lying, but of saying the *whole* truth, of sacrificing oneself *for* the truth, to the very limits of innocence" (Margel 23–24). What happens in the literary work of fiction, then, is not a claim to truth but an effort to question unequivocal, univocal truth by transforming the text into a space where multiple truths lie, where subtle, complicated truths prove to be all the more convincing precisely because of this paradoxical structure.

WHERE THE TRUTH LIES

In *Paroles suffoquées* (*Smothered Words*), French philosopher Sarah Kofman reflects on the seemingly impossible task of testifying after the horrors of the Nazi concentration camps, arguing that even "if no story is possible after Auschwitz, there remains, nonetheless a duty to speak, to speak endlessly for those who could not speak because to the very end they wanted to safeguard true speech against betrayal. To speak in order to bear witness. But how?" (36). She refers to the risk that testimony will be "impaired by the introduction, with fiction, of attraction and seduction, where 'truth' alone ought to speak," but nonetheless upholds Robert Antelme's *The Human Race,* a memoir of the author's year in a German labor camp, as a work that "underscores the need for fabulation, for the selection of events and therefore of writing, when trying to communicate unbearable truths" (36–37).

Kofman hints here that a work of literature can never hope to tell the whole truth because of the simple and obvious fact that writing inevitably involves selection. As Serge Margel puts it: "Rousseau's *Confessions* aimed to tell the *whole* truth. But which truth?" (26). In writing, certain elements are privileged at the expense of others, and it is as impossible to include every single aspect of a life in an autobiographical text as it is to valorize every version of the truths communicated therein. As Derrida puts it in another context: "There is not *one* truth on this matter" (*Sur parole* 107).

Of course, frequently a particular spin is placed on a story, in which a certain angle of any given event is emphasized at the expense of other interpretations, as Derrida reveals in his comments on the politics of the media: "It is obvious that the filtering of information, its selection, the fact that certain details are marginalized while others are placed at the forefront, can be interpreted as a sort of falsification that renders the concept of lying uncertain from the outset" (*Sur parole* 98). In these situations, it is not a question of presenting a reader or a viewer with false information but with framing the story in a certain way that is determining, and not entirely forthcoming. This precision points to the notion of intention: "I can easily propose a false enunciation because I believe it, therefore with the sincere intention to tell the truth, and I cannot be accused of lying simply because what I say is false" (*Sur parole* 94). In other words, if I didn't mean to lie, then I cannot be accused of lying. A crucial distinction arises between what is true and what is veracious: "When I testify, I promise to tell the truth, whether it is before a tribunal or in everyday life, and it is thus necessary to dissociate from the beginning truthfulness [*la véracité*] from the truth [*la vérité*]. When I lie, I do not necessarily say something false and I can say something false without lying" (*Sur parole* 93).

If something false can be communicated without the communicator being a liar, it is because intention is such a crucial part of the equation. Intention doesn't determine whether what is said is true or false, it only reflects on whether the speaker hoped to tell the truth or a lie. When it comes to literature, then, it is interesting to apply the question Derrida asks, that of *when* the work of fiction can be considered a falsehood: "It is this notion of fiction that is interesting, for when fiction is brought into the discourse, at what point can this fiction be called a lie?" (*Sur parole* 96).

A reader of any written work is almost unavoidably curious *to know,* eager to establish connections between the text and the outside world, between the fictional characters and the real-life persons they seem to depict. If the reader adheres to Derrida's belief that every text is autobiographical, then he or she is even more anxious to find the links between the writing and the writer.[1] But part of what we refer to as testimony—and, by extension, life—consists of learning how not to know, how to let go of absolute certainty and embrace probability, plausibility, even possibility. It often means relinquishing the desire for mechanical, objective proof in exchange for individual, subjective conviction.

Derrida situates testimony outside the confines of "knowledge," insisting that "what is essential to the avowal or the testimony does not consist in an experience of knowledge. Its act is not reduced to informing, teaching, making known" ("Sauf le nom" 38–39). These affirmations have something in common with Shoshana Felman and Dori Laub's reflections on this "crucial mode or our relation to events of our times": "As a relation to events, testimony seems to be composed of bits and pieces of a memory that has been overwhelmed by occurrences that have not settled into understanding or remembrance, acts that cannot be constructed as knowledge nor assimilated into full cognition, events in excess of our frames of reference" (5). Testimony in these definitions appears to be associated not with what is established and known but rather with what is fresh, unrecorded, unpublished. It cannot be chalked up to a history book or a how-to manual but is made up instead of a groping into unforeseen, unexplored territories, in search of what is true but goes beyond what we know as truth. Cixous's comments on learning how "not to know" are in accord with these definitions of testimony: "One of the first lessons about living is the one that consists of *knowing how not to know,* which does not mean not knowing, but knowing how to not know, knowing how to avoid getting closed in by knowledge, knowing more and less than what one knows, knowing how not to understand, while never being on the side of ignorance" ("The Author" 161). It is significant that Cixous upholds "not knowing" in light of her essay's title, "The Author in Truth," a reflection on a particular publication by the Brazilian writer Clarice Lispector. Truth may be communicated textually in indirect ways, Cixous's analysis suggests: "The author is in reserve—and inasmuch as she is true, the truth is reserved. Being an author in truth is being in reserve. On the side. Text not without reserve. Rich in truth, but obliquely" (145–46).

Cixous's close examination of Lispector's work sheds light on the ways in which personal truths come through in the literary text. Cixous as reader, and as literary critic, may wish to know Lispector, "but like any truth she is kept secret, guarded unknowable. But could she simply slip by us? We know only that she is there like a heart in a breast, we hear her beating the rhythm of life. And what is the truth of Clarice Lispector?" ("The Author" 146). As an unusually attuned, attentive reader, Cixous reaches for "the impossible truth that can't be justified before a philosophical tribunal, can't pass the bar of monological discourses or mass-mediatized imaginations," ascertaining what lies far out of reach, not only for the untrained jury but also, and especially, for the lie detector, the polygraph. Cixous reads for us, with us, training us to become readers of her caliber, able to discern truths on a different level: "It is the inexpressible, indemonstrable truth, which can be said only in parentheses, as a subtitle, set back, among several layers of beings, one working on another" ("The Author" 146). What Cixous helps her readers to discover, in the end, is how to appropriately take the witness stand.

ALIGNMENTS: POSITIONING ONESELF WITH RESPECT TO/FOR OTHERS

When a writer "takes the witness stand" in the text, she necessarily adopts a stance. She assumes a position that is inclined toward others, taking them into account as she bears witness, seeking to be respectful in particular toward the others who are implicated in her writing. Testimony is, therefore, by definition, other-oriented:

> To bear witness is to take responsibility for truth: to speak, implicitly, from within the legal pledge and the juridical imperative of the witness's oath. To testify—before a court of law or before the court of history and of the future; to testify, likewise, before an audience of readers or spectators—is more than simply to report a fact or an event or to relate what has been lived, recorded and remembered. Memory is conjured here essentially in order to *address* another, to impress upon a listener, to *appeal* to a community. To testify is always, metaphorically, to take the witness stand, or to take the position of the witness insofar as the narrative account of the witness is at once engaged in an appeal and bound by an oath. To testify is thus not merely to narrate but to commit oneself, and to commit the narrative, to others: to *take responsibility*—in speech—for history or for the truth of an occurrence, for something which, by definition, goes beyond the personal, in having general (nonpersonal) validity and consequences. (Felman and Laub 204–5)

The idea of community is essential to understanding how the act of bearing witness occurs in the literary text. The "consequences" of the written work extend "beyond the personal," as Felman and Laub explain, to influence a potentially large public, an entire group of readers, a collectivity.[2]

What relatively recent research on written testimony has revealed is that taking the witness stand—and adopting the appropriate stance that goes with it—is not limited to the writer. The reader must also assume a suitable position with respect to the written work. Approaching the text with an open mind-set from the beginning is critical, if we consider Derrida's comments: "If avowal cannot consist in declaring, making known, informing, telling the truth, which one can always do, indeed, without confessing anything, without *making* truth, the other must not learn anything that he was not already in a position to know for avowal as such to begin" ("Circonfession" 55). In his detailed analysis of Rousseau, Serge Margel demonstrates that reading is an act that can only be effective if it does not attempt to decipher the text, to define it, to determine its exact meaning and ascertain its single strict interpretation: "For Rousseau, every destined or designated reader, every interpreter, every expert would necessarily produce a partial reading, unfaithful as well as biased, tendentious, and interested" (22–23). Margel makes a convincing case for moving away from other understandings to viewing *reading as testimony;* in other words, to read is to testify: "For readers, now idle, *to read* can no longer mean *to interpret* or *to compose* an oeuvre, but only *to testify* to their inability to act [*désoeuvrement*] through an avowal of their innocence" (25). Rousseau himself invites us to read in this way: "According to the epigraph to the *Confessions,* it is the reader who must first bear witness" (Margel 26). When readers approach the written work not from a superior position, that of a judge, for instance, but rather from an equal situation in which they too are called to bear witness, to actively take part in the textual testimony, truth is seen from a new angle that depends on recognition: "The truth value of confessions would now depend directly on the acknowledgement [*reconnaissance*] of the witness" (26).

Margel affirms that Rousseau's *Confessions* call for a new type of reading, "a reading whose engagement is purely testimonial, like an unending work of memory" (60) and insists that such a reading goes hand in hand with an awareness that each text contains elements that cannot be "read." It is therefore necessary, for the reader, to appreciate what is unreadable in every literary work: "the 'illegibility' of confessions, 'that which exceeds' or 'that which resists' all judgment, all interpretation, all implementation and therefore all identification with authority" (60). As Cixous maintains, some confessions are impossible, and this very impossibility is what leads to literature: "The inclination for avowal, the desire for avowal, the yearning to taste the taste of avowal, is what compels us to write: both the need to avow and its impossibility" (*Three Steps* 45). When he reads Cixous's work, Derrida concentrates on the secret that is inherent to her writing: "Therein lies literature's secret, the infinite power to keep undecidable and thus forever sealed the secret of what it/she [*elle*] says, it, literature, or she, Cixous, or even that which it/she avows and which remains secret, even as in broad daylight she/it avows, unveils or claims to unveil it. The secret of literature is thus the secret itself" (*Genèses* 18). Even when Cixous avows, what she avows remains secret, in many senses. This is why her works of fiction call for another sort of reading:

> This other reading, this reading of the illegible, purely testimonial, would consist of reading, in the confessed discourse, not the *story* of a life, its joys, its sufferings, its errors, its desires, but the *sacrifice* of a life and its authority. As we have already noted, to confess oneself, according to Rousseau, is to dedicate one's life to truth, it is to sacrifice oneself *for* the truth. And this sacrifice comes from a precise economy. While confessing myself, I *give* myself entirely to be read, raw, openly and totally, until death. I give myself there where, before God, I am the most vulnerable, where my authority is without shelter, without secret, at this place in my discourse where, absolutely naked, I am at once the most fearful and have nothing left to fear. It is at the moment when I give totally and mercilessly, when my story becomes illegible, that the partial perspective of the reader is transformed [*se désoeuvre*] into testimony and my innocence is commemorated as infinite mourning and the last avowal of the reading. (Margel 63–64)

Like Cixous, the other women writers from Algeria in this study have arguably made great sacrifices, have given their all for literature. The only appropriate response for the reader in search of textual truth is not to judge but to testify in turn.

If we learn to read in these terms, then we can truly come to literature— as writers and/or readers—with the hope of reaching an *"alignment between witnesses,"* as Felman and Laub articulate this special alliance (2). This is a configuration between writer and reader similar to the one evoked in Doris Sommer's examination of Latin American women's *testimonios*, which have the capacity "to raise the reader's consciousness by linking her to the writer's testimony" (130). This intimate connection means that when readers open themselves to literary fiction, they can be truly affected on a deep level: "A 'life-testimony' is not simply a testimony to a private life, but a point of conflation between text and life, a textual testimony which can *penetrate us like an actual life*" (Felman and Laub 2). This happens in part because it is not just the truths conveyed in the literary text that touch us; it is the way in which they are communicated that makes these texts unforgettable, inimitable, *exceptional.*

Cixous may appear to accuse herself of illegitimacy in the writing process when she says, "False signatures you're using there, I told myself not long ago" ("Coming" 46), but she knows that the truths behind these plagiarisms are much greater than the form they take on. What makes their impact especially strong is that these truths can escape the machine's detection, thanks to this subterfuge. The creativity Cixous employs when she signs falsely is part of a larger project of giving voice to an experience in ways that are indispensable to its survival. Though it may seem "impersonal" to use a false signature, nothing could be more distinctive. This is how testimony works: "But if the essence of the testimony is impersonal (to enable a decision by a judge or jury—metaphorical or literal—about the true nature of the facts of an occurrence; to enable an objective reconstruction of what history was like, irrespective of the witness), why is it that the witness's speech is so uniquely, literally irreplaceable?" (Felman and Laub 204–5). I believe that the women whose written work is honored throughout this collection are also "uniquely, literally irreplaceable."

BODY LANGUAGE: CREATING TEXTUAL IMPRESSIONS

In an aforementioned quotation from Derrida, the philosopher addresses the usefulness of what he calls "fictionality" to "try to thematize the 'essence' or the 'truth' of 'language'" (*Acts* 49). When he places loaded terms like *truth* or *language* in quotation marks, he is not only drawing our attention to the difficulty of defining them, he is also highlighting their critical importance to our thought as a collectivity. What, indeed, is the truth of language? How can language truly speak, and how can it speak truthfully? Is language inevitably bound to fall short of the truth, is it doomed to fail from the outset to truly tell what it should, since it is by nature a faulty construct, something that is not fully functional, since neither I nor my reader totally "possess" it and we can therefore never be sure that meaning is made in a manner faithful to lived experience?[3] When he tackles the heavy question of truth's supposed opposite, Derrida asserts that untruth is innately related to language: "The lie is an aspect of language [*une chose du langage*], all the rhetorical effects, the tropes, the ambiguities tied to the fact that I do not say exactly what I want to say how I want to say it" (*Sur parole* 95). We can imagine that, since it is characteristic of the human experience in general to not always say exactly *what* we want to *in the way* we want to, such an expression of inadequate communication skills would be magnified in the experience of an illiterate, uneducated woman from Algeria. When Djebar or Sebbar or any other author seeks to translate such a woman's life and words into the French-language text, she cannot help but underscore the difficulty and the risk inherent in this act. She may also indicate her hesitancy with respect to this great challenge, but she will indicate that it is worth it, that she must go ahead with this task and answer the calling, the vocation of taking down, of paying homage to, aspects of the other's life. And, naturally, she does not represent the experience of the other, of others, without being affected herself.

Djebar eloquently describes the ways in which her whole being is moved, literally and figuratively, by the voices she introduces into her literary text: "Yes, to bring back non-Francophone voices—guttural, feral, unsubmissive—in the French text that finally becomes mine. These voices have transported within me their turbulence, their turmoil, more in the rhythm of my writing than in the narrative style that I don't really choose, or the non-visualization that I find tempting, or the framing of the bodies" (*Ces voix* 29). Djebar's comments lead to the conclusion that we can conceive of the body on several levels in writing. The writer's body is not only influenced by what she writes, but it is also involved in the writing process: the written text is itself influenced by—and perhaps, somehow, reflective of—the body behind the text. In addition, the writer is putting bodies into the text, "framing" them in certain ways, if we take up Djebar's own language. Writing is, in her view, an extension of the body that is visible to all: "From the moment it springs, writing is a silent word in movement, that prolongs the body, as visible to others as to oneself" (*Ces voix* 28). The fact that the body does not remain indifferent to what is placed in the written work recalls the possible workings of a polygraph machine that seeks to detect the telling of lies by measuring the speaker's pulse, heartbeat, blood pressure, body temperature, pupil dilation, and respiratory movements. After all, the body is presumed to communicate on many levels, and the lie detector is a medical machine that measures the body's responses as evidence of false statements. But the body may not always respond the way we might expect it to, and this is why innocent people are sometimes unfairly "proven" guilty when hooked up to the machine and why elaborate websites titled "How to Cheat a Polygraph Test" are in full swing. What is interesting, even gripping, for the reader is, once again, not to judge the truth of a text by submitting it to such an analysis but instead to explore and enjoy the various idiosyncratic bodily rhythms and sensations that make each text—and each corpus—vibrate to its own beat.

It is not anecdotal that some prominent women writers continue to write by hand, even in a technological age. Sebbar is someone whose beautiful penmanship has led to every one of her texts; Cixous is another who has composed page after page by hand, and even made inroads into literary forms by publishing her handwritten words in certain highly creative works, such as *Portrait de Jacques Derrida en jeune saint juif* (*Portrait of Jacques Derrida as a Young Jewish Saint*). The connection between a personal writing style and the very breath of the written text is captured quite persuasively in Moroccan writer Abdelkébir Khatibi's reflections on his own manner of writing in *Le scribe et son ombre* (The scribe and his shadow): "My writing is slanting, cursive, tangled. Confusion and fluid identity are in the gesture, the trace, the moments of hesitation, as well as in my behavior and the making of small decisions. The body is a syntax of gestures, which to a greater or lesser extent grant access to writing, to painting" (28). Khatibi could be said to be engaging in a sort of "autographology" in this passage, examining his own personality from characteristic patterns or features of his writing. He is effectuating this unique metatextual commentary for the benefit of readers who do not have direct access to his handwriting, and who only come to the text after it has been mediated through the machine, so to speak. He reads his own body, as a writer, in order to give us another angle on the written text, as readers. He is delivering to us what does not always come through as clearly as it could, once the written work has been spell-checked, typeset, and formatted to fit the page: body language.

In an essay titled "The School of Roots," Cixous brings up the possibility of reading the body, of reading another's body, in terms that we often refer to as body language: "reading the signs of the body: not those of the unconscious, which is already speaking—the unconscious is a language—but the body signs that are of the same order as those of the unconscious, though before language" (136). In her analysis, the body can be read outside of traditional forms of communication, "beneath thought, form, or codes" (136). Learning to read the bodies of others, training our ears to hear other forms of expression, is a vital part of contemporary writing by women from Algeria. As Derrida has suggested, testimony may come in ways the courtroom has not allowed for: "We are dealing with expressions, with testimonies that are not necessarily spoken, that can be cries or that can be silent, and that can have the effect of dissimulation or falsification, whether useful or not" (*Sur parole* 98). The writers whose works are examined in this book often pay close attention in their texts to unconventional testimonies, revealing truths that exist outside language, or that are conveyed in manners that test our understanding of language. In order to accomplish this, they have to open their own bodies to other experiences of truth. As Cixous puts it, "I seek the truth, I encounter error. How do I recognize error? It is obvious, like truth. Who tells me? My body. Truth gives us pleasure. It makes us burst out laughing, trembling. Blushing. It's hot" ("Without end" 29). According to the theorist who has made a number of noteworthy remarks on the body and its relation to writing, truth strikes the right chord within her: "Truth strikes us. Opens our heart. Our lips. Error makes us sense the absence of taste. Drops us like a dead person apathetic tongue, dry eyes" (29). And the truths of interest to her are international; they are not limited to the places she knows, to the countries that define her own trajectory. Her body—and, therefore, her work—is open to the entire planet, and the many others who inhabit it: "History has fertilized my geography. I travel: where people suffer, where they fight, where they escape, where they enjoy, my body is suddenly there" ("La venue à l'écriture" 47). As Cixous affirms, body and spirit are both involved in these ongoing journeys: "Worldwide my unconscious, worldwide my body. What happens outside happens inside. I myself am the earth, everything that happens, the lives that live me in my different forms, the voyage, the voyager, the body of travel and the spirit of travel, and all of this with such suppleness that I go in and out, in and out, I am in my body and my body is in me, I envelop myself and contain myself, we might be afraid of getting lost but it never happens, one of my lives always brings me back to solid body" ("La venue à l'écriture" 47). It is curiously compelling that what might be described as a disembodied experience involving global travel and a "worldwide" "unconscious" is transformed here into a tangible ("solid") experience located in the flesh-and-blood being that is the writer.

POLYGRAPHIES AND CALLIGRAPHIES:
TRACING A WRITTEN PATH

The French word *polygraphe* refers to a writer whose works deal with a variety of subjects and belong to several different domains; the term has been used for such erudite men as Aristotle and Voltaire, while it has also been employed pejoratively in reference to journalists today who attempt to address a variety of topics about which they have no expertise. It might be applied to the women writers in this study in a very positive sense, valorizing the many innovative ways in which they disrupt conventional divisions of literary works into different categories with strict definitions. As Susan Suleiman notes with respect to a collection of Cixous's essays, the strength of this writer's work is that it does not adhere to tired groupings of texts under specified headings: "Is this poetry? Critical commentary? Autobiography? Ethical reflection? Feminist theory? Yes. One wall these texts most definitely get past is the wall of genres" (xi). Many of the texts under study in the present book do not fit into a single, easily identifiable literary genre. The especially "polygraphic" nature of these more or less autobiographical works opens them up to a number of possible readings, many of which are true, justifiable, and testimonial.⁴

The French *polygraphe* is also a *détecteur de mensonges,* as we have already seen, a machine that is meant to determine, by measuring physiological responses to questions, whether an individual is telling a truth or a lie. In the neologism *polygraphies,* I intend to evoke the multiple genres that characterize the writing of a *polygraphe*. I also hope that the prefix *poly-* may point toward the plurality of voices and (their) stories present in the single-author text, as well as the possible insertions of various other tongues in the French-language literary work. Several of the authors in this book are bilingual or trilingual, possessing linguistic skills that arguably qualify them as polyglots, and when they include words or expressions (in the original or in translation) in their work, the result is an enriched *multilingual* writing in French. But what I propose most fervently with the title *Polygraphies* is that the many texts by women writers from Algeria help us out of the dichotomy proposed by the polygraph machine, moving us well beyond the true-false binary presumed by the lie detector to a wealth of possible truths, all communicated in writing. I underscore the *written* aspect of these texts, not in an effort to dispense with the orality that is so crucial to them, but to highlight the multiple forms of writing that women writers are now inventing.

The adjective *francophone* is not one that many of these writers readily embrace to describe their person or their work. Cixous argues that she has a problem with both the first and the last half of this term, and finds it especially inadequate to describe writing: "It concentrates too much on the 'franco'—and the 'phone.' That always worries me a bit, the 'phone.' Attention should be paid to the written aspect, that of the trace."⁵ Rahmani indicates that there is a very pejorative connotation that often accompanies this label; potential readers automatically assume that a Francophone text is not very literary. She adopts the critics' voices when she says: "Francophone authors don't think about literature; they have Francophone topics."[6] By proposing to call these women's texts "polygraphies," I recommend that we leave behind a debate about whether or not the works should be called Francophone. I suggest that we place the term to the side and shift our emphasis—taking our cue from Cixous—from speaking to writing, as we seek to appropriately read these *literary* works. Djebar, who also hesitates to call herself francophone, makes a move in this very direction when she affirms herself in other terms to be "a writer of the French language, I certainly take part in 'Franco-graphy'" (*Ces voix* 29; "franco-graphie").

Cixous is well known for exhorting women to write, for extolling the virtues of the written word, and for bringing to light the lasting impact of this form of communication. In her oft-quoted essay "La venue à l'écriture," she specifies in ardent, exclamatory language that it is the written text that has a unique capacity to endure: "Speaking (crying out, yelling, tearing the air, rage drove me to this endlessly) doesn't leave traces: you can speak—it evaporates, ears are made for not hearing, voices get lost. But writing! Establishing a contract with time. Noting! Making yourself noticed!!!" (15). In a similar manner, Djebar also indicates that the writer has the important ability to leave a trace: "to therefore be a writer for the trace, for the virtue of the trace" (*Ces voix* 216). Djebar is aware that she is not the only one to want to make a visible mark, to provide evidence of occurrences, such as those concerning the Algerian War. Indeed, a plethora of traces remain from this conflict: "Traces of all sorts are multiplying with respect to the 'Algerian war': images, photographs, special reports with retrospective fragments" (*Ces voix* 156). But Djebar is equally attentive to the fact that her written impressions may differ in their emphasis from the many existing artifacts: "Faced with this sustained graphomania, I think of the women from our homeland who partake in a meal of *semoule* and a few dates on graves" (*Ces voix* 156). Placing women, with their activities, their customs, the details of their daily activities, along with their rituals, their survival techniques, and their coping mechanisms into the text is a vitally important gesture in Djebar's writing. In her various texts, she puts what is often denigrated, or almost always undervalued, into the equation by including details from women's experiences, and she *questions,* asking the powers that be to answer for mistreatment, for violation, for ignorance.

This is the motivation behind the act of writing: "For suddenly there is a surge in the need to interpellate, this need that lies, latent, in every written birth" (*Ces voix* 208; dans toute naissance de l'écriture). The words Djebar carves out in her work can be seen to adhere to a definition of "trace" as a line drawn by a recording instrument, such as a cardiograph. But in her textual creations, the writer listens to her own heart in order to turn the machine on its head, restructuring, reordering, and reconsidering what those in power deem normal and abnormal, right and wrong, true and false.

Polygraphies is a word that resonates with *calligraphies* and therefore evokes the fine handwriting skills often associated with the Arabic language. Bringing more to mind than a practice of penmanship, calligraphy also carries with it the idea of great aesthetic value, suggesting that words are not only meant to convey meaning but are also filled with tremendous beauty in their very presentation. In a recent study, Dina Al-Kassim engages in an in-depth analysis of calligraphy as more than an attractive way of writing, focusing on the work of Abdelkébir Khatibi and Abdelwahab Meddeb to show that calligraphy is "a reference point for these avant-garde projects of decolonization, critiquing both the continued hegemony of French and France as well as the forms of auto-colonization at work more generally in Maghrebian culture" (223). Al-Kassim recommends that we consider calligraphy "as a practice that has deep roots in the languages and life of the region from which one might extract a performative model for producing new forms of social connection and critique" (211). It is not unconnected to the questions of power that are present in Djebar's critiques: "As a figure for the writing of a modern Maghrebian literature, the calligraphic trope raises the pragmatic questions of who is empowered to write, in what language, and according to what balance of lucid reason and a wilder creativity" (223). Perhaps most important when it comes to women writers from Algeria is the conception of calligraphy as a space of new creation within the French language and larger mind-set to which the language belongs. What Al-Kassim lauds in Meddeb's work is the invention of a personal signature that also can be detected in many of the writings examined in this book: "Meddeb has crafted a literary style that reinvents the narrative 'je'/'I' to re-create features of an 'Islamic' calligraphic textuality within the confines of the French and, one might add, 'Western' writing system" (211). Indeed, such a style might give rise to another neologism: auto-bio-calligraphy.

THE AUTOBIOGRAPHICAL SPRINGBOARD: LAUNCHING THE I-PAD

The first of this book's four sections, titled "The Autobiographical Springboard," is devoted to further exploration of what has been briefly addressed in this introduction: the autobiographical nature of contemporary French-language writings by women from Algeria. Chapter 1 delves into the writings of Hélène Cixous and Assia Djebar, analyzing the ongoing autobiographical strands in these corpuses. While both writers have inevitably been influenced by Saint Augustine and Rousseau and the European tradition of the confession, I argue that it is much more appropriate to apply the term *testimony* to these writings. Cixous and Djebar are devoted to bearing witness to the events and situations that have affected them and others in their common country of origin, as well as in France and around the world. Their texts shed new light on what it means to be a witness today, and they therefore illuminate a different worldview by testifying to wrongs committed on many levels, rather than by focusing solely on confessing the sins of the singular self.

Chapter 2 turns to a newer voice, that of Maïssa Bey, whose 2009 text *L'une et l'autre* (The one and the other) constitutes a unique autobiographical essay, allowing the author to explore her multiple identities. From the outset of this indefinable publication, Bey places herself in relation to others, a move that will not surprise those familiar with her work. She examines her nationality, sex, religion, and age in highly personal writing, in an effort to find solidarity as well as singularity, and a deceptively simple text turns out to reveal complicated philosophical truths in every category. Like chapter 1, this second demonstrates how the autobiographical serves as a springboard for literary composition that is unusually attentive to others. Writing the "je" or the "I" in the text is just the beginning; this act sets up the introduction of experiences that go way beyond the personal, as the intimate written text becomes a launching pad for fiction that implicates many others, on a grand scale.

The second section, "Takeoff Points," focuses on Algeria in the written text. The writers in my study have differing reactions to this native country, this "homeland." Many of them have felt attracted to, but estranged from, their birthplace from the very beginning, while others have found, because of varying circumstances later in life, that they cannot remain there. Only one—Bey—still resides there. But all have strong feelings toward Algeria; not a single writer exhibits indifference to the land in which she spent her early years. In chapter 3, I examine representations of Algeria alongside portrayals of the mother in the work of Marie Cardinal, Cixous, and Djebar. I explore these writers' complex relationships to the country of their birth, the situation of each woman complicated by her experience in the French educational system. It might seem at first glance that Djebar would have a more "natural," unproblematic love for Algeria, since both sides of her family come from this land, but the strained relation between this writer and her country has much in common with the difficulties experienced by Cardinal and Cixous. I pay special attention to the exclusion and prejudice Cixous encountered as a child in Algeria, as these experiences influenced the development of a consciousness that is open to victims of all races and social classes. Since she experienced firsthand what it was like to be "other," Cixous is a writer who takes it upon herself to denounce all evils committed against others of every category. For her, the personal has truly led to the plural. For all three authors, Algeria and the mother both serve as takeoff points, both literally and metaphorically, to find their own transnational spaces in writing.

Chapter 4 focuses on Albert Camus as a "frère de terre," to quote Maïssa Bey. Bey and Djebar both analyze the works of Camus in their relation to the French author's native land. Djebar draws a parallel between Camus and Saint Augustine as men from the same part of North Africa who composed autobiographical works. Bey and Djebar are similarly interested in Camus's textual representations of Algeria, as well as of the mother, particularly in his unfinished, posthumously published *The First Man*. And Bey is especially attuned to the discreet portrayals of various women in Camus's corpus in a country where women have not often had the possibility of speaking, much less of writing.

The two chapters in the book's third section, "Embodiments," address the writing of the body. Chapter 5 explores Cixous's evolving treatment of the form, beginning with some of her first publications and continuing up to the present. In recent essays and works of fiction, the author associated with the term *écriture féminine* still upholds the writing of the body, but her emphasis is less on the feminine jouissance of her early texts than on the pleasures, and pains, of corporal existence. Writing the body often goes hand in hand with *reading* the body in these later works, and the image one sees upon close observation bears visible traces of suffering, and of aging. The specific staging of the self, the other, and the mother in the written text changes over the years, and the implications of Cixous's personal insights extend to address the expectations for and condition of women in Algeria, as well as in France and the larger world.

Chapter 6 focuses on sexuality and sensuality in texts by Bey, Djebar, Malika Mokeddem, and Leïla Sebbar. These four authors valorize the expression of the female body as sexual and desiring in their literary compositions, describing characters that have a healthy sensuality that allows for the expression of love in several languages. My analysis of the various depictions of the female body, and the myriad corporeal configurations of the text, draws from comments by postcolonial critics on the concept of hybridity to show how race and sex emerge in crucial ways when lovemaking is present in the written work. For these women writers who grew up in Algeria, undressing, or perhaps "unveiling," the female body in the text is a meaningful and significant gesture. In various publications, these writers depict the negotiations women must go through in order to assume their own bodies and establish their own identities, whether in their homeland or in other geographies.

The final section, "Reverberations," focuses on depictions of interpersonal relationships in the written text. It begins with an acknowledgment of the premise that our interactions with others have a lasting impact on us, that the words and gestures that characterize our experiences will have effects, whether we are completely conscious of them or not. And when we go through something that truly shakes us up, the aftershocks will undoubtedly have a great influence on us and those with whom we come into contact, perhaps long after the initial "earthquake." Chapter 7 focuses on love relationships in Djebar's novels in an effort to decipher the meanings of the breakups that frequently occur in these works. The end of a love affair in Djebar's writings is portrayed as a positive occurrence, opening up to movement and possibility. Literature ultimately proves to be the place of revisiting the past and reconnecting with the other, with a multitude of others, for the author whose autobiographical works indicate that sentimental splitting presents the only solution to continued creativity in her own life.

In chapter 8, I concentrate on a novel by Malika Mokeddem that depicts a budding relationship between an Algerian woman and a Frenchman with an organ transplant whose donor was an Algerian woman. The text alternates between the first-person voices of these two principal protagonists, providing us with their different perspectives as each travels to Algeria, Vincent for the very first time and Sultana in a return after leaving her homeland behind when she immigrated to France. The love that grows between these two individuals shows how people can overcome racial and sexual differences if they open their hearts and minds to one another. This amorous relationship is framed within a novel that repeatedly addresses the condition of women in Algeria, and my conclusion indicates that female solidarity is possible, even across national borders.

In chapter 9, the work of Zahia Rahmani reveals the fraught relationship the daughter of a *harki* has with her father, as well as with her "Muslim" heritage. Born to an Algerian whose countrymen considered him a traitor because he sided with France during the war for independence, Rahmani has composed various texts that grapple with the difficult status she has inherited because of her father. She has never felt completely at home in France, where she has lived since the age of five, and yet she cannot claim Algeria as her homeland either. The written text allows her to express the pain of her personal experience, to find words for the distress her father was never able to articulate. Her writing project seeks to remedy his silence by giving voice to the complexity of her own experience alongside that of others.

Chapter 10 turns to a novel by Maïssa Bey, *Cette fille-là* (That girl), in an examination of the young main protagonist's relationship to the other Algerian women with whom she lives. This work of fiction makes deeply insightful statements about the history and present experiences of women in Algeria when the title character Malika's life story gradually unravels in fragmented form among the threads of other biographical accounts belonging to the women around her. The diverse nature of their disjointed narratives combines to dispel any single prevailing stereotypical image of an "Algerian woman" and effectively unveils the multiple competing forces that make life challenging for many individuals in post-independence Algeria. I draw a number of parallels between Bey's work and Djebar's, demonstrating that both writers are especially gifted at putting their characters in relation to others and arguing that their attentiveness to the unwritten stories of women is crucial to the establishment of an equitable national narrative in Algeria. This final chapter further explores themes developed in this introduction as it focuses on the crucial role of fiction, in a narrow and a broad sense, in creating affiliations that ultimately lead to the uncovering of profound truths.

Readers will note that the chapters in *Polygraphies* are of two different lengths that reflect their nature and content. Longer chapters are devoted to more than one author, and to more complex elaborations of innovative theorizations and conceptualizations of these authors' works. Shorter chapters are generally devoted to single authors and are written "in dialogue" with—or as responses to—the other chapters in each section. For instance, chapter 1 is an in-depth study of Cixous and Djebar that brings out some of the significant points their autobiographical writings have in common, and it is, partly for that reason, twice the length of chapter 2, which examines a rich, concise autobiographical text recently penned by Bey, an author whose work is in many ways a response to the oeuvres of Cixous and Djebar. This pattern, with longer chapters concentrating on multiple authors and shorter chapters focusing on specific topics related to the themes developed within each section, can be found throughout this publication.

Polygraphies is the first book to bring together in a comprehensive and cohesive study the works of seven of the most prominent women writers in French today. It forges new ground by placing a strong emphasis on the works of Hélène Cixous as intimately connected to her birthplace, and thus establishes a connection between this influential thinker and the multiple works by other French-language women writers from Algeria. The tremendous notoriety of Cixous, illustrated by a large three-day colloquium held at the Bibliothèque nationale de France on the occasion of the inauguration of the Cixous archive in this symbolic location in 2003, is perhaps matched by the illustrious reputation of Djebar, who was elected to the Académie Française in 2005. Both Cixous and Djebar have exerted—and continue to exercise—an undeniable influence on younger writers, but each of the authors included in this study can hold her own, so to speak. They have all proven to be prolific, publishing a number of significant works that define them as possessing a singular voice that is making an indispensable contribution to contemporary literature in French. As the following chapters illustrate, their special relationship to both Algeria and France, to the contentious countries that have marked their experiences and defined their itineraries, has stimulated the creation of inimitable oeuvres in French. While similarities can be drawn between these writers, their differences abound, and that is why a book containing this variety is crucial to understanding women writers from Algeria today. The diversity of their ethnic, racial, and religious backgrounds comes to play in their literary works, as every one of these writers could echo the epigraph of Zahia Rahmani's *France, récit d'une enfance* (France, narrative of a childhood): "In [her] case, wouldn't having recourse to 'I' be the only possible fiction?" (9). Each in her own way, and collectively, Bey, Cardinal, Cixous, Djebar, Mokeddem, Sebbar, and Rahmani are taking contemporary autobiographical writing to new levels, demonstrating that fictions in French are potential places of real impact because they are open to the paradoxical position of being the location where the truth lies.

PART I The Autobiographical Springboard

CHAPTER 1 | Le moi à plusieurs reprises | From Confession to Testimony in the Autobiographical Writings of Hélène Cixous and Assia Djebar

> *There is autobiography circulating through all the transfers of meaning. The circulation of readability, of iterability, is the circulation of a deviation and of autobiography as always already the autobiography of the other. Or, in still other terms, one could say that there is autobiography of a "we" given by the division, the deviation, and the sharing of voices.*—Peggy Kamuf, Signature Pieces

Hélène Cixous and Assia Djebar have composed prolific oeuvres that are quite different, but that have in common recurring autobiographical elements. Cixous, in works both theoretical and fictional, repeatedly comes back to personal topics, establishing a veritable "myth" surrounding her history and her family as they are presented from different angles in the written text. Djebar has also often returned to idiosyncratic themes, especially in the three volumes of the projected autobiographical quartet, as well as in her 2007 novel titled *Nulle part dans la maison de mon père* (Nowhere in my father's house). These various autobiographical texts provide readers with multiple perspectives for examining how testimony works in contemporary works by women writers from Algeria, and this first chapter will engage in an exploration of the ways in which bearing witness to events experienced in their homeland takes place again and again in the literary text.

Both Cixous and Djebar have addressed questions of the autobiographical in their writing and made provocative statements that challenge our conceptions of the term. In *Rencontre terrestre* (Terrestrial meeting), Cixous claims that she avoids the word altogether, asserting that all literature begins with personal experience: "'Autobiographical' is a word I avoid. I have always been it, not more or less than Montaigne and every *littérateur*" (31). Cixous's resistance to employing the term is partly due to her belief that the self is always in relation to the other, particularly when it comes to the "translation" of the literary text: "'The self' ['*L'auto-*'] is always already other, translation has always already begun" (31). She goes on to argue that while some texts are more or less autobiographical than others, the three grammatical persons always come back to the first person pronoun "I":

All begins with the experience of the subject, a fact Montaigne firmly established in French literature. Just like Scève, Louise Labbé, François Villon, Viau, Proust, and Stendhal. I don't see how anyone could write differently. Novels that don't begin with personal experience are fakes [*sont du toc*]. The distance between the source and the text is larger or smaller, and the period of writing changes, like in painting, that's all. But I is always all three persons, first, second, third, it is the second who is the first and the third who comes back to begin. (31)

It is interesting that Cixous neglects to name Jean-Jacques Rousseau among the great writers mentioned in this passage, especially since he has had such a strong influence on her work. She often cites him outright, though she occasionally makes more subtle intertextual references to his writing. It might be that she wants to avoid in this instance an immediate association between her writing and the *Confessions*, since she is arguing precisely against a strictly, canonically autobiographical understanding of her work. But it would be hard not to appreciate the blatantly autobiographical aspects of Cixous's many publications, especially when one text seems to respond to and build on an earlier text in an ongoing search for adequate written representations of the intimate.

When Assia Djebar turns to the "violence of autobiography" in an essay of that title published in *Ces voix qui m'assiègent* (These voices that besiege me), she cannot avoid the confessional model: "In sum, the 'I haven't told you everything,' a little like in the visiting room of the Catholic confession. I have never found myself in a confessional, but there is of course something of the confession of the penitent in the autobiographical text. In this place, in this situation, once you have avowed a fact, a detail, nothing can be taken back: it's too late! Your word, your text, are uneffaceable" (110–11). Even as she addresses the indelible nature of the printed word, she admits that the opportunity to continue writing, and to publish again, always adding to the previous volume and complicating it, providing nuance and admitting change, seems to repeal in some ways what Djebar calls "the irreversibility of the autobiographical act" (110). This is how she explains it: "On the contrary, doubtless thanks to this encounter, autobiography offers a continuous unfolding. It can continue uninterrupted in the form of a journal until the last day; until the last word, as long as it remains lucid, and even beyond, the writer could, sometimes, behave like a sovereign" (111). The emphasis Djebar places here on the possibility of unending autobiographical writing offers an alternative to the singular, all-defining "autobiography" by hinting that the author of numerous written works is engaged in a continual search for textual truths that may change from one year to the next, from one publication to another.

If Cixous shies away from the use of the word *autobiographical* to describe her writing, it may be because of the word's close association with *confession* and the muddy definitions and outcomes for this loaded term. In *Troubling Confessions: Speaking Guilt in Law and Literature,* the critic Peter Brooks articulates this lack of clarity: "The fact remains that our sense of what confession is and does hovers in a zone of uncertainty that has much to do with the multiform nature of confession and its uses for cleansing, amelioration, conversion, counseling, as well as conviction" (87). While it is unlikely that she would object to its "multiform nature," Cixous would be reluctant to embrace all of the outcomes in this list. Brooks hones in on what he calls the "notion of transparency" in Rousseau's *Confessions,* identifying the "desire to abolish all veils between" the writer and his readers as "a repeated motif" in his seminal eighteenth-century tome (161). Brooks points out that a concern with total openness can easily lead to what he calls the "tyranny of transparency," created by "an imperative to confess" that leads to "the abolition of all zones of privacy around the individual" (163).

In her deeply personal work of fiction *Les rêveries de la femme sauvage* (*Reveries of the Wild Woman*), Cixous presents the reader with a powerful "primal scene," in accordance with the book's subtitle, that reveals the pain of forced confession. When a friend's mother forbids her to attend a planned outing, it is the first-person narrator who claims responsibility for the misdeed: "Grant me one day with my fiancée I admit my crimes I'll admit whatever you like, the pen I know it, I lost it myself, don't punish me tomorrow" (74). Cixous makes it evident that she who confesses her crimes in this passage is not guilty, that she admits to losing a pen herself in order to absolve her friend of this wrongdoing, in the hope of regaining her company at the next day's event. This scene illustrates very effectively two problematic ideas that are bound up with the idea of confession in the autobiographical text. The first is in the person of the confessor to whom one admits wrongdoing. In the hierarchical confessional scene, the confessor is the one with the power. This binary relation places the confessor in the superior position, able to judge the guilt of the confessant. The second troublesome concept in the term *confession* is that of implied guilt. It is assumed that one is confessing one's sins, and that one has been naughty and must be punished before one is exonerated.

It is my conviction that to address the autobiographical writings of contemporary writers like Hélène Cixous and Assia Djebar we must make a shift in terminology, moving away from the idea of confession toward an understanding of testimony as it operates in their work. I am certainly not arguing for eliminating *confession* from our vocabulary, because it is a crucial and unavoidable concept for this autobiographical writing. But I ascertain that an oscillation characterizes the movement of these texts between confession and testimony as two different models for writing the self in contemporary autobiographical fiction. While confession is an inevitable point of reference for reflections like those by Djebar cited above, testimony presents a pertinent counterpoint for readings of this innovative writing that does not hold to static concepts of truth, sincerity, and authenticity. As Leigh Gilmore contends in *The Limits of Autobiography: Trauma and Testimony*, contemporary works demonstrate that a "culture of confession" and a "culture of testimony" can "coexist," albeit "with a certain tension" (2). When I argue that women's autobiographical writings in French are moving toward testimony, this understanding does not therefore preclude confession but seeks instead to explore the tension between these terms, the tension inherent to current autobiographical writing in French, at once in line with a tradition of "autobiographical" texts from Montaigne to Rousseau and in harmony with postcolonial women's writing.

In their autobiographical writings, Cixous and Djebar do not seek forgiveness. In fact, they seldom admit to any crime. One notable exception is found in the occasional shocking avowals of Cixous, but even in these textual moments, she proudly claims her act and even defends it; she does not want to be absolved, asserting that great literature results from such transgressions. In a number of texts, notably *Three Steps on the Ladder of Writing*, Cixous indicates that expiation is not the goal of her writing project, and warns that atonement is something to be avoided, not sought: "The moment we avow we fall into the snare of atonement: confession—and forgetfulness. Confession is the worst thing: it disavows what it avows" (45).

When Derrida asks if there has ever been an autobiography unmarked by confession, he just may be pointing to this "crossing of borders" toward a new term, *testimony*, that occupies much of his work on the law, on hospitality, and on the law(s) of hospitality. Derrida locates confession geographically and chronologically, indicating its emergence—and persistence—as a distinctively Christian phenomenon: "Is there . . . an ancient form of autobiography immune to confession, an account of the self free from any sense of confession? . . . Autobiography and memoir before Christianity, especially before the Christian institutions of confession?" ("L'animal que donc je suis" 21). While he seems to be searching here for a confessional form situated outside the confines of religion and its history, Derrida does not seem to be pushing for a simple "secularization" of confession.[1] Rather, he is gesturing toward a horizon with different premises, distanced from "our culture of subjectivity" ("L'animal que donc je suis" 271),[2] on the other side of the "border" between self and other, in line with this movement described in "Sauf le nom": "For Augustine does not respond only to the question: Why do I confess to you, God, who know all in advance? Augustine speaks of 'doing the truth' (*veritatem facere*), which does not come down to revealing, unveiling, nor to informing in the order of cognitive reason. Perhaps it comes down to *testifying*" (39). If testifying is defined here as contributing to the communication of truth apart from the revealing of information appealing to cognitive reason, then Derrida is effectively describing the works of such writers as Cixous and Djebar. But his analysis reveals that this understanding of how testimony works in the written text is not new. In fact, the transition from confession to testimony is present in the very *Confessions* of Saint Augustine: "He responds to the question of public, that is to say, written testimony. A written testimony seems more public and thus, as some would be tempted to think, more in conformity with the essence of testimony, that is also to say, of its survival through the test of testamentary attestation" ("Sauf le nom" 39).

TESTING TESTIMONY: STANDING UP TO THE SYRINGE

The words *témoignage* and *témoin* appear with remarkable frequency in both Cixous's and Djebar's texts. In Djebar's collection of short stories titled *Oran, langue morte* (*The Tongue's Blood Does Not Run Dry*), we find narrative voices expressing their status as witness, affirmations that are curiously rendered as *bystander* in the English translation: "I believe that I am an invisible bystander, omnipresent" (28; je me crois témoin invisible, omniprésente [42]); "I felt myself turning into a pure bystander" (74; Je me sentais me muer en pur témoin [125]). In *L'amour, la fantasia* (*Fantasia: An Algerian Cavalcade*), an evocative passage on mothers and daughters in Algeria introduces the crucial idea that one can witness one's own life, in a sense, and in this case the English translation is slightly more faithful to the original: "Ainsi se déroule le théâtre des citadines assises qui se font témoins, tant bien que mal, de leur propre vie" (175) (So these city ladies sit

Le moi à plusieurs reprises 31

there and bear witness, as best they can, to the unfolding drama of their own lives [154]). While a witness may be a bystander, in many cases she is much more, precisely because of her capacity to speak, and to therefore turn a passive visual act into an active verbal one. In this text, as in others by Djebar, the author is in essence taking down the testimony of other women, noting in literary form the stories that her Algerian countrywomen have told her in their native Berber tongue and that she has rendered in French in the text. In a somewhat similar manner, Cixous has often listened to the narratives of others and turned them into literary works, whether in plays, essays, or in what she calls "fictions." Perhaps the greatest inspiration to her comes from her inimitable mother, the German Jew who worked for years as a midwife in Algeria and whose unfailing energy comes through in the autobiographical text. Cixous indicates in *Benjamin à Montaigne: Il ne faut pas le dire* (From Benjamin to Montaigne: It shouldn't be said) that the maternal muse works in a particular way: "Now, I noted, I have stopped wanting to collect her memory. It is time that I judge my mother's testimonies and trophies more for what they summarize than for their panoramic art of the extravagance of their opinions" (207). While the use of the concept of testimony comes through in many passages in these writers' work, perhaps the strongest example can be found in a similar episode that occurs in two different autobiographical texts.

In *L'amour, la fantasia,* Djebar depicts the scene of an attempted suicide. The narrative voice recounts in the first person this eventful day in detail, which I am abbreviating here: "I am seventeen. . . . We have had a trivial lovers' tiff, which I make into an issue; I hurl a defiant ultimatum at him; an invisible breach occurs and spreads . . . Frenzy, impetuosity, exhilaration of the all-or-nothing; I rush headlong down the street. Even though I have put nothing into words, probably planned nothing, except to let myself be borne along by this pure spontaneous impulse, my body hurls itself under a tram as it turns a sharp corner of the avenue" (113). Fortunately, the tramway driver was able to stop the vehicle in time, and the narrative voice speculates about a gesture the driver must have made toward those who had seen the traumatic event: "He must have held up his hand to show the crowd of witnesses what had saved me by controlling the speed of the tram" (114). Djebar goes on in this chapter to address another incident in which a stranger plays a significant role: the first-person narrator describes herself as an older individual walking along a Parisian street at the end of a fifteen-year love relationship and screaming without realizing it, until a stranger draws her attention to the piercing cry she is letting out and gently begs her to stop. These crucial incidents in her personal itinerary are introduced with the following two sentences at the outset of the chapter: "Two men, two strangers intruded so intimately into my life as to seem for a few brief moments to be of my own flesh and blood: we engaged in neither philosophical discourse nor in polite or friendly conversation. Two complete strangers crossed my path, each close encounter accompanied by a cry, a scream—it is of little significance from whom it came, from one or other of those strangers or indeed from myself" (113).

This portrayal of the other as *témoin,* as a witness even closer to her than she is to herself, is a striking element in Djebar's autobiographical text. While she observes herself from the standpoint of the outsider ("I perceive this nauseating sling of sounds as a nearly indifferent witness" [131]), those who see her distress in these moments seem to feel as intensely as if the pain were their own.³ Djebar says that she responded to the man on the Parisian street with a soft tone, so surprised was she by "the emotion shown by the stranger" (132). In her own textual testimony, she is bearing witness to the witness of the other, in a circle of witnessing that itself bears witness to how even anonymous observation is not "innocent" but filled with meaning for all those involved. When it comes to the possibility of witnessing, spectators are never disengaged from the action they observe but instead are inevitably concerned, caught up in the scene simply because of their presence. This is what Cixous's testimony reveals, but before we turn to her memorable experience with a tramway, I would like to examine the suicide attempt depicted by Djebar in greater detail.

It is significant that the identity of the man who saved the seventeen-year-old girl's life is revealed through his voice: "I was struck by one detail which assumed a curious importance: the 'Poor White' accent of the man who was so upset that he cried over and over again, 'My hand's still trembling. Look!'" (*L'amour* 114). The narrator reveals that this resonant voice inspired her to open her eyes and contemplate this being who had made such a decisive movement in her life, and maintains that she has since forgotten everything about him, except this voice that still echoes within her: "the timbre of his voice, in the midst of that crowd, still resonates within me" (*L'amour* 130).⁴ In her 2007 novel *Nulle part dans la maison de mon père,* Djebar returns to her impetuous plunge before the moving tram, a near-fatal movement that she qualifies in this text as a "self-murdering gesture" (379; geste auto-meurtrier). When Djebar revisits this pivotal, defining moment from her past in this later work, she provides a great deal of background information, retracing her thoughts and steps leading up to the *acte,* turning around it, repeating it in textual terms, and then reflecting on it. Instead of devoting less than two pages to the event, as she did in *L'amour, la fantasia,* she has dedicated to it the entire third part of the latter novel, as well as the epilogues, approximately 150 pages of a 400-page text. Rather than serving as an anecdote, a word Djebar herself employs to hint at the role it might be considered to play in *L'amour, la fantasia* (130), this attempt to cut her life short has arguably become the central preoccupation of Djebar's most recent publication.

In *Nulle part dans la maison de mon père,* the narrative voice describes in the first person what took place within her immediately prior to the "accident": "In a split second, I catch sight of the tramway barrelling toward me. The machine is launched, bounding forward, a blissful monster! My goal, in the end: to annihilate myself there, where the sea is so far off, to sleep.... The rails: I'll lie down there! And everything will be over more quickly" (358). The narrative perspective shifts from the first to the third person following the fall:[5] "Cries. Turmoil. A loud hubbub mixed with the stridency of the crowd. Several minutes later, removed from beneath the engine and spread out on her back, the young girl emerges little by little from her unconsciousness. The voice of a man—that of the conductor (undoubtedly shaken up)—ululates, obsessed, panic-stricken, above the body with its eyes closed: 'She threw herself . . . it was she who threw herself! Look: my hand is still shaking!'" (359). In the later version, the tramway driver's voice is filled with emotion, as in the earlier account of this event, but his insistence in this passage on the agency with which the seventeen-year-old girl acted is significant. This important figure whose quick reaction saved the girl's life is *insisting on his innocence,* making it clear for all that he was not at fault for the near-death incident in which he played such a crucial role. Amid the noise of the crowd, the "collective clamor" that surrounded her limp body, it was the voice of this man that stood out, that indelibly made its mark on Djebar's mind: "The voice cries out, its echo extending to the point that it becomes ingrained in me" (363). Despite an obsessive focus on the conductor's voice in *Nulle part dans la maison de mon père,* no mention is made of the man's accent in the lengthy revisiting of this scene. This seems unusual, since this is precisely the detail that made the voice so memorable, according to the earlier account: "The only thing that clung so closely to her was that accent from the poor European districts of the city, that way of speaking which had made her most aware of the tram-driver's voice" (*L'amour* 114). The foremost witness of her suicidal act stood out because of his particular form of speech. While Djebar does not elaborate on the meaning this accent held for her, we might assume that it identified him as a part of a less affluent class, even if he could be said to belong to the more "privileged" category of European in a bifurcated colonial society.

It is noteworthy that Cixous should describe a scene very similar to Djebar's tramway incident in *Les rêveries de la femme sauvage*. It is written in the first-person singular as well, but it is not the "je" who jumps under the moving vehicle in this case:

> I am seven, I've been Jewish for a few years they tell me. The wheel turns, the little carriages swing back and forth. In front of me a man leans over and hugs a girl in a veil. Suddenly like a lunatic on fire she jumps like a girl who has caught fire she jumps. She is all you can see. French Algeria leaves the stage. The veil gets caught in the slats of the ride. The girl is yanked after her veil her body is trapped like a piece of meat in a grinder, she can't extract it. Her scream rings out right to the port, right to the tip of the cathedral, if a scream could halt fate, everything would stop dead. But the wheel must turn, two more times it rolls over the screaming body, a scream never before heard in the City of Oran. Everything stops now. The girl has finished screaming. Her body cut in two through its middle wrapped in the veil falls like a stone to the ground of the square to the relief of the spectators. A dreadful feeling of release runs through me. My existence has been cut in two. It is from having seen and looked at the torture that no human being should have to see, that no human being should turn away from, riveted as we were in the little carriages, the one completely given over to death the other outside it is from having heard the most piercing human scream and what's more feminine rising from the pit of time in a single uninterrupted gush, as if I had heard life accusing death while spilling its blood to the very last drop. The fault grips me, here, in the little carriage. The fault, its terrible mystery. I did nothing. I was there. I am still there. I saw. I lived it. I am not dead. There is a fault. And it is my fault, somehow. (81–82)

This eyewitness account is framed in intriguing terms. The seven-year-old girl who sees this horrific scene transpire in front of her watches this other woman die with an awareness of a specific identity that comes to her from external sources: others call her Jewish. She doesn't indicate that this designation distinguishes her from the veiled woman, but readers might immediately jump to the conclusion that such a separation exists between these two individuals from different ethnic and religious backgrounds. There are many possible interpretations of the feeling of guilt, of having committed a "fault" that the first-person narrator expresses as she observes another perish before her eyes. Unlike the tramway driver who, in Djebar's account, was able to apply the brakes and stop the machine in time to save the seventeen-year-old Algerian girl's life, the young Cixous is powerless to act on behalf of this Algerian woman. However, like the tramway driver, she is perceived by the Algerians as coming from the "other side of the tracks," so to speak, as a "European," hailing from the more favorable side of the colonial dividing line. While the fact that she is a Jew considerably complicates this belonging, it is undeniable that she suffers from what Ronnie Scharfman has termed "the painful freedom of privileged difference" (97).[6] In response to a scene in which she was unable to change the outcome, Cixous has turned to writing the incident, testifying to its tremendous impact on her, as it effectively split her existence in two, separating her life into a "before" and "after" this tragic scene in which a body was severed right in front of her, and a striking, strident cry forever recorded itself on the soundtrack of her memory.

What is most remarkable about this passage is that Cixous does not separate herself from the other whose fate she has seen firsthand. This fusion with another being is illustrated in the phrases juxtaposed without any punctuation in the text already quoted: "the one completely given over to death the other outside it is from having heard the most piercing human scream and what's more feminine rising from the pit of time in a single uninterrupted gush" (81). These phrases run together in a fashion that resembles a total melding with the other, an idea and a written style that can be found again in the first part of the following quotation: "In spite of myself I am the bearer of a girl in a veil who is not me, I have within me a veiled girl cut in two the deadly veil the cut because I am a girl the victim's witness, cut off from the victim. I go home. I do not run. I feel that *that happened to me*. Since that accident something inside me is veiled to me" (82). In both of these examples, the sentences that lack punctuation are followed by short, deliberate sentences that seem to represent a desire on the part of the narrator to regain control, to take account of the situation in real terms, and to make some sense of it. What these passages reveal is that the witness has internalized the incident to such an extent that years later, in the present of the writing of this text, she asserts that she carries the young veiled woman within her. She has not become the other, but the other has entered into her consciousness in such a definitive manner that she will never be the same again. Even though she was a bystander, she was completely and utterly involved in the event. When she avows this, Cixous may inadvertently be telling her readers what it really means to be a witness to an event, whether we are present at an accident in a public place, or reading a work of fiction: to truly witness means to internalize to the extent that what has taken place for another has irrevocably *happened to us*.

These similar scenes in Djebar's and Cixous's works of fiction test the limits of testimony by implicating the autobiographical authors themselves in gestures of absolute desperation. These two writers have comparable composed accounts of urgency and anxiety in their native Algeria that communicate the ways in which women are ensnared, feeling they have no other way out of certain situations than to commit acts of great violence against their person. Their candor in revealing unfathomable anguish in and through this bloodshed is self-contained, in the sense that it does not appeal to a reader for judgment in the way a confessional text presumably would. In her subtle reading of Derrida's "Circonfession," Peggy Kamuf indicates that the reader has the power to handle a book like a syringe: "A word or a phrase can bleed [*saigner*] before it signs [*signer*] or signifies [*signifier*]. It is in the symptom of blood, by which the circonfessional account gives itself to the other who holds the book in his or her hands like a giant syringe. It is the other who has to invent me, to tell me if I told the truth, or not. This is the great risk that is run: to exhibit the symptom by which writing cuts itself off from literature and its games of hide-and-seek" ("Seringues" 399; cachotteries). Cixous and Djebar may tell the truth about these events; they may have really experienced them as they describe in the text. But they do so in works that are not cut off from literature. To the contrary, they make these occurrences the very stuff of literature. If, as Kamuf asserts, "A confession should not belong to literature" (402; Une confession ne devrait pas être de la littérature), then Cixous and Djebar are right to turn to testimony, to test it and try it out for its literary potential. They move away from the trap of the mechanics of confession, in an effort to get rid of the machine that is meant to detect the truth from a lie and assign blame to the author: "We dream through writing to get rid of the instrument that collects blood little by little, but at a great cost" (400; par petites prises, mais non à petit prix). As it participates in this dream and its realization, testimony vibrates to a decidedly different tune.

WITNESSING THE SCENES OF THE CRIME: THE TRIALS OF THEATRICAL PRODUCTIONS

In her own analysis of Derrida's "Circonfession," Cixous indicates that this text illustrates how the Algerian-born philosopher found inexhaustible inspiration in crime and its avowal. "But that's what writing is: taking the pen to increase the pain. So he writes the crime [*il écrime*]. And does it again. *Circumfession* avows and as quickly forgets its avowal in order to reavow and revive the avowal with its inexhaustible facets and figures. He considers his avowal, his crime, his avowal as crime-written-down, as if he hadn't yet committed it hadn't properly commenced" (*Portrait* 91). In a personal essay titled "Obstétriques cruelles" (Cruel obstetrics), Cixous reiterates her conviction that crime serves as a continual source of rejuvenation in written creation: "If I had to experience the state of crime in spite of my innocence, it wasn't so I could regret it but so I could benefit from the bloodshed" (112; en tirer tous les saignements). Circling back again and again to revisit the scenes of crime and allowing the blood to flow metaphorically from lived traumatic episodes contributes to powerful literary creations.[7] That is why, in Cixous's view, crime is to be treasured and sheltered from absolution; it must be kept intact or it will lose its ability to tell us our truth. If the crime is absorbed into the order it violates by definition, if it becomes a part of the law it defies, then it is threatened with permanent forgetfulness. Unlike Derrida, who continually "forgets" his avowal in "Circonfession" only to return repeatedly to the crime in new ways, the criminal who has served a sentence and paid the debt for the crime loses his crime forever. This final, authoritative loss would be tragic, in Cixous's analysis: "What finally emerges from the earth of the narrative is that *we need the scene of the crime* in order to come to terms with ourselves: we need the theater of the crime. We need to be able to expose the crime and at the same time to somehow keep it alive" (*Portrait* 45).[8]

Cixous's comments in "Writings on the Theater" reaffirm the human need for the theater of crime by asserting that the theater is the place where crime is best contemplated: "For the Theater is the place of Crime. Yes the place of Crime, the place of horror, also the place of Forgiveness. What does it give us to see? The primitive passions: adoration, assassination" (*The Hélène Cixous Reader* 154). The forgiveness contained in the theatrical experience differs from the social and legal forms of forgiveness that erase the crime.[9] The forgiveness that takes place on stage preserves the act from oblivion. The narrative of the spectacle is memorable because of its repeatability; the crime can be returned to (in a literal and figurative sense) because it is embedded in sight and sound. Because spectators are *witnesses,* they take part in both the crime and the forgiveness that follows, *and they don't forget:* "Why do we love so immediately, so eternally, certain works of the theater or opera? Because by showing us our crimes in the Theater, before witnesses, they accuse us and at the same time they forgive us" (154). The "primitive passions" enacted on stage are crimes to which all humans are naturally drawn, in spite of social and legal interdicts.

The spectacle makes theatergoers aware of their own propensity to carry out the misdeeds incarnated before them: "And there are moments when the monster discovers his humanity. There is always the moment of hesitation, and of temptation: and if I were to kill? And if I were mistaken? And if I were a monster? And if I were blind?" (155). The series of questions posed here indicate that all humans are subject to impulsive action, that all people are tempted to commit crimes, and that the theater unveils the crucial, pivotal moments on which fate hinges. Everyone must struggle with a sudden urge to carry out a "crime of passion" at one point or another: "This moment is given to us at the Theater, it is the tragic instant when everything could be changed. . . . For between good and evil, the step is blade thin" (155). Treading the fine line between good and evil, between acts that are condoned and those that are condemned, is an integral part of the spectator's experience. Cixous maintains that spectators identify with both the criminal *and* the victim of the crime; as witnesses to the complexity of any given situation, viewers cannot easily pronounce judgment. They recognize themselves as caught in a precarious position on the thin border between right and wrong. And they realize that they are occupying this position *together.*

Theatergoing is a communal experience, in contrast to the solitary activities of reading and writing. In the theater, individuals are part of a larger collectivity, and they are brought together to see the same events at the same time. Witnesses to the crime in the theater are therefore multiple, an aspect of theater that is indispensable to what takes place there. In the work of fiction *Benjamin à Montaigne: Il ne faut pas le dire,* the narrator informs us of the danger of being "without witness": "I am without witness, it is an infernal circle I just got killed and I myself am guilty of my own murder" (24). In this phrase containing crime carried out against oneself, there is a notable absence of emotion. The "infernal circle" in which the narrator is caught leads to a singular, solo, senseless death, devoid of the sentiments of fear and pity that are essential to catharsis.

In some senses, Djebar believes that she is "without witness," when she returns to the scene of her suicide attempt. Just as Derrida repeatedly forgot the crimes he had already confessed and therefore confessed them again in "Circonfession," according to Cixous's astute analysis, so Djebar has no recollection of having already written about her brush with death when she devotes herself to this event in her most recent novel. This forgetfulness is specifically related to the form of narration that the author has chosen, according to Mireille Calle-Gruber. The critic stipulates that the first version of events is written in such a way that it is not particularly memorable: "The narrative is written in a single sitting, in one episode, an event a pronouncement; it minimizes and self-ironizes; the scene can be recounted and then forgotten, the narrator forgets herself" ("La servante du texte" 205). In contrast, the second text necessitated the creation of a "singular form of writing," unprecedented in its cyclical structure.[10] If this text is unusual in its circling back, in its rhythmic returns to the same instance, much in line with the aptly titled "Circonfession," it is nonetheless in step with Djebar's oeuvre as a whole, according to Ernstpeter Ruhe's understanding. In his words, Djebar's "creative method" recalls the workings of the ultrasound, with all of the rich resonance the French term contains: "We would like to call it an *'échographie,'* in accordance with the exploratory medical procedure of the same name, that uses the reflection of ultrasounds by organic structures to visualize organs" ("Enjambements" 39). Conceiving of her written creations as influenced by the connotations of the *échographie*—by the bodily movements that make a woman at one with the other (or others) she carries within her, as measured by a machine that gently touches this intimate relation—allows us to see Djebar's work in several dimensions. While the autobiographical texts respond to each other with various echoes that reflect "the story of an ego, which untiringly probes itself" (Ruhe 39), they are also in harmony with a larger body, with a collectivity that is found within and surrounding the writing.

What is particularly remarkable about Djebar's revisiting of her suicidal gesture in *Nulle part dans la maison de mon père* is that she continually refers to it in theatrical terms, as if this moment from her past had been scripted and staged, as if she were simply an actor hired to play a specific role. This reference to the theater takes place explicitly, but it also occurs obliquely, as in this opening question to the tenth chapter, leading up to the monumental moment: "Ten minutes or a bit longer before the 'act'... what act" (341). Obviously, an act can refer to an action, and in this case it is pointing to an irrevocable gesture. But an act can also apply to a division of a play, and this meaning is apparent when the narrator draws a clear connection between her lived past and a dramatic production: "Like at the theater. . . . Two ghosts who thrash about" (345). Several pages later, the narrator repeats this conception of characters as phantoms, emphasizing here the capacity of beings to switch roles, to adopt different identities on the stage: "I had become an other? Change of roles, of masks, of ghosts?" (350). What finally emerges in this use of the theatrical metaphor, however, is the pre-scripted nature of her interaction with her fiancé on this day: "'Here I find myself in a play that I have not chosen, in a bit of very bad theater...'" (351). This statement leads us to believe that Djebar's desperate attempt to end her life may be tied to a desire to escape from the prescribed nature of her interactions with others in the Algeria of her adolescence. Perhaps the seventeen-year-old girl judged that the only possible way to escape the strictures of her society was to jump off the stage, literally and metaphorically. This seems to be what Cixous suggests happened when she saw a young woman throw herself in front of the tram: "L'Algériefrançaise sort de la scène" is a sentence that envisions another background; it is a declaration that a certain location can be exchanged for another and that an opening up toward the universal is possible, if the stage is appropriately set.

When Mireille Rosello turns her attention to the piece titled "Annie and Fatima" in Djebar's collection of short stories *Oran, langue morte,* she highlights the fact that Djebar has adopted a new strategy in this written work: "It is certainly significant that Djebar, who has always been fascinated by the model of the palimpsest and the process of successive rewritings (especially on monuments), should abandon that particular image and turn, instead, to the universe of theatrical performance where actors and mimes reenact the past" (Rosello 14). Indeed, the meeting between the eponymous mother and daughter is represented in theatrical terminology, and this carries consequences in Rosello's analysis, for it "suggests that when two individuals meet, two narrative scenarios suddenly come into contact and sometimes clash: a double individual destiny imitates national history, the latter functioning like the scenario of a play in which the characters must perform their role according to the preexisting script" (13). It is worth noting that *Oran, langue morte* was published in 1997, the same year as *Les nuits de Strasbourg* (Strasbourg nights), a work of fiction that also accords a significant place to the theater, especially as it evokes Maghrebian youth in France who are preparing for a performance of *Antigone*. Following ten years later, *Nulle part dans la maison de mon père* effectively brings together both the "process of successive rewritings," as its own cyclical nature suggests, and "the universe of theatrical performance," as we have already seen. What becomes painfully clear in this work is that the real-life outcome of the autobiographical event is not entirely fulfilling, and therefore the narrative voice, which occupies the role of playwright, indicates a desire to take some liberties with the text: "I rewrite the script, unsatisfied with its very real ending: 'a failed ending!'" (*Nulle part* 389). It is precisely the search for different scenarios that characterizes the "performative encounters" that Rosello explores so brilliantly in her study of France and the Maghreb. Such an encounter was impossible between the young Djebar and her father, and it was the fear of his condemnation, of his pronouncement of the death sentence (354) that drove her to seek an abrupt end to her life. Her flight was precipitated by the impossibility of standing trial before him, by the inability to testify in his tribunal: "If I am brought before my father's court ... I will kill myself!" (370).

In Cixous's reflection, the theater provides a place to perceive and conceive of *death,* to come face to face with its reality and to deal with the conflicted emotions it creates: "I go to the theater because I need to understand or at least to contemplate the act of death, or at least admit it, meditate on it. And also because I need to cry. And to laugh: but laughter is merely the sigh of relief that bursts forth at the scythe's passing: it missed us by a hair!" (*The Hélène Cixous Reader* 154). The tears and laughter that death evokes at the theater are noticeably missing from the quotation taken from *Benjamin à Montaigne,* in which the narrator is guilty of her own assassination. When it represents death, the theater introduces *emotions* into the equation, and these emotions are capable of bringing about change in the spectator: "The Theater doesn't give us death brutally like a blow to the back. No, it doesn't assassinate us. Because essentially, the Theater pities. It gives us one of the most rarefied times in the market of our everyday existences, the time of pity. We have become capable of no longer crying before the little Asian beggar who has lost his legs, isn't that true? Fortunately the Theater stops us and strikes us in the heart and brings us to tears" (155). For people who have become numb to the suffering that surrounds them, and even to the suffering within them, witnessing a play can awaken feelings and elicit a response. Cixous praises the particular necessity for two noble sentiments a worthy play will inspire: "Yes pity, fear, remain the most precious emotions in the world. They are love. And they so need to be rekindled in the hearts of our epoch" (155).[11] Feeling *for* and feeling *with* the other, experiencing the crime of the other, and identifying with both sides (the victim and the perpetrator) of the illicit act are important theatrical experiences that can carry over into life. This is

Cixous's hope in composing plays for contemporary production. Perhaps the pity experienced in this unique setting will influence people's actions in other settings, and perhaps those who have experienced crime together in the theater will take compassion together on those in need. Perhaps learning to feel in the theater will teach us to feel in the world. Most important, perhaps the theater will bring us out of selfish individualism, if only for a moment, in order to save us from what Cixous labels the worst of all crimes: complacency.[12]

Cixous is certainly not a complacent writer. She is far from being self-satisfied in an unreflective way; to the contrary, she is demanding and exacting with respect to her creative output and critical thought. But she is nonetheless skilled in the art of self-satisfaction in a larger sense. While some writers see their vocation as laborious and painstaking, Cixous derives pleasure from literary production, and the enjoyment she finds therein contributes to her innovative style and widespread appeal.

Cixous is an avid reader of Maurice Blanchot, a philosopher whose conception of literature as a place where one can "say everything" has influenced Cixous's autobiographical work. Writing is a space of infinite possibility, where *anything* can happen: "'everything' can be done, 'everything' can be said (*L'espace littéraire* 52; "tout" pourra se faire, "tout" pourra se dire).[13] According to Blanchot's affirmations in *Le livre à venir* (*The Book to Come*), the *tout* that can be communicated through literature is dependent upon the immediacy and truth of its expression: "What matters is thus not the whole as it unfurls and develops in the story, if it be that of the heart; it is the entirety of the immediate, and the truth of that entirety" (46). This precision takes place in Blanchot's reading of Rousseau; the confessional genre owes much to the emphasis this eighteenth-century writer places on the sincerity of his autobiographical project. Rousseau's desire to tell all, in Blanchot's analysis, means to divulge not only the less noble aspects of his existence but also the less interesting details of his life: "In his Confessions, Rousseau necessarily wants to say everything. 'Everything' is first of all his entire story, his whole life, that which accuses him (and which alone can excuse him), the ignoble, the base, the perverse, but also the insignificant, the uncertain, the null" (*Le livre à venir* 45). In order to be exhaustive, to truly reveal everything, one must confess the base and the boring. As Djebar has so convincingly shown in her latest work of fiction, one must also confess that which may be the most shameful, and certainly the most painful, episode of one's existence. As Mireille Calle-Gruber asserts, "This book is neither an autobiography nor a confession but the writer's grave, where she finds the sources of writing and the strength to go off" ("La servante" 209). Indeed, the narrator of Djebar's latest work indicates the agony involved in this elaborate process of "bleeding out," in these revealing personal, textual exsanguinations: "It is here that fiction tears itself, wears holes in itself. Here is where the drops of blood form, despite the ink spilled so many times. Here is where the author bears all.... Only because the father is dead? The beloved and sublime father? The father who is judge, even though he is also the liberator and necessarily a strict judge?" (*Nulle part* 384). For Djebar, true testimony is possible only outside of the father's tribunal, far from his harsh judgment, only after he has disappeared from the scene of the trial.

When Djebar refers to her story as a confession in *Nulle part dans la maison de mon père,* she makes sure to qualify her use of this term by remarking that she is from a different tradition: "the Muslim culture of my origins is unaware of or distances itself from this unveiling, at least in front of a priest" (401). Confession is foreign to Cixous's upbringing as well. The narrator of *Les rêveries de la femme sauvage* claims that her mother's confidence always kept her from confessing her sins: "... says my mother whose trust has always dissuaded me from owning up to my sins [*confesser mes péchés*]. Each time that I am about to admit my shameful suffering along with certain utterly scandalous and still vivid deeds I shut up" (37). And yet, the mother is often the figure for whom the child commits crime, whether in search of affection or punishment: "First a small sexual transgression nothing at all. Immediately we are called criminal. Small cause great consequence. That is how we become *recriminal:* we repeat tirelessly in writing this brief moment of glory that dazzled mama with surprise and anger" ("Obstétriques" 106). In repeating the crime in writing, in returning to the scene of the crime and continually composing new texts, Cixous is a criminal, knowing with Blanchot that the project of telling all necessarily entails condemnation.[14] Given the fact that she has been "condemned in advance" due to factors like her ethnicity and her gender, Cixous decides to revolt, just as she did as a child when her friend's mother prohibited their outing: "I revolt. Already on the scaffold I dispute it. I am as good as dead. I pick myself up. Confront the obstacle again. Impotent before a pen" (*Les rêveries* 73). No longer impotent before the pen, no longer powerless before the law, Cixous appropriates the writing utensil and uses it as an instrument to play—and sing—a different tune, one that is in harmony with the positive possibilities of testimony. As Ronnie Scharfman has noted, writing has offered Cixous a productive way to speak specifically of and to her place of origin, especially in recent years: "By bearing witness, she can share in the country's tragedy, neither imprisoned by it nor excluded from it" (97). After the "internal exile of childhood trauma" that Cixous suffered from in Algeria, composing works of written testimony "is this coming home of solidarity" (97).

In their collaborative publication *Testimony: Crises of Witnessing in Literature, Psychoanalysis, and History,* Shoshana Felman and Dori Laub identify the power of testimony to accomplish things, to bring about change and exert an influence not only on events but attitudes as well: "Testimony is, in other words, a discursive *practice,* as opposed to a pure *theory.* To testify—to *vow to tell,* to *promise* and *produce* one's own speech as material evidence for truth—is to accomplish a *speech act,* rather than to simply formulate a statement" (5). In this critical work, as in others that deal with "testimonial" writing, events are not remembered in a logical, coherent manner; this is a form that allows for representation of reality in step with the unreasonable, discontinuous nature of its experience, and its memory. Gayatri Spivak defines testimony as "the genre of the subaltern giving witness to oppression, to a less oppressed other" (7). It is significant that Felman places emphasis on the address to the other that is inherent in the act of testifying: "To testify is thus not merely to narrate but to commit oneself, and to commit the narrative, to others" (205). Rather than being bound up solely with the self, the "testimony" of the autobiographical works in this study signals a commitment, a dedication, and an acceptance of profound responsibility toward a community, toward an entity that extends beyond the individual. These writers are producing works in the wake of unjust acts committed against people in their common country of origin, Algeria. The personal emphasis of traditional autobiography (which is meant to be "universal" but in an arguably selfish manner) has turned outward to encompass families, clans, indeed to embrace entire groups of people who have been wronged. Such writing does not seek to expose sin and have it forgiven—and forgotten. It seeks instead to testify, to bear witness, to give testimony.

CHAPTER 2 | La singularité de l'altérité |
Self-Portraiture and the Other in Maïssa Bey

> *Writing myself? Yes, it isn't about telling the truth, or joyfully making things up about myself, or lying true, superbly true. No, it is an exercise in alterity and going toward the other.* —Abdelkébir Khatibi, Le scribe et son ombre *(The scribe and his shadow)*

In 1993, Maïssa Bey accorded a substantial interview to Martine Marzloff, and their conversation was published as part of a book five years later. The interview came at a critical moment in her life, as Samia Benameur had recently decided to take up a pen name, and take up the pen in a new way, writing now for public consumption instead of for her private enjoyment. She explains in the appropriately titled *À contre-silence* (Against the silence) what it meant to bring an end to her silence by becoming a writer:

> At the end of a whole life of silence and self-compromises, you feel—maybe because you can no longer put it off—that reality is there, tragic, terribly tragic, and that there is a necessity to really find words to express what has been buried deeply within you for so long. The motivation is solely that of breaking the silence and confronting your fears. And you write with the feeling that you are giving birth to yourself. It is the movement from writing for yourself to writing for others that implies a renunciation, a baring [*une mise à nu*], an unveiling. And thus a commitment. To allow yourself to be seen, because that's how it is for me, to find yourself open to looks, judgments, when you have spent your whole life up to that point trying to preserve yourself. When you take the plunge, you go through an ordeal that makes its mark on you. (29)

Bey knows very well that she is not the first Algerian woman to engage in autobiographical writing, and her use of the phrase *une mise à nu* recalls Assia Djebar's own formulation: "Speaking of oneself in a language other than that of the elders is indeed to unveil oneself, not only to emerge from childhood but to leave it, never to return. Such incidental unveiling is tantamount to stripping oneself naked" (*L'amour* 156–57). Bey has drawn inspiration from Djebar on many levels, but following in this predecessor's footsteps is nonetheless a challenging task, a meaningful, even monumental undertaking that the younger author does not take lightly. She realizes that she must be faithful not only to herself but also to others, and she will be forever changed because of this textual engagement.

Nearly two decades later, in 2009, the accomplished author published an unprecedented text that seems to elude all possible categorization: neither a novel, nor a narrative, nor a short story, *L'une et l'autre* is an innovative autobiographical essay, a self-portrait in which the author gives herself over to an exercise of self-analysis and self-presentation in a weaving of humble and subtle words. Maïssa Bey describes herself in this text as both a host and a guest: "I am your host/guest [*hôte*] today. At once she who is received and she who welcomes. You receive me in your home and I welcome you in my dwelling of words, at the threshold of which I remain, doors open" (12). As this quotation suggests, these words were initially pronounced aloud on 20 November 2008, at one of a series of lectures organized in the French city of Roubaix under the title "Rencontres du nouveau siècle." The encounter with the other, with others, that characterizes this precise moment in the career of this Algerian novelist resonates in a text that hopes to explain numerous aspects of the personal life of a writer who has always shown herself to be deeply devoted to others.

LECTRICE

Her relationship to others is at the heart of the multiple self-definitions Bey provides in her reflections. Indeed, the most important aspect of her own training, and the gesture that undoubtedly remains her principal source of inspiration, is reading: "The words of others taught me about the world. They taught me to live. I am a reader" (25). Books have allowed her to lead an entirely different life, to travel far from the locations of her childhood and adolescence: "I was a rebel without knowing how to or being able to say no. I had traveled the world, sailed the seas, visited all the continents and even beyond, without ever having gone outside my neighborhood" (26). This act of rebellion propels her far from her familiar surroundings, creating connections to people far away, as she explains: "My companions were adults, characters on paper who were closer to me than my loved ones, women and men who confided in me their most intimate thoughts, who shared with me—as if in a fraternal community— their bread and salt, the words and the truth of their being" (26). The voices of narrators and characters that speak through the written page are so compelling that these individuals become even closer to Bey than her family members, in her assessment. When she highlights this incredible community that is created through literature, through the corresponding acts of writing and reading a fruitful text, she calls attention to the intense importance of her own creations. Inspired by the words and the truth of the beings in the books before her, she is acutely aware of the possibility that her writing will spark similar reactions in her readers and provide a sense of solidarity among them.

L'une et l'autre is a work that presents these readings, that contains "the words and the truth" of those whose books Bey has frequented. These are the words she repeats, that she quotes in order to express herself in the intertextual wealth of dialogue with others. This intertextuality is present beginning with the epigraph, attributed to Adonis: "Chains are my steps, however my body is horizon." In the first paragraph, Bey focuses on a work by Henri Michaux, devoting her attention to a long quotation that opens up the question of singularity and difference(s). The author underscores her own method by affirming the following: "You will have noticed, of course, that I begin by having recourse to the other" (11). This is why she proceeds in this manner: "If I allow him to give me authority, it is in order to place myself under the sign of the other from the outset" (11). The others who express themselves in this text are numerous and varied, including Jean Cocteau, Édouard Glissant, Milan Kundera, and Octavio Paz, as well as Ibn Khaldoun, Lucienne Saâda, and Mostefa Lacheraf. Bey makes use of very different writings to address the multiple aspects of a life that cannot be reduced to a simple definition.

Bey's use of epigraphs in this text recalls Djebar's creative insertion of epigraphs in her novels. As Anne Donadey suggests, the "complex system of epigraphs" that Djebar creates in her written works "can be seen as a cartography, a type of road map providing guideposts by which to read and interpret the texts" (*Recasting Postcolonialism* 63). But Djebar's innovation must also be understood as belonging to a larger tradition, as Donadey points out: "In grounding her text in the works of others before her, Djebar inscribes herself in a long Arabic, even Koranic, tradition in which one must quote someone else in order to support an assertion, to legitimate one's report" (66). What is important about Djebar's "appropriation" of "other discourses" is that it "transforms their context of production, underscoring both the tensions inherent in her writing project and her desire to bring out women's voices, even at the risk of death" (Donadey 92).[1]

Bey is also aware of the multiple risks wrapped up in writing in her homeland, and in the 1993 interview she specifically mentions the "moral and religious constraints" that make writing a dangerous "double transgression": "*to dare to speak,* but also, and this is even more serious in our society, especially for a woman, *to dare to speak of oneself,* to unveil oneself" (*À contre-silence* 28). Writing works that are assumed to be fictional does provide some sense of protection, and Bey takes advantage of this categorical cover to tell of herself and those she has known, from the beginning of her writing career: "The will to express—with all of the freedom that the alibi of fiction can provide—the lived reality of women in Algeria. Even or especially if this reality appears unbearable, such as in the tragic time that we are going through" (*À contre-silence* 26). Therefore, from the very start, fictional and autobiographical writing have been inextricably intertwined for Bey: "First the need to express here and now my being, even if, because I chose fiction, 'I is an other' [*Je est un autre*], this other is still and always I" (27).

In *L'une et l'autre,* Bey affirms with the voice of experience that she is completely aware of the difficulty of drawing her own portrait in words: "A perilous enterprise therefore, is the one which consists of being the subject and the object of discourse. A discourse which, you will see, has an enlarged scope [*champ élargi*] that goes well beyond the borders of the self" (12). An attention to life experience that extends beyond herself is what makes so many of Bey's novels and short stories so gripping. The inspiration she finds in her personal life only leads to a consideration of a larger "field," in her terms, one that is much larger than the self. Bey astutely eschews what could be considered a strictly autobiographical text by immediately denouncing the danger of such a written undertaking. Her concerns go much further than the individual life and text.

COLONISÉE

Bey describes the moment of her birth in 1950 as significant in the history of Algeria, for her life began at a pivotal moment, as she puts it: "at a transitional period in the history of my country" (12). She witnessed decolonization in her formative years, and the fact that she had lived before this historical event is of undeniable importance to the writer: "I belong to a generation with a rather remarkable itinerary. Or, at the least, it is complex. I have to add that the languages and cultures tied to this history cohabit within me" (13). Colonial domination in her homeland is *the* determining factor in her life, in Bey's assessment. It is what has provided her with a worldview and given her direction, in every sense of the term: "It is colonization that forged my representation of the world and that without the slightest doubt provided direction (both meaning and orientation) for my commitments as an adult" (36). Her writing is motivated by and inevitably influenced by this history.

The oppression that characterized French rule in Algeria is something Bey does not hesitate to denounce in *L'une et l'autre*. She reminds us that colonizers showed tremendous ignorance, demonstrated inexplicable prejudice, and utterly failed to distinguish among the different peoples who inhabited the conquered land: "The administrators and historians from the colony . . . lumped together the Berbers, Kabyles, Chaouias, and Arabs under the generic term 'indigenous Muslims,' highlighting their belonging to a land, a religion, and morals that they didn't hesitate to call 'barbarous'" (18–19). The widespread use of the pejorative term *barbares* infuriates the author, who attended French school in Algeria and therefore knew the rules with respect to language within the walls of this establishment: "At the time of the French occupation, we didn't have the right to speak Arabic at the secular, republican school. In the name of cultural and linguistic colonial hegemony" (21). The fact that she had to endure and even respect this "colonial hegemony" motivated the young Maïssa Bey to learn everything she could about the other(s) who dominated her: "That is what gave me an even stronger desire to become familiar with the culture of the others, to appropriate it, and therefore to better understand who they were, those who in the name of the ideals of civilization, had taken appropriated my country" (41). As a consequence of this desire to fully understand and even *appropriate* the other, Bey attained a certain form of mastery over French culture and language that has undeniably propelled her writing career. The strength of her written texts arguably depends on her full familiarity with both of the cultures she grew up in, with France and with Algeria.

Questions of belonging, of appropriation, of property and propriety on a national level emerge with gusto in the lived experience of the writer, who admits that she believed for years that she was French: "For a long time I naively believed that I was French—at least until 1962—because of my birth in a French department" (34). In other words, as a young girl, Bey naturally assumed that if Algeria was officially a part of France, then she who was born in this land would also be French. But when she consulted the history books in order to understand the difference the French administration had established between nationality and citizenship, she learned that she and her family, as well as many others, did not have the legal status she had imagined: "I learned that the indigenous were French subjects and not French citizens" (35). In *L'une et l'autre,* these precisions are made with clarity and simplicity, as the author re-creates a chronology that the Caribbean francophone writer Édouard Glissant argues has been obscured over the years: "It became murky when it was not obliterated for all sorts of reasons, especially colonial ones" (13).

ALGÉRIENNE, ARABE, MUSULMANE

When she details her identity, there are certain factors Bey simply cannot ignore, and she lists them as follows: "First, the criteria of an established identity. Incontestable. The most visible. The one that figures on my papers. Let us enumerate, in no particular order: Nationality. Gender. Religion. Age" (12). It is above all Algeria that comes to mind when the writer analyzes herself: "First of all, I am a place. Algeria. A land that one can hardly say is blessed by the gods today. A land shaken by multiple earthquakes, where the vehemence of light is in harmony with the vehemence of men" (14). This is not only the land of her childhood; it is the place where she continues to reside today, and the choice to stay there, to remain in this country rather than to live in exile, contributes to the validity of her ongoing textual testimony.

But "Algerian" is not sufficient to describe Bey, for not all Algerians share the same roots: "Algerian then. But also Arab, by origin. By my familial ancestry" (14). It is this genealogy that ties her to the conquest undertaken by the Beni Ameur, whom she explains came to Algeria around the eleventh century from the distant lands of Arabia and Egypt and contributed to the Arabization of the North African region (15). It is also this genealogy that ties her to the resistance of the "gesture of conquest," as she puts it: "the tribe of the Beni Ameur, the one I come from, is one of the tribes that, according to the historians of the colonial period, resisted the French conquest most fiercely" (17). Bey thus indicates that her ancestors participated in conquest *and* resistance, suggesting without commentary that they are neither on the good side nor the bad, but rather on both sides of the same human desire to occupy and dominate. She turns to the question of defining *arabité,* seeking to distance the term from the prejudices that exist in certain dictionaries by taking into account genealogy, language, and culture, as well as other aspects of daily existence: "the set of daily practices of a group: manners, habits, attitudes, and beliefs" (18). She calls attention to the crucial difference between the adjectives *Muslim* and *Arab*—terms that are often used interchangeably in France but are not synonymous: "To be of the Muslim religion does not necessarily mean to be Arab, even if Islam, revealed in the Arabic language, played an essential role in the formation of Arab identity" (18).

Arabic is Bey's mother tongue, the language that shaped her world, as she eloquently articulates it: "The language that, from the first dawns, sketched the contours of the world for me" (20). It is a language that is at first oral for her: "the mother tongue, Algerian Arabic or spoken Arabic, in opposition to the written language" (20). But it is also a tongue that cannot be dissociated from Islam: "Arabic, the sacred language of Islam" (20). Indeed, those in favor of Arabization in Algeria are opposed to the use of dialectical Arabic in school: "They judge the mother tongue, their mother tongue, to be not pure enough, too bastardized, precisely by these 'foreign' presences" (21). When faced with this irony, Bey poses a question: "How can you feel like a foreigner in a language that they tell you is yours?" (23).

Religion also figures in the self-portrait of the writer who esteems herself "deeply influenced by the Muslim culture and tradition" (19). But she insists on specifying how she sees her religious belonging, in a personal perspective that reflects the believers around her: "I would like to evoke Islam as I have always seen it practiced around me" (19). According to Bey, *this* Islam is the following: "An internalized practice, locating its source in a faith that is serene, not ostentatious. It is rooted in a secular tradition, free from resentment and rejection, marked by tolerance and openness" (19). This positive definition does not exclude a certain critique of women's place in Islam, present in this quotation taken from Assia Djebar's acceptance speech for a literary prize in Frankfurt in October 2000: "I was raised in the Muslim faith, that of my ancestors for generations, that shaped me affectively and spiritually. But I avow that I am in confrontation with it because I am still caught up in some of its interdicts" (19–20). The interdicts Djebar makes reference to are interdicts that Bey does not mention explicitly, but she directly addresses the status of women. "Inscribed in the body," being a woman is a "reality" of extreme importance because it constitutes the foremost trait in a list of belongings. This reality constitutes the core of her being: "that which makes up my own essence, my essence woven with light and dark, the essence of my being in the world" (44).

FEMME

If Bey's oeuvre focuses especially on women, on those who haven't had the opportunity to express themselves, to tell their stories and share their experiences with others—such as those who occupy center stage in *Cette fille-là* (That girl)—it is because the writer is very attentive to the destiny of women in her country. She does not wish to play into stereotypes or exaggerate the depth of their suffering, as she says before an audience that may have many preconceived ideas when they hear the words "Arab woman": "I say an Arab woman, and immediately you hear the deafening sounds of chains, immediately centuries of oppression are unfurled, immediately blinding walls go up and bodies are shut up behind closed doors, immediately piles of silence are beaten down, that bury piles of dreams that have already drowned under layers of interdicts" (45). When confronted with these ideas, Bey wants to provide a certain historical perspective, finding support in the Orientalism of another period that depended on the same formulation: "These same words, 'Arab woman,' not so long ago, or in other circumstances, could have brought up other images. Images of the Orient, the Arab women featured on the postcards of Orientalist painters, shrouded in mystery and erotic suggestion" (46). Differentiating herself from the women described in these two circumstances, Bey affirms that she is an Arab woman but that she is also a *"femme écrivant, écrivain"* (45), a writing woman who possesses the capacity to say what others have had to keep silent for years.

Bey is especially attuned to the plight of women who are not much older than she is, such as the aunts who have not had any agency, who have lacked even the ability to *imagine* something different for themselves: "Serene. Accepting their condition without even being able to imagine another life, other horizons than the walls that surround them. Can one desire what one doesn't know?" (48). Everything they do revolves around others, particularly the men in their lives: "Their occupations are all centered on a single objective, the satisfaction of the needs of their men: first the father, then the husband, and finally the children. Concern for the other, pushed to point of caricature" (48). Their priorities seem to be entirely different from those of the writer, who is nonetheless a wife and mother, but with another worldview: "All of that seems to me to be so far removed from what I am, from what I live, that I have a hard time realizing that only one generation separates us" (48). She asks if those who should be so close are actually strangers: *"Étrangères, elles?"* And she responds as follows: *"De l'une à l'autre"* (49). She juxtaposes this reflection and another that extends to her own daughters, indicating that they are not free from restrictions: "these young girls who grow up today in a space covered with

La singularité de l'altérité

constraints" (49). When her girls seem surprised that their mother's dress code at their age was more permissive than their own, the writer concludes in the same fashion: "From one to the other" (50; De l'une à l'autre).

Bey is convinced that in the contemporary context women who are Arab, Muslim, and Algerian occupy a role of inestimable importance. This crucial configuration of descriptors, this timely convergence of ethnicity, religion, nationality, and gender make of her and other women who share this fourfold set of belongings undeniable centers for questioning identity today: "Here we are today, we, Arab women, Muslim women, Algerian women, at the center of all of these questionings. At the center of the identitary escalation" (51; la surenchère identitaire). She explains that it is women—and their bodies—who incite so many interrogations and worries: "For woman, unwillingly, is at the heart of all these preoccupations. It is without a doubt because even when she is absent, even when silent, she incarnates desire, but also the hatred of this desire" (51). Bey points out that the question of the veil, which has received so much attention in France, is not at the heart of the struggle of Arab women: "You have to be wary of any easy interpretations—that are all too frequent—that would turn clothing into the very symbol of women's struggle" (50). She insists that women wearing the hijab were among the first rows of demonstrators against fundamentalism and terrorism in Algeria in the 1990s: "Algerian women must be situated, in my view, within this complexity" (50). This text contributes to the creation of a nuanced portrait not only of the writer herself but of other women who may have slightly different self-images but who share Bey's desire for understanding and harmony.

L'UNE ET L'AUTRE

When she contemplates the distance that separates her from both the preceding generation and the following generation, Bey ends up posing a different question: "From one to the other. The distance is great. Then why not one and the other?" (52). We recognize the title in this question, of course, and we perceive the numerous possible interpretations of the phrase *l'une et l'autre*. Born to a father who had studied at the French *École normale* for teachers at Bouzaréah, the writer's childhood gave her access to two universes: "I was born in an environment where two languages, two cultures, and two ways of life coexisted, without that posing a problem. And I went naturally from one to the other, without ever being aware of any incompatibility or antagonism" (23). Thanks to this exposure to two different ways of life, Bey adopted a unique perspective, marked by what she calls a "double impregnation," "that determined my behaviors, my view of the world, my affinities, and my tastes" (25). But these two worlds proved not to be as compatible as she had initially hoped when she experienced "the feeling of being on the edge of two worlds between which the distance continued to grow, due to a war whose echoes buzzed in my ears" (40).[2] She became an orphan at an early age, having lost the one who had taught her to "read in the language of the other" (26) precisely because of the distance that separated these two universes: "For me, as a child, the first encounter with the other took place violently, with the noise of military boots that had come during the night to look for my father" (39). Bey dedicated an earlier book (*Entendez-vous dans les montagnes . . .*) to her father, and *L'une et l'autre* is a touching compliment that gives us additional information on the person who so influenced and who has been so missed by the writer: "I write in the language that my father, the teacher, left me. Language-legacy" (23).[3]

In *Le scribe et son ombre,* Abdelkébir Khatibi describes the particular gesture that is autobiographical writing in evocative language: "I owed it to myself, in writing myself [*en m'autographiant*], to give birth to myself [*m'engendrer*], to develop myself in the language of the other" (29). Bey also describes her writing as a birth of sorts: "a birth, a painful birth to oneself, because too often when the desire for self-affirmation is realized, it is accompanied by a strange feeling of foreignness" (53; un sentiment étrange d'étrangeté). Khatibi affirms that writing about oneself entails separation, "an intimate alteration" (29). Bey seems to echo this reflection in a rich, resonant passage that reads like poetry:

> To write while forgetting the self . . . but at the same time while discovering the other within the self. Prodigious contradiction!
> One and the other.
> I am other, because I write, carrying the word, I have gone to meet the other, all others. (56)

In *L'une et l'autre,* Bey engages in the exploration of the diverse, and sometimes contradictory, facets of her being to show that she incarnates not only the other, but all others: "I chose to go to meet all the others I carry in me" (57). These others are made up of those whose stories she unveils, of the characters who people the moments of writing: "Those I carry in me, whose voices, silences, and wounds are present at the center of my solitude. For I deeply believe that writing is also, and especially, listening to the heartbeats of our fellow humans; it entails solidarity" (58).

Albert Camus—the Algerian-born French writer whose influence on both Djebar and Bey will be the focus of chapter 4—is the writer she cites to reinforce the connection between these two concepts: "'Solitary and in solidarity,' wrote Camus" (58).

There is no doubt that Maïssa Bey's writing is an exercise in solidarity, but it is also a movement of singularity. In *L'une et l'autre,* she attests to the daring nature of this enterprise, in an affirmation that echoes sentiments she expressed in the 1993 interview: "Here it is a question of me. Of the one who dared to speak, who dared to speak of herself" (*À contre-silence* 55). The attempt to paint a self-portrait is all the more courageous if we consider that the writer is Algerian: "I am other because I live in a society that aspires to obscure individual identities" (53). When she turns to the "multiple belongings," the "identity traits that are not exclusive, the roots and branches with complex ramifications" that "situate her in the eyes of others," Bey brings together in a rich text the strands that ultimately make her singular—a woman who can be one thing and its opposite, at once *l'une et l'autre*—to open herself up to the differences in herself as well as the differences that single out others, all the others who find their place in her works of fiction. It is a courageous attitude, and an indispensable position for the writer who is Maïssa Bey: "I refuse to make mine the rejections and exclusions, imprecations and stigmatizations that are so quick to designate all those who are singular, who stand out" (54). The author who praises singularity in this way concludes her essay as she began it, giving place to a beautiful quotation. This one is taken from Édouard Glissant "to live an alterity starred with inheritances and horizons" (59). To be an exceptional writer, Bey shows us that it is necessary to be an extraordinary reader.

The specific location from which Bey writes, this precise place that is Algeria, has arguably had an overwhelming influence on the reader—and writer—she has become. While she is the only author in this study to still reside in Algeria at the time of this book's writing, this common birthplace has played an undeniable role in shaping the sensitivities of all French-language women writers born in Algeria during the time of French colonial rule. This land was characterized at this time by tremendous diversity, and yet by a total absence of the possible benefits that can come from such a rich mixture of customs, histories, languages, and religions, as Sebbar laments in *Lettres parisiennes,* Algeria was "a country where the French, Jews, Arabs, Berbers, Spanish, Italians, Corsicans, and Maltese are all gathered together, but where none of these communities of different confessions and cultures enrich themselves by intermingling" (82). It was undoubtedly this exposure to unprecedented possibility and the accompanying frustration of restrictive rules that brought these women to engage in a certain kind of innovative autobiographical writing, one that speaks of and seeks to break free from the ubiquitous limitations that prevented them as girls and young women from enjoying the cultural enrichment they so avidly sought in their country of origin. Despite, or perhaps because of, the negative aspects of their upbringing there, Algeria provided them with the takeoff points for composing unique testimonies in French, and the next section of *Polygraphies* will focus first on *pied-noir* author Marie Cardinal's work as it interacts and intersects with that of Cixous and Djebar, in textual explorations of the complicated relationships between the young autobiographical self, the mother, and the country of origin.

PART II Takeoff Points

CHAPTER 3 | La Terre Maternelle | Algeria and the Mother in the Work of Marie Cardinal, Hélène Cixous, and Assia Djebar

> *Every mother is wild. Wild in that she belongs to a memory older than she is, to a body more original than her own body.*—Anne Dufourmantelle, La sauvagerie maternelle *(Maternal savagery)*
>
> *Yes, that's it, my body is my mother ... I have the impression that my body belongs to my mother.*—Marie Cardinal, Autrement dit (In Other Words)
>
> *My beautiful land, my mother, my progenitor, how lowly and basely I lost you!* —Marie Cardinal, Au pays de mes racines *(In the country of my roots)*

La terre et la mère—the native land and the mother—arguably constitute *the* subjects of reflection at the heart of Marie Cardinal's oeuvre.[1] While homeland and family are central to most autobiographical works, these two themes of predilection are particularly striking in the case of this woman writer from Algeria. As a *pied-noir* child, born in 1929 to a French bourgeois family in Algiers, the young Cardinal lived for years between the two very different cultures that surrounded her, feeling part of neither one and yet earnestly desiring acceptance from both. The external environment of the multilingual, multiethnic "mother country" she inhabited clashed with her biological mother's distinctly "French" way of life and its complex value system related to class and religion. The competitive coexistence of these two mothers (one metaphorical, the other physical) is perhaps most salient in *Les mots pour le dire* (*The Words to Say It*), a novel that depicts the connections between a personified Algeria and the mother in explicit terms, as Françoise Lionnet demonstrates in detail in *Autobiographical Voices* (201).[2] While Cardinal's personal struggle to find her own identity in relation to these conflicting forces is unique, it is not the only one of its kind. As Colette Hall asserts, "This bi-culturalism, source of joy and conflict, is a sentiment Cardinal shares with other French writers from Algeria" (12–13). For diverse reasons and in different ways, Cixous and Djebar have also paid considerable attention to both mother and land, and Cardinal's work takes on new light and new resonance when placed alongside their essays and novels.

The autobiographical writings of these three women born in Algeria to very different mothers reveal that, whether their maternal lineage stems from France, Germany, or Algeria itself, Algerian-born women writers in French have relations to their native land that are complex and difficult to define. This birthplace is not exactly a "homeland"; instead, it is a place where not one of them has managed to fit in, where scholastic, linguistic, and political conditions have definitively barred "entry" into this elusive country. While it is certainly not the only reason these writers cannot gain access to this geographic site, the fact that they are *women* renders even more difficult the challenging task of belonging to this land. Despite its inaccessibility, all three writers claim that their roots are undeniably located in this tumultuous North African territory under French rule during their early years. For each of these writing subjects, it is in relation to land and mother that the complex underlying questions of nation and sex play themselves out. This chapter will address the specificity of the experience of each of these three Algerian-born women writers in an effort to determine in what ways the women's experience of the country in their formative years gave rise in each case to an inimitable autobiographical oeuvre in French.

In *Les mots pour le dire,* the narrator describes two worlds that seem diametrically opposed. There is the external world of the street, and the internal world of the mother. The narrator makes reference to the "harmful father planet" from which she is distanced in an upbringing limited to contact with women (63). But the ordered, regulated "mother planet" she inhabits as a youngster is not only different from the world of men; it can also be placed in contrast to the bustling, disorderly street. It is outside, walking the roads, that Marie comes into contact with the people, the sounds, and the smells of her native land that clash so vehemently with her education. Trekking to school each morning entails a trip between two worlds, as this passage reveals: "The traffic, the honking, the streetcar bells, the conductors who cursing each other out. . . . The street that has to be crossed in all this turmoil. . . . Paying attention to everything except to where I'm going, constantly bumping into the fig trees planted right in the middle of Rue Michelet. Getting to school, groggy, losing my balance, the contrast was too great! What I was taught did not correspond to what I saw. Charity, good habits, hygiene, manners! I understood that there were two ways of living, our own and theirs" (133–34). Later in the text, the narrator revisits the street to evoke her solo promenades at the age of ten: "That was the time when I was dizzily discovering the streets, knocking against the fig trees on the Rue Michelet because I didn't know how to walk by myself" (252).³ The lively street from these quotations stands out in marked contrast to the hygienic environment of home and school, and the difference is enough to make the young girl's head spin.

In recollections that bear a resemblance to those of Cardinal, Cixous evokes the particular environment of the French school in Algeria by indicating that she also was forced to live in what she calls "FrenchAlgeria," a single word that translates an attitude as much as a territory in *Les rêveries de la femme sauvage:* "In Algiers I fell into FrenchAlgeria, and that was the Lycée, my high school, against which I was powerless" (80). This scholastic experience is marked by separation and exclusion from the outside world. In Cixous's text, we find an echo of the "two lives" of Cardinal's description of a hermetically sealed academic atmosphere in a similar lack of reference to the outside world and a parallel mention of the exclusion of external surroundings in the tightly closed French school: "Never in the powder-puff Lycée did anyone mention the Algerian being. The word Algeria never sets foot here. Here in the Lycée, it is France, that is it was one great raving lie, which had taken over the whole place of truth, thus becoming the truth" (*Les rêveries* 84). Racial distinction is in this passage only alluded to with the addition of the adjective *poudré,* but the hygiene to which Cardinal makes reference in *Les mots pour le dire* extends beyond a simple cleaning to (an attempt at) complete erasure of ethnic and racial differences in the powdered Algeria of French creation, in the whitened FrenchAlgeria.⁴

The passages on school in Algeria are important to these autobiographical texts not only for what they reveal about the personal experience of education but also and especially for what they disclose about the educational project of the French in Algeria. For, if young students like Cardinal and Cixous felt alienated from the Algerian land of their birth, it is in large part because of the schooling they received. Attending French school meant adopting specific, prescribed precepts and exposing oneself to a single, rigid worldview, as the narrative comments of *Les rêveries de la femme sauvage* make clear. School served as a training ground for "French" citizens, and the process of inculcating certain national values in the context of the colonized Algerian territory was complicated and often ineffective, as expressed in the troublesome personal accounts of Algerian-born writers.⁵

In her short story "L'Affrance," whose title is a neologism, Cixous testifies to an awful reminiscence of humiliation and presumed guilt from her school days, a scene that in retrospect appears to be a trial with religious overtones: "The passwords are whispered before me: alms, missal. I don't dare say them. I am stuck to my chair and I have just gone pee-drop-by-drop unable to raise my hand. Holy water fount upside down. A pond. My neighbor denounces me, in a very Christian manner, to the authorities. Madame she is peeing. I want to die, but I cannot" (97). Unable to pronounce the appropriate words to acquit herself, not familiar with the language of expiation, she is condemned to soil herself, to commit this particular crime in front of a number of witnesses, and to be declared at fault immediately and publicly. Here it is a question of possessing the right vocabulary, of mastering the appropriate terminology, to be allowed to move from the public space to the private one devoted to relieving oneself. But this is a tongue that proves foreign to the young Cixous, who does not have the training—or the practice—to claim her rights and find her place in a French school system that is not without prejudice, and the narrative voice poses a probing rhetorical question that places Christianity in a continuum with the national motto of France: "Isn't France libertequalityfraternitychristianity?" (102).

In a reflection devoted to the relation between government and education,[6] Pierre Bourdieu addresses the way schools serve to structure mental processes, define and transmit culture, and create a national society: "The creation of national society is accompanied by the affirmation of universal educability: all individuals being equal before the law, the State must make them its citizens, endowed with the cultural means to actively exercise their civic rights" (*Raisons pratiques* 115). In this comparative study of national educational systems from Japan to England, Bourdieu ascertains that the French are less likely than others to openly address their ambition to communicate national values through education, preferring rather to mask the nationalist dimension of culture behind "universalist" principles (116). If the hidden national emphases of French educational enterprise described by Bourdieu are fraught with difficulty even within the hexagonal borders of contemporary France, they are practically unthinkable in Algeria. The "national" values taught at school are often in flagrant contradiction with the world the students inhabit, and it is this discrepancy that leads to identity crises not unlike those explored by Abdelmalek Sayad in *La double absence,* a careful analysis of the disillusionment and suffering of Algerian immigrants in France. Sayad's thoughts on nationalism and domination are relevant to the complex situation of the French presence in Algeria during the period of colonization. For, as he points out, education—understood in part as the transmission of national culture—quite literally makes an imprint on the educated person on numerous levels: "name, language, accent, and on a greater scale, all that is called 'culture,' a mark that is at once hidden and visible, that is inscribed in the body as well, in its gestures, postures, its ways of 'carrying the body and behaving with the body' (Bourdieu), the body being that which gives body to culture. The unease that we feel in our body and through our body finds its equivalent in the unease that we feel in our nationality or through our nationality" (*La double absence* 368). Sayad is addressing the specific situation of the immigrant, but his comments have meaning for those born in Algeria who experience similar dilemmas with respect to nationality. Sayad's attention to the ways in which a learned culture plays itself out in corporal terms is key, for the body is the site of visibility that reveals differences, whether racial, sexual, or cultural. In Cardinal's personal account of madness, the manifestation of her mental illness is *visibly visceral,* and it provides a crucial example of how she has inappropriately incorporated the lessons her mother—and her mother's culture—sought to inculcate in her. Before exploring the daughter's bodily dysfunction, however, I would like to examine the way the role of her mother echoes that of the educational system.

MATERNAL PERCEPTIONS AND PROJECTIONS:
LONGING FOR OTHERS

In *Les mots pour le dire,* Cardinal depicts the mother as an earnest Frenchwoman who fervently teaches her daughter the unbending rules of her belief system in terms that blur their social and religious origins. Some things are not done because members of the bourgeois class cannot stoop to such actions, and other things are not done because Catholics cannot betray their faith. Seemingly endless prohibitions are communicated through a simple, dismissive phrase: *"Ça ne se fait pas."*[7] This expression doesn't provide the young protagonist with any clarification as to the reasons behind these strict behavioral codes. And it is not just behavior that falls into this system of categorization, as the narrator explains: "The entire universe was definitively labeled, sorted and classified. By all means, don't reason or reflect, or call into question these values, since it would be a waste of time as it was impossible to end up with any other categories. Bourgeois values were alone in embodying the good, the beautiful and the intelligent, to such a point that I didn't even know they were called bourgeois values. For me, quite simply they were the only values" (242).[8] The need to define the world, to put things in their appropriate place and avoid unnecessary complications, is not only a bourgeois impulse; it is especially illustrative of the *mission civilisatrice* of the French colonizers who sought to bring religion and education to the indigenous peoples. These well-intentioned invaders hoped the colonized would benefit from their intervention, but *only to a point.* Complete integration into French society was never the goal—and certainly not the result—of colonization. If equality was supported in theory, it was never engaged in practice, and *Les mots pour le dire* provides evidence of ongoing exclusion.

While the mother's charitable activities provide her with a deep sense of purpose in Algeria, the extent of her magnanimity is limited. When Marie asks her if it would be possible to invite some Muslim children to their home, the response is unequivocal: "You do have a talent for asking stupid questions. What would people like that find to do here? They would be bored. They wouldn't feel at home." (116).[9] As well-to-do landowners in Algeria, Marie's family provides people with employment and assurance, but no more: "The workers were entirely under our protection. We shared everything, save blood, money, and land" (126). Workers living in such close proximity to their employers could not be called "family" or "countrymen," since they shared neither blood nor land. The complex resulting relationships of unacknowledged interdependence create strained relations among the "French" and the "Algerians."[10] This tension underlies two provocative instances of "maternal" longing that we will explore in a moment in the writings of Cixous and Djebar.

As she undergoes a psychoanalytic cure, the daughter in *Les mots pour le dire* comes to realize that her rigid mother is not "naturally" inclined toward self-abnegation and piety. Therapy inspires her to see her mother as a sensual being who suffered tremendous unexpressed pain and suffering due to years of stifled sexuality and repressed desires following her early divorce. Just as Cardinal insists in *Autrement dit* on the artificial, socially constructed nature of the abstract idea of "mother"[11] in the Western world, so the complete denial of the passions that characterizes the concrete, particular mother in *Les mots pour le dire* is an artifical imposition that is socially enforced. It is of little surprise in this familial context that the daughter's difficulties should manifest themselves corporeally.[12] Marie's perpetual bleeding is a bodily revolt not only against a stifling patriarchal system but also and especially against a woman's limited place within that system and the impossibility of breaking out, of forging new ground, of creating one's own territory.

The narrative voice in Cixous's *Les rêveries de la femme sauvage* speaks nostalgically of an unfulfilled desire to "enter" the country of her birth, to finally "arrive" in Algeria: "The whole time I was living in Algeria I would dream of one day arriving in Algeria, I would have done anything to get there" (3). Like the mother in *Les mots pour le dire,* the foreign-born mother depicted in *Les rêveries de la femme sauvage* has found a niche for herself that consists of serving the Algerian people. The activity she has chosen is a specific one; as a trained midwife running a clinic, she comes into contact with new life each day. A woman who lives in exile without the slightest remorse for her "rootlessness," this German mother is unaware of the pain her children feel in this country that is not their own: "my mother . . . did not see, structurally, that we were crazed and ill with our need of Algeria, with the inner reality of the country that was the country of our birth and not ours at all" (32). In contrast to this well-adjusted and industrious biological mother, a well-rounded and kindhearted adoptive mother stands out as the object of the young protagonists affections. Aïcha takes on mythic proportions in the text, and while these proportions admittedly have some problematic interpretations, they are nonetheless important to examine in Cixous's autobiographical work.

The portrait of Aïcha in *Les rêveries de la femme sauvage* is multifaceted. Cixous paints this woman first of all as much more "feminine," indeed more "motherly" than the young girl's own mother or grandmother: "it's a woman who is-the-woman and there is no other woman but Aïcha, neither my mother nor Omi being women, my mother is girlish with a touch of boy, Omi is an Osnabrück lady from a distinguished family of photographs, there is no woman among us that's why for my daily woman I wait for the fruit that comes to ripen every morning from the City of Algiers" (52). While her mother and grandmother are not "really" women, Aïcha is "fully" woman. From the perspective of the young girl, this individual embodies femininity in ways that her female relatives do not. Aïcha is also mysterious, since she is unable to speak more than a few words in French and therefore has recourse to other means of communication, notably that of *body language:* "a woman of great beauty who knew a few French words all the other words were in her eyes in her hands in her laughter" (53). As an Algerian woman, Aïcha represents her land, and her openness to the young girl's caresses leads to the following statement of equivalence: " the person of Aïcha, for that is the only Algeria that I was ever able to touch" (51). In the analysis of Verena Andermatt Conley, Aïcha is indeed a figure for Algeria itself: "It is through the character of Aïcha, the cleaning help, that Algeria slips into the text. The country as geographical space is metamorphosed into a woman . . . Woman-body, she is the only Algeria the author ever knew" (51).[13] Aïcha is the tangible incarnation of the "untouchable" country, a meaningful and complex mother figure whose identity blends with Algeria. Rather than constituting a simple preference for the more shapely form of the Aïcha, the positive portrayal of this individual reflects an overwhelming desire to know Algeria, a country that has affected the writer to the core of her *corps*.

The passages focusing on Aïcha as a contrast to the women of her own family—among whom "a discreet virility" holds sway (90)—take on special significance if we read them in the context of Cixous's larger oeuvre, for they reveal a complicated, evolving relationship to women's bodies in Cixous's textual creations. While it would be easy to assume that this depiction of the character named Aïcha risks falling into the trap of exoticism, I would argue that a much more complex process is involved in Cixous's representation of this beloved woman. Cixous is knowingly framing her portrait of this individual in Orientalist terms, most obviously in her comparison to a piece of fruit in the previous quotation, and a work of art, as in the following assertion: "What is left of 'Aïcha' who died long ago: volumes and volumes. Art. 'Algeria' as a name caressing the untouchable" (*Les rêveries* 52). But this text problematizes this perspective by revealing a deep desire to really know *this person*. She is recognized and appreciated for her singularity as well, and is not seen simply as a member of a larger group, or a resident of the particular location she hails from. While Aïcha is indeed the closest connection to the elusive country for the young girl who ardently wishes to become familiar with this place and its people, she is *not only* important to Cixous because of this status. Ronnie Scharfman has explained the significance of Aïcha in the context of the writer's personal experience as "perpetual outsider" in the Algeria she longs to know intimately: "This fact of birth, the mark of the perpetual outsider desiring to be fused with Algeria, with the Algerian Other, with Algeria as Mother's body, contributed to Cixous's eventual feminist stance its passion that is both ecstasy and suffering. For the young girl, this passion is displaced onto surrogate female figures expressed in her wanting to possess the family's housekeeper Aicha, the one Arab woman in her life with whom she shares a physical, if not erotic, intimacy" (98).

It is true that little is known about this fascinating person, and the narrative voice reveals a deep regret over what remains secret about her. An important "corrective" occurs in this work, when Aïcha's name turns out to be a wrong redressed at a crucial point in her textual (re)presentation, for it is only now that the narrator discovers that she didn't even know how Aïcha was called: "Now we all know that Aïcha was really called Messaouda. But too late" (*Les rêveries* 53). This moment of revelation as to the real "identity" of the other mother, of this desired woman, this indication of her true name points to the veritable goal of the writing project. Aïcha is evoked not as an idealized mother whose attributes are imagined, but as the other as *truly other,* someone whose attributes will never be fully known (in the same way as Cixous's biological mother's characteristics are never completely understood, and serve as literary inspiration in text after text). The written work is not intended to "essentialize" this "other mother" as an exotic being who is just the same as any other from her country. It is instead meant to highlight the particularities of a woman who played a special, unique role in the consciousness of the narrator as a young girl. Perhaps it is not too late to learn the real name of this person after all, for her name is preserved in the writing of the text, and the wrong of the misnomer is rectified in the sincere autobiographical account.

It is important to note that Messaouda, the true name of the woman Cixous depicts as such a sought-after figure in her autobiographical fiction, is also the name of a significant individual in Assia Djebar's textual explorations of Algerian women in her collection of short stories titled *Femmes d'Alger dans leur appartement* (*Women of Algiers in Their Apartment*). In the short story "Regard interdit, son coupé" ("Forbidden Gaze, Severed Sound"), a young girl named Messaouda "spurs the fleeing men of her village to turn around and fight the invading army by involuntarily exposing her body to the would-be conquerors" (Weber-Fève xxvi). What is especially meaningful about Messaouda's heroic gesture in the insightful analysis of Stacey Weber-Fève is that it allows Djebar to "call into question the cultural erasure of representations (or social constructions) of Algerian women beyond that of the mother" (xxvi). Djebar thus inserts the story of the *Song of Messaouda* into her text in order to move beyond the mother, in a sense, and "tease out multiple theoretical interrogations of women's contemporary representations, ideologies, subjectivities, and identities" (xxvi), and this is made possible in part thanks to an understanding of "the importance of communal language (or oral discourse) as these songs and legends are passed inside traditional, indigenous female communities" that Djebar explores in her literary work (xxvi).

It could be argued that Djebar has a greater claim to the country of her birth than Cardinal and Cixous, due to the fact that her ancestors inhabited this land long before her. But this argument might be difficult to uphold, and it could be counter-argued that Djebar's relation to her native land is just as complicated as that of others, perhaps more so. The difficulty she experiences in writing (of) Algeria is expressed in such statements as "I do not call you mother, bitter Algeria" (*Vaste est la prison* 358) and such questions as "how to write violent Algeria?" ("Le roman maghrébin francophone" 197). Immersing herself in the French language and steeping herself in French culture ultimately separated her from her own people, in many senses, transforming her into *"la visiteuse," "l'invitée,"* or even *"étrangère"* among her own, as she reveals in the account of her return to the city of her childhood in *La femme sans sépulture* (The woman without a sepulcher).

The strained relation between Djebar and her native country is perhaps best illustrated in a story that echoes the longing for another mother, for a mother "other," similar to the desire expressed in Cixous's writing. The narrator of *Vaste est la prison* reminisces about a night of bombing in her hometown: "That night when the tumult was unable to wake me up completely, that night became one of transmutation. The mother and her boy, the 'French,' were of course neighbors on the same floor but also the closest representatives of 'the other world' for me: 'they,' this couple sprung from the dark and stretched out there in the open for me to see, had taken my parents' place!" (268). Just as the young "French" girl of *Les rêveries de la femme sauvage* is fascinated with Aïcha because this substitute mother represents the "other world," so the young "Algerian" girl is mesmerized by this substitute French mother who is suddenly, miraculously brought closer by the breaking down of barriers. The excitement of this replacement is enhanced because, as in Cixous's work of fiction, this new mother possesses more "mature," "matronly" characteristics than her original, biological counterpart: "The excitement of an unknown world, a new mother (the neighbor did of course seem older, more of a 'matron' than my mother, who was then scarcely more than twenty), no, that is not familiar either. The nearness of this twelve-year-old boy with whom I would sometimes play in the afternoon in the park and who seemed to me a young man, this unexpected familiarity provided an ambiguity and keen pleasure that I can deal with more readily" (*Vaste est la prison* 268). This woman fulfills the young girl's dream of a mother, incorporating all the values taught in school and serving as the living representative of France itself.[14] Anna Kemp points out that "what is particular to France" "is the way in which a certain idea of the French woman is married to national interests, and indeed to national pride" (55). While this observation pertains to the current climate within France, Kemp's argument that the "desirable

French woman is an established part of the French brand" has relevance for the excited way in which Djebar views this "new mother" who is suddenly thrust into the intimacy of her home.

As Ania Loomba reminds us in her work on colonialism and postcolonialism, "national fantasies" often "play upon and with the connections between women, land or nations" (215). While these passages taken from works by Cixous and Djebar seem to subscribe to the idea that women are equivalent to "national emblems" (216) and as such are usually cast as mothers or wives, the conclusions we can draw from these passages are not so simple.[15] To the contrary, complex processes are at work in the imagined "reversals" of mothers and the girls' embrace of the "other" as "mother" constitutes a conciliatory gesture of acceptance and understanding in the midst of a highly divided, racially complex situation in Algeria. The desire for reconciliation in the form of physical proximity and affection as expressed in motherly touch is a powerful reaction to the tense relations in this fraught land.[16] Cixous and Djebar, in their different treatments of a similar theme, are ultimately reacting in their writing against what Pierre Bourdieu, influenced by Thomas Bernhard, refers to as *"corps 'étatisés,'"* bodies formed and governed by the nation ("Preface" 12), by pointing out how their own bodies were codified and categorized, and expressing their desire to transcend these divisive classifications by becoming intimately familiar with other bodies, as close as they would be with a mother.

In *Les mots pour le dire,* the daughter does not wish for another mother. Unlike the girls in the autobiographical fiction of Cixous and Djebar who dream of maternal figures who at once represent the unattainable land of the "other," and who possess more "feminine" characteristics in accordance with interpretations of that other, the girl in this autobiographical account imagines *herself* as other. She envisions herself as more obedient, as a better student, as a more acceptable daughter. Instead of desiring a more "feminine" mother, she strives to be more "feminine" herself, in accordance with strict, arbitrary rules that declare for instance that mathematics is not a subject in which girls should excel.[17] The impossibility of attaining unrealistic ideals of femininity according to the class and religion of her mother leads to her ongoing corporeal rebellion in the form of constant blood loss, of continual menstruation. Given her guilt and remorse for failing to attract the affection and attention of her mother, and given her attribution of this failure to an inability to live up to rules, the resulting bodily upheaval seems perfectly predictable. It constitutes, in a metaphorical sense, a rejoining of the earth, a reconnecting to the native land where so much blood has been shed in the course of French colonization, and where so much blood will flow during the war that will rock the country after Marie's departure.

What the infamous bleeding from Marie Cardinal's intimate story suggests is an innermost desire for *movement* that is best expressed not in passages where she walks the streets but rather in textual moments that evoke the sea. The French homophone for mother represents the possible connection between Algeria and the mother, the imagined fusion of self and other, as well as resolution of the conflicting forces that tear the narrator in different directions. A poetic invitation to slip into the sea reveals how the body of water allows the human body to move freely and simply, without restriction: "Come, look at us, don't take your eyes off me. We are going to go into the waves. I know a passage made of white sand where you won't get hurt, where you will just be able to let yourself go. Remember, my soft one, my beauty, that the sea is good if you are not afraid. She only wants to lick you, caress you, carry you, rock you, allow her to do it and you'll like her. Otherwise she will scare you" (218). The relaxation, the letting go that is an integral part of this evocative passage is something that the young Marie was never allowed to indulge in. Careful curbing of her every desire constantly pulled her from the pleasures that her native country had to offer, the bodily pleasures described here, in this fleshly contact with the sea. Shut up within the walls of school, church, and home, she was unable to take full advantage of the natural environment around her, of this *"pays chaud"* where *"volupté"* reigns. Bathing in the Mediterranean has whetted her palate for the joys of giving in to physical pleasure: "the sea, the beach, the warm wind, the freedom of the body that gives itself to the sea, allowing itself to be caressed and carried by her" (212). It has provided her with a foretaste of the delights of writing, an activity that engages the body in rhythmic reflection, as this poetic passage demonstrates. While the mother is arguably *present* in this writing (both thematically and linguistically), textual composition is something that goes *beyond* the mother, that leaves her behind in a certain sense, since the mother herself never wrote. In this way, Cardinal joins the other two writers in this study in treading new ground, in venturing into the unexplored land of literary creation that extends beyond the mother's reach and forms an identity outside the realm of familial control.

The sea is a recurrent metaphor in Cardinal's work—as evidenced in the very title of her first novel, *Ecoutez la mer* (Listen to the sea)—that carries with it the hope of eliminating borders, breaking down walls, and facilitating passage.[18] Indeed, moving between countries and cultures became a way of life for Cardinal after leaving her native Algeria. Subsequent to this departure, Cardinal cannot be said to have "settled down," nor can she be said to have "settled" for any single stable national adhesion. Instead, she moved about, becoming a woman of "double exile," if one is to take seriously the words of a critic for *Le Monde*.[19] It seems that, like Assia Djebar, who describes herself in *Vaste est la prison* and *Ces voix qui m'assiègent* as a "Fugitive without knowing it" (*Vaste* 171), and Hélène Cixous, who proclaims "The fugitive. It was I . . . the fugitive was she was I" ("La Fugitive" 82; la fuie moi), Marie Cardinal is also a sort of "fugitive" whose roots are terrestrial, leading back always to the place of birth, but whose flight is, if not celestial, one that nonetheless always leads to new heights. The wings of the pen create a sense of belonging that exceeds that of national, sexual, or even familial classification. These three writers, in unique ways, draw from their experiences of land and mother to carve out their own transnational spaces. Their diverse autobiographical works find inspiration ever new in two places summed up in the words of Assia Djebar: "Writing and Algeria as territories" (*Ces voix* 274).

GENDERED IMMOBILITIES OR VULNERABLE VELOCITIES: BREAKING AWAY FROM THE PAST

In her careful reading of Djebar's oeuvre published under the significant title *Assia Djebar: Out of Algeria,* Jane Hiddleston pinpoints the importance of movement to the writer's work, explaining the "evocation of the fugitive as a common motif" as follows: "Feminine identity is not rooted in a specific place but is endlessly mobile and subject to renewal. Characters derive a sense of self not from habitation and belonging but precisely from their ability to break away from home and roots" (100). Djebar's privileging of the fugitive is related to a childhood marked by restricted movement, even though her education allowed her to circulate outside the home long after the age when her female cousins had been sequestered. The fact that she could not move about outside as she pleased is most powerfully illustrated in her recollection of a particularly striking incident from her early childhood.

In *Nulle part dans la maison de mon père,* Djebar reconstructs a scene from a peaceful location, a particular square where the children of schoolteachers had the unique privilege of being able to run and play together, in the "temporary ignorance of their differences" (47). This idyllic reconstruction is disturbed by an annoying noise, according to the narrative voice, when she recalls her desire to climb onto a bicycle for the first time, at the age of four or five, and what is a positive recollection then becomes "wound, scratch" in Djebar's terms (48; blessure, griffure). Seated on the bicycle, the young girl's efforts to learn to pedal were curtailed when her father's voice erupted, from out of nowhere: "I do not want my daughter to show her legs while riding a bicycle!" (49). Just as with the scene of the attempted suicide, this aborted effort to learn to ride a bike is returned to in textual terms in a cyclical manner, and the narrator testifies to the fact that she is still standing trial for her actions in her father's tribunal: "He hails me at present. He calls me before the ancestral tribunal of the interdict against the fair sex, at the age of five—or three, or four—until puberty, until the wedding night, when this heavy right will be given over to the first husband, to the second if need be, but he will finally be able to breathe, the father, each other. He will put down the obscure, obscene burden of the necessity of invisibility. In my case, it was that of my little legs filled with desire to spin the wheels of a bicycle" (55). The rhythm of the long, single sentence that makes up most of this passage seems to be in accord with the breathless, frightened state of the girl who has been indelibly affected by her father's verbal outrage. In this portion of the text, she puts together fragmentary strands of a willowy sentence that speaks of her subjugation first to her father, then to her husband, in a system that shut off all possibility of fluidity, of freedom of movement that her little legs so desired.

This autobiographical reminiscence reveals that Djebar has "scrupulously respected the patriarchal interdict," and has never attempted to ride a bicycle again (52), but the text testifies to a yearning for mobility that revisits the forbidden bicycle and allows her to transgress more than one rule in an emancipatory ride:

> Oh yes, I am free, and my legs are not only carrying me, making me run, but they are activating a machine, a *velocipede,* a bicycle not even for a girl, for a boy, that finally takes me across the city and its big street, that allows me to cover the main street in every direction, in front of the Moorish cafes at one end to the brasseries full of European men at the other, yes, rolling like this in front of them all, from the school to the town hall, from the town hall to the train station and, while I'm at it, continuing to pedal again and again, crossing, this time on a professional vehicle, all the villages of the Sahel, one after the other, until I reach Césarée, the ancestral city, the door of my maternal grandmother, rue Jules-César! (58)

Here again, we find a single sentence that extends well over one hundred words, revealing the jubilation of the rider, and writer, who declares her freedom at length, in an exclamation of joy caught up in the movement of the wheels that propel her past all the boundaries, especially those connected to gender. For her relationship to her father was forever changed when he denied her the right to move her legs in this manner: "All that I retained from his resonant phrase, like a steel arrow resounding between us, were two words in Arabic: 'her legs'" (49). Because of the incident with the bicycle, her connection to her father—and her homeland—was critically altered.

It is significant that in Cixous's autobiographical account it was a bicycle that suddenly disrupted her close relationship to her brother in an Algeria, where neither one felt they belonged. As we have already seen, the particular circumstances of her Algerian childhood excluded Cixous from any community. Every articulation of the word *nous* was unpronounceable: "I note: I am on the outside of my house, I am nostalgic for what will never exist, there is no judgment, I am outside all the us's, all the us's go by like tanks crushing earthworms with their treads. If I survive, I shall tell all—to no one" (*Les rêveries* 65). The lack of solidarity in this lamentation of the young protagonist points toward the *new* solitude she is now condemned to experience. She had not always been completely alone in this Algeria that she claims excludes her from *"tous les nous."* Before, there was the tight *nous* of the brother-and-sister, of this young couple of accomplices who sought to discover their country together, as two inseparable beings. But a barrier has come up between the young girl and her double that will forever separate them with respect to Algeria: "Between us the gate. Us? I mean that other us that the gate began separuniting into those small daily agonies which are for us—my brother-what's-left-of-the-Dog-and-me-the-spirit-or-the-genius-of-the-Clos-Salembier—and for me the epitome of my Disalgeria" (*Les rêveries* 39). This remarkable passage is filled with innovative textual gestures that illustrate the point Cixous is making. The creation of a neologism in the contradictory verb "separuniting" (*sépareunir*) finds its parallel in the brother-sister pair composed of hyphenation that both separates and unites the various descriptors that make them up. The separation that splits in two the formerly singular entity of the young girl and her brother finds form in a fateful gift that is destined for both of them: a bicycle. This vehicle, this mode of transportation, these wheels that promise movement, displacement, travel through the unknown country, have a defect that provoke the brother's dismay: it is

La Terre Maternelle 75

a *girl's* bike. The ironic nature of this present consists in the fact that the brother ends up accepting it and using it whereas the sister deprives herself of it: "This bike was our lot: to my brother it gives Algeria, from the very day after the famous day, to me: nothing" (*Les rêveries* 29). It is the paradoxical gesture of not wanting to appropriate an object obviously destined for someone of her gender that deprives the young female protagonist of the mobility the gift was meant to bestow.

When the adult brother speaks of this critical aspect of their past in this work of fiction, he insists that this simple machine gave him freedom along with an intimate knowledge of the country, while his sister's refusal kept her from making any discoveries outside the home: "From that day and during those final years all you ever did was work, work, I told myself and not live and I from the vantage point of the Bike I knew I was soaring over the Clos-Salembier and our common and respective chains. And Algeria I knew it" (*Les rêveries* 12). In this brief passage, we see a characteristic lack of punctuation in the first sentence fragment that seems to reflect the message of movement and continuity that the bicycle gave to the brother who knew how to ignore its prescriptive nature and take advantage of the possibilities it offered for freedom beyond the restrictions of his and his sister's native land. It allowed him to discover their mutual birthplace in obvious ways that immobility did not. The retrospective analysis of the narrative voice agrees with the brother, for instead of living with the wind in her face, the young protagonist isolated herself in total solitude: "That bike really drove a wedge between us, I thought, up to then we were just one brother with an internal sister and vice versa now I was nothing but a sister with no internal brother, and as my brother says I for my part burrowed deeper and deeper into *my solitary reveries*" (30).

SOLITARY REVERIES: THE INTERSTICES OF FICTION AND AUTOBIOGRAPHICAL WRITING

The words Cixous places in italics, *rêveries solitaires,* do not leave any doubt as to the title of her novel, *Les rêveries de la femme sauvage.* Instead of carrying the name *Le ravin de la femme sauvage* to refer to a geographical location in Algeria,[20] a slip of the tongue, a *lapsus,* has given place to an intertextual reference to the celebrated book by Jean-Jacques Rousseau. The ravine yields its place to the text, and the real landscapes blur into the background as dreamed landscapes take over the Cixousian imagination. Indeed, the solitary reveries of the great admirer of Rousseau are influenced as much by interior promenades that consist of reading as by the exterior views that she renounced when she declined to make use of the bicycle. The first words of Rousseau's well-known work find a place in Cixous's fiction in the following paragraph, where they are surrounded by a context that is far removed from that of the work's origin:

> But what does Jewish mean wondered the Dog, and Arab, and dog, friend, brother, enemy, Papa, liberty nothing exists save injustice and brutality. *Here I am, alone on the earth, having no more brother, sister, no father nearby, no friend only my solitude for company. The most sociable and loving of beings is unanimously outlawed. I am caged as in a dream and I don't sleep anymore. And I, detached from them and tied to a strand of wire, what am I?* And I, I thought, I never shone any light on his darkness. . . . I only thought about fleeing this country of chained-up creatures, that chain of chainings-up, the unleashing of the chained-up who in their turn start chaining. (*Les rêveries* 44)

The discrimination suffered by all of those excluded from Algerian society resembles the ostracism Rousseau deplores. The solitude the philosopher experienced on the Island of Saint-Pierre finds an echo two centuries later in the miseries of the multiple victims of prejudice in Algeria. When the narrator evokes the circles of chains in this tautological passage on the country of her childhood, she shows that she has traits in common with the singular writer who indicates that he loves to "define himself" in a specific way in *Les rêveries du promeneur solitaire* (*The Reveries of a Solitary Walker*): "a man who loves to circumscribe himself; for I am perhaps the only one in the world whose destiny has made this a law" (Rousseau 85).[21] Cixous's personal experience, as it is presented in her work, shows that Rousseau is not the only one whom destiny has influenced. Her writing also shows that he is not the only one who likes to "circumscribe himself": Cixous "turns around" the details of her own life in numerous publications in a manner that is reminiscent of Djebar's circular textual creation in *Nulle part dans la maison de mon père*, as we have already seen.

Cixous finds literary inspiration not only in Rousseau's *Les rêveries du promeneur solitaire* but also in his *Confessions*. Nonetheless, in contrast to the search for real sins and crimes actually committed that are related with care in this founding text of the autobiographical genre, the author of the essay "Coming to Writing" confesses to crimes that are only imagined: "I beat up children. The Enemy's little ones" (19). She goes even further in this textual violence to make avowals of acts that, though unthinkable, are nevertheless a part of the cruel Algerian environment that surrounds her:

La Terre Maternelle

"I killed. I tortured. I struck, cheated, stole. In dreams. Sometimes in reality. Guilty? Yes. Not guilty? Yes. Colonized, I decolonized. Bit, ate, vomited up. And was punished, punished. Spanked. My curls shorn, my eyes put out" (19).[22] Her confession of guilt here—even if she refers to transgression that only took place in her imagination—is touching, especially in its resonance with her testimony with respect to the aforementioned tramway scene. The intense culpability she experienced upon witnessing another commit suicide may be connected to a more general feeling of responsibility for a situation that is nonetheless beyond her control. Since she considers herself punished without having committed a crime, Cixous mentions wrongdoing that is clearly made up, thus obscuring the boundaries between what is real and what is imagined. Cixous may find encouragement for this gesture in Rousseau's reflections on his afternoon walks: "Finally finding myself brought back by degrees to myself and to what surrounded me, I could not mark out the point separating the fictions from the realities" (*The Reveries of a Solitary Walker* 70). This difficulty in separating fictions from realities is an undeniable aspect of Cixous's oeuvre, one that Derrida celebrates in a number of reflections on her work. In particular, he identifies one of Cixous's numerous neologisms, *rêvexiste*, as crucial to understanding her literary innovations ("H. C." 138). By employing this conception of *rêvexistence* in her writing, Cixous shows herself to be very close to Rousseau, for whom reveries were often more memorable than real events.

Derrida is right to emphasize the inscription of the dream in Cixous's oeuvre. The mixture of real and dream in her texts is exemplary of a writing that dares to engage seriously with the imaginary, crossing over borders and denying all generic classification, as Derrida observes: "The nullification of the border, this passage of the forbidden between the public and the private, the visible and the hidden, the fictional and the real, the interpretable and the unreadable of an absolute reserve, like the collusion of all genres, I believe, is at work at every moment. It is the very work of her writing, its operation and its opus, which, although literary through and through, also goes beyond literature, just as it goes beyond autobiography" ("H. C." 12). If these writings do not conform to any categorization, it is in part because they yield to what is often removed from the literary text: reveries. But the enormous importance of these cerebral activities, of these mental promenades that marked her childhood, planted the roots for fertile creation: "I do not deny that not having taken advantage of the extraordinary opening on the world that the Bike held I did not in fact get to know Algeria, while maintaining that I never stopped dreaming of exploration and discovery" (*Les rêveries* 13). Her incessant dreams served as an apprenticeship for an imaginary life that transcends reality.

After long digressions on the bicycle that allowed the boy to explore the country while the girl devoted herself to work and to dreams, the narrative voice poses the question hidden behind this entire conversation between the grown siblings: "But what does it mean to know—I say—Algeria, sitting beside my brother, tracking his silences" (*Les rêveries* 51). She testifies to the fact that even a lack of memory constitutes a sort of memory, to the hope that even a faulty knowledge can be a kind of knowledge: "That which doesn't remind reminds, I say and not-to-know Algeria is also to know it" (51). The complexity of truly knowing the country of her childhood is also tied to the fact that everyone may know this land differently, for there are a number of *Algerias* in Algeria (89). The frustration the narrator feels as a girl stems from the fact that the country and the city she dreams of knowing are off-limits to her: "I wanted to be on their side . . . I only wanted their City and their Algeria" (24). This dream remains unrealized, for the doors in front of the young Jewish girl are always slammed in her face.

Instead of blaming those who exclude her from Algerian society, the young girl feels guilty, blaming herself beyond measure for being on the wrong side of the door in the neighborhood where she spends her teenage years in Algiers: "How far can one go with the blows one administers oneself with respect to a closed door is something I experienced almost every week in the Clos-Salembier" (*Les rêveries* 65). Despite many refusals, despite repeated disappointments, she remains optimistic and spends her childhood dreaming of eventual entrance into the country of her birth: "Heart pounding I don't give up even today I keep watch perhaps a door will open in the City of Algiers if I rap hard enough at my mother's memory even now I skirt the wall, I run my fingers over it and I dream of entering into the country of which I am the stubborn abortion" (*Les rêveries* 55). The lack of punctuation in this sentence reveals the obstinacy—and the breathlessness—with which the first-person narrator insists on her passionate attempts to finally gain entry into the place she so desires to intimately know. She has experienced rejection innumerable times, but the hope is still alive that she will finally find herself within the walls that prematurely expelled her, in the womb of her country.

Cixous's mention of abortion in this powerful passage, and her reference to herself as a child who has been aborted in Algeria, immediately brings to mind Cardinal's written account of her mother's literal attempt to abort her in *Les mots pour le dire*. The first-person narrator explains that her mother's confession enabled her to take an important step during her psychoanalytic cure. Thanks to this crucial piece of information about her prenatal past, she is able to return to a time when she was still in her mother's womb, in order to come to terms with the deep-seated feelings that caused her panic and paralysis: "Without my mother's acknowledgement I might never have succeeded in going back to the womb, returning to that hated and pursued fetus, which, without knowing it, I had found when I curled up between the bidet and the tub in the obscurity of the bathroom" (140–41). The insight her mother's avowal provided her is arguably the focal point of Cardinal's autobiographical text, and the author addresses the writing process in the lengthy interview-turned-book titled *Autrement dit*. She explains that what occupied a larger part of her sessions with her psychoanalyst was a preoccupation with her mother's physical abuse during her early years; her mother had dealt her real blows, and had harmed her body on various occasions, and this part of her past was more detrimental to her, in her estimation, than the unsuccessful abortion attempt. What is noteworthy, however, is that that this attempt became much more significant when it came to the book: "in writing about it, it became enormous, it occupied a formidable place" (21). Cardinal made the abortion attempt the central focus of the book, even though it did not occupy this status in her own mind. In her reflections on this choice, she demonstrates that she is aware that remaining entirely faithful to lived experience does not necessarily make for compelling works of literature. She asserts that her autobiographical text is much more moving because of its emphasis on the attempted abortion than it would be if she had chosen to concentrate on the beatings she received, even if these were ultimately more difficult for her to overcome. For her, the failed abortion carried greater symbolic weight: "It best marked the rejection of the daughter" (21).

Reflecting on the selectivity and the focus she has chosen for *Les mots pour le dire* gives Cardinal the opportunity to make a statement about autobiographical writing in general: "We are already far from the truth, and yet fully within it. When I write, I always begin with something that I know, that I have lived, then it transforms, opens up, rambles; the 'I' could become 'she,' but 'she' is more myself than 'I.' 'I' is a mask" (21). Cardinal's provocative assertion that the "she" is more herself than "I" reveals a great deal about autobiographical confessions, and the covers that authors may choose to dissimulate certain truths that can possibly emerge just the same.

In her opinion, she occupied a particular stance with respect to her own past when she wrote this book: "It is in the persona of the writer that I saw this story, not in the persona of the witness" (20). It may be accurate that she desired to make the text more "literary" than strictly testimonial, but Cardinal's text nonetheless bears witness, relating in literary terms her deeply painful early experiences in a particular familial situation within colonial Algeria. While it might not constitute a valid statement for a witness stand in a court of law, this written work is a powerful testimony that just may change the way we read history, in accordance with Sebbar's assertion that works of fiction have unusual staying power: "I hang onto that memory by transporting it into fiction, so as not to lose it. Fiction becomes a landscape unaided by history" (*Lettres parisiennes* 98).

Cixous's personal geography is rich with the history of a dispersed people, as she affirms in "La venue à l'écriture": "I have no roots: from what sources could I take in enough to nourish a text? Diaspora effect" (15). The rhetorical question she poses here finds its answer in numerous textual reflections on the two geographical poles her parents hail from. In her comments on her family history, Cixous explains that her father is from the west. In *Photos de racines* (*Rootprints*), she indicates that this Spanish point of reference provides her with a unique sense of direction, reorienting her with respect to her birthplace: "Geography of my genealogical memory: I stand at the edge of North Africa. On its beach. To my left, that is, to the West, my paternal family—which followed the classic trajectory of the Jews chased from Spain to Morocco" (182). Despite his undeniable role in her life, this paternal "genealogical memory" does not occupy as consequential a place as that taken up by the writer's mother, whose role as a midwife takes on special significance in light of the literal and metaphorical importance of abortion in works by women writers from Algeria. In Cixous's autobiographical text, this woman's past materializes in the reveries of her daughter's childhood to such an extent that the landscapes of the mother's native country merge with the landscapes that surround the girl in Algeria.

The country of Cixous's birth, where both her person and her writing originated, has two faces for the writer, made up of two sets of memories that are almost contradictory, and yet, somehow, complementary: "I have a childhood with two memories. My own childhood was accompanied and illustrated by the childhood of my mother. The German childhood of my mother came to recount and resuscitate itself in my childhood like an immense North in my South.... Consequently, although I am profoundly

Mediterranean of body, of appearance, of jouissances, all my imaginary affinities are Nordic" (*Photos de racines* 181). This passage reinforces the point to which Cixous is influenced by the "dreams" of her childhood. The double landscape of these early years contains climactic extremes, ranging from the heat of her native land to the cold of her mother's country: "On the one hand there was North Africa, a powerfully sensual body, that I shared, bread, fruit, odours, spices, with my brother. On the other hand existed a landscape with the snow of my mother" (196).[23] In Oran, the young girl inhabits two cities at once: "I was the child of two cities. Oran my native city which I adored. Osnabrück, city of the childhood of my mother, native city of Omi. I imagine Osnabrück" (201). The dream of the maternal city is so vivid that Cixous admits that she doesn't know if she has actually been there or not: "I have a memory problem: I do not know if I went to Osnabrück or if I did not go" (201). During a visit to Germany with her grandmother, it is possible that the fifteen-year-old adolescent stepped foot in this city imagined so many times, but it isn't certain: "I have the feeling I went to Osnabrück with Omi. I seem to see the streets. But I do not know if I dreamed it. Everything seems to me. . . . Osnabrück—if I went—remains dreamed. I cannot know" (202). In her view, the dream saves us from the necessity of knowing: "But there are dreams, this marvelous ruse that saves us from faith from knowledge and from reason" (*Portrait* 46). Cixous underscores in these reflections the impossibility of knowing, but this lack of certainty does not remove in any sense the powerful impact of these images of the German city. The experience of the young girl shows that our reality is not limited to the places where we have lived; memory is made beginning with a compelling mixture of things seen with the naked eye and things seen in a dream, of events witnessed in person and events we have only heard about. In Cixous's writing, the place accorded to reveries provides a glimpse of the extent to which our lives are composed of these moments that exist outside the strict boundaries of "logic," of these incalculable instants found on the border between being awake and asleep, between life and death.

The multiple prejudices that inhibit her in the colonized Algeria of her childhood make Cixous perceptive to victims of every race and every social class, in every society, in her writing. Cixous has experienced racism not only on a personal and social level, but also on an official, governmental level. If the first years of her life as she describes them appear to be a piece of paradise, all of that changes with the loss of her French citizenship in 1940 under Vichy. Suddenly, school is off-limits to her: "In Oran, I had a very strong feeling of paradise, even while it was the war and my family was hit from all sides: by the concentration camps in the North, by Vichy in Algeria. My father was forbidden to practice medicine, we lost French nationality, we were excluded from the public school" (*Photos de racines* 196). The *nous* in this quotation, this collectivity banished from the French school, is suddenly larger than her family. This "we" does exist, finally, even if it makes its appearance at the most painful moment, and this is what inexorably ties Cixous to Derrida, who also experienced this *"Désalgérie"* of Jews born in Algeria: "former children of said-to-be-Jews-born-in-Algeria whose book of memories had been inaugurated by similar events, events of war" (*Portrait* 4).

As she explores all that they have in common in *Portrait de Jacques Derrida en jeune saint juif* (*Portrait of Jacques Derrida as a Young Jewish Saint*), Cixous draws attention to the "stigmata," to the "scars" that have made an indelible imprint on them. Indeed, Cixous's exploration of the body (both hers and Jacques Derrida's) and its relationship to Algeria has become a recurring theme in her recent work. It is important to note that the ills from which she suffers during her childhood are not purely physical, of course; the *"maladie algérie"* she describes in *Les rêveries de la femme sauvage* also affects the heads of the young girl and her brother, as they are driven mad by the circumstances of their surroundings (16). In a personal itinerary that moves from Oran to Algiers, it is this second urban space that represents the apogee of the incurable sickness that is synonymous with this country for Cixous: "According to my mother Germany is incurable, according to me the City of Algiers as crowning point and metaphor for all of Algeria is the incurable one" (*Les rêveries* 22). Despite her definitive departure, her final flight, Cixous cannot leave behind her country of origin. She can leave Algeria, but Algeria will not leave her: "I can't stop coming from Algeria" ("La Fugitive" 79). The repetition of this idea underscores its importance, and her luck: "I come from. I want to come from. I come from Algeria. She gave me points of departure and I took them" ("La Fugitive" 76). She has made the most of what was in many ways a negative point of departure, in order to have a more lucid appreciation of her environment in France: "It's not that I think I see what I don't see, it's that I think what I see and I see what the French do not see" (*Les rêveries* 64). By her own account, the unique vision of Hélène Cixous finds its roots in Algeria. It is in large part thanks to this birthplace that the writer has such a new perspective on the world, marked by insightful and penetrating points of view.

In her writing, Cixous draws inspiration from dreams of paradise in an effort to create a different world. He who came from the same garden explains it best:

> In the memory of our common childhood, and although we never went there together, note that it is a blessed garden. . . . in her book with Mireille Calle-Gruber, to whom we owe so much, *Photos de racines,* more precisely in her 'Inter Views' with Mireille, a page is entitled 'We Are of the Same Garden.' . . . Everything leads me to guess that it is in Algiers, not far from the sea, very near the shore, a big botanical garden whose avenues are lined with all the living trees of the world to which the heaven and earth of our country can offer their hospitality. This Garden has a name dear to all the inhabitants of Algiers: the Jardin d'Essais. (151)

In *Les rêveries de la femme sauvage,* the writer confirms her friend Derrida's supposition in a certain sense: "I never had a bit of luck, no matter how hard I tried. I searched I didn't find. I started from the beginning, the whole time I was living in Algeria, I tried-all-the-same" (26). Essayist, playwright, and author of works of fiction, Cixous has composed a vast and varied oeuvre: each new publication continues to open doors exposing the rich complexity of human existence(s). This gesture always inevitably overcomes obstacles, whether they are based on race, religion, sex, or nationality. In order to find the courage necessary to keep writing, to keep trying and to keep putting herself on trial in written work that pushes the limits of autobiography, this multifaceted writer obeys her reveries in order to think *differently,* and to reflect difference, outside the confines of accepted conventions and expectations. She is arguably able to do this because of her complicated background in Algeria: "the unbelievable place-lessness [*atopicité*] to which France and the French had condemned its Algerian uncitizens, the France its cross and its sword, we were its exorcized, I was from both sides. I reflected but I was not reflected on" ("La Fugitive" 80).

It is significant that Cixous is not the only individual who felt without a place in Algeria, as the writings of Cardinal and Djebar have revealed in this chapter, and as the writings of Bey, Mokeddem, Rahmani, and Sebbar also make clear. Each of these individuals seems to emerge from a particular background that means that they cannot be easily "reflected on," or "conceived of," with all of the rich connotations these expressions carry. While this situation of singularity initially means that they struggle with their "identity," it has ultimately meant that they have been able to connect with others on multiple levels, particularly on the written page, and their plural "identifications" have opened up new ways of writing in French. While *Nulle part dans la maison de mon père* bears a title that could be interpreted as a lament for a lost home, the work points to Djebar's challenging but productive position of exile that leads to poignant, probing literary creation. In the next chapter, I turn to another individual whose birth in Algeria has not often been understood as important to his corpus, a man whose background has frequently been overlooked, possibly to the detriment of potential interpretations of its import for his written work. The fact that Bey and Djebar have turned their attention to Albert Camus in relatively recent explorations indicates that their common birthplace is significant. Exploring their reactions to and interactions with the great "French" writer's work, especially his posthumously published autobiographical novel, has implications for our understanding of how women from Algeria represent their own early experiences in the written text, as they seek at once to bring to the forefront an idiosyncratic personal history with a specific takeoff point, and turn themselves outward to accurately depict the stories of others who often possess vastly different beginnings.

CHAPTER 4 | "La célébration d'une terre-mère" | Albert Camus and Algeria according to Maïssa Bey and Assia Djebar

> *What makes me feel close to the man is his relationships, not those he maintains with others, but with himself. Complex relationships, tied to an untiring quest, not for the truth, which we know is many-sided, but for an authenticity, the truth of your being, that you alone are able to define.* —Maïssa Bey, L'ombre d'un homme qui marche au soleil *(The shadow of a man walking in the sun)*

The quotation that makes up the title of this chapter is from a unique publication by Maïssa Bey, a work initially written for a talk delivered in the heart of Paris, at the Centre Pompidou, on the occasion of a colloquium entitled "Albert Camus and Falsehood." Bey's reflections in this text are both academic and personal in nature. Catherine Camus, the daughter of the celebrated author to whom the two days of this 2002 conference were dedicated, was deeply touched by Bey's speech, as she explains in her preface: "Listening to Maïssa, I found my father again. Not a famous writer, no, my father, a human being with his solitude, his courage, and his heartbreaks. And it was an Algerian woman who, in her solitude and her heartbreaks, had the courage of such luminous intelligence" (7–8).

Catherine Camus also wrote the introductory words to her father's last work, the unfinished autobiographical text titled *Le premier homme* (*The First Man*). This publication attracted the attention of many readers who sought to become acquainted with the human being behind the impressive oeuvre, and especially to understand his relationship to Algeria, the country of his childhood. Albert Camus's representations of his native country and his mother have found a place not only in Bey's recent comments but also in the writings of Assia Djebar. The focus in the previous chapter on these women's autobiographical depictions of their native land and mother figures will find an echo in the first part of this chapter, as I turn to Camus's autobiographical text to examine his portrayal of his own fragile position with respect to the mother country, Algeria, and the mother, both relationships marked by a simultaneous distance and proximity.

In *Albert Camus, Alger,* Algerian-born literary critic Christiane Chaulet-Achour engages in a detailed study of the connection between Camus and the place of his birth. The very title of this publication, with its juxtaposition of the author's name and the capital city, indicates much about its content. Chaulet-Achour concentrates first on *L'étranger* (*The Stranger*) before turning her attention to other works by the author in order to highlight a number of important details regarding the place of origin as it emerges throughout Camus's oeuvre. If many readers have not paid attention to the significance of Algeria in his writings, Chaulet-Achour argues convincingly that a renewed reading of the renowned author is called for: "A new reading of Camus appreciates, analyzes, savors what he had to offer and then integrates it into a dialogue with other Algerian texts" (187). As she demonstrates in her erudite analysis, a number of readers born in Algeria find in this writing something of this land they have in common: "This writing sensually connected to the soil remains the secret garden of a number of Algerian readers who discover in Camus a brother from their land" (177; un frère de terre).

Bey appears to subscribe to the idea of calling Camus a *frère de terre* in the aforementioned text. She finds a certain complexity in his writing—and in his very being—that stems from the precise place where he spent the formative years of his life: "What makes me feel close to the man is his relationships, not those he maintains with others, but with himself. Complex relationships tied to an untiring quest, not for the truth, which we know is many-sided, but for an authenticity, the truth of your being, that you alone are able to define; especially if it is inscribed in a place that one could categorize as forever marked by the tragedies of its history, a land 'inhabited by gods' and that continually pays the price of some obscure curse" (*L'ombre* 25). The truths that Bey seeks to uncover in her work are fashioned by an understanding of the complexity of truth as *multiforme*, as taking on many shapes in the writing and the personal experience of the one who was influenced by his birthplace, just as she was in his wake: "He was initially and above all informed by the drama and the excess of the land where he was born, to the extent that he lost his taste for solitude and the clear mornings of his country. His country, which is also mine, Algeria" (24). When Bey places her own experience alongside that of the writer whose life and work she addresses in this intimate text, she is establishing a connection that has very few literary precedents to date. While such a rapport may seem "natural," it is not at all a "given" for a woman born in Algeria to turn to the work of Camus.

It wasn't until 1995 that Djebar gave an invited lecture at the University of California, Berkeley, in which she evoked an unprecedented "encounter" between herself and the writer with whom she shares "a common native land" (*Ces voix* 224): "We meet.... The man, the 'pied-noir,' the child of Belcourt (above all the 'first man' coming forward at once as fictional and real). I, the Arab woman, without a veil, from Césarée very close to Tipasa, but emerging uneasily in early 1995 from autobiographical writing..." (*Ces voix* 225). Djebar is aware that she has been invited to speak on this occasion to an audience of university professors and students as an "Algerian woman." This specific invitation to deliver a talk is what motivates her to finally "come" to the work of the 1957 Nobel Prize laureate, as she attests in a later publication, *Le blanc de l'Algérie* (*Algerian White*): "Hours after that lecture, I understood that I had spent a long time justifying, as an Algerian woman, never having paid any serious attention to Camus, as if not knowing that this time I was going to the other end of the earth, as though by duty, in spite of myself, to meet him, in this work in progress, which marks a renewal of his novelistic art" (28). It is noteworthy that Djebar mentions "this unfinished novel" (ce roman inachevé) in her explanation, for it appears that the autobiographical nature of this text opened the door, in important ways, to the readings of Camus's "compatriots," or "half compatriots," according to Djebar's formula: "Camus my almost compatriot or half compatriot through land and the space of childhood" (*Ces voix* 226). It is as if this "new" work titled *Le premier homme* that appears in print in 1994 describes the relationship between the character who is the author and the essential elements of his existence, a relationship that illuminates all of his writing.

Reading *Le premier homme* inspires a strong reaction in Djebar, who describes the experience as follows: "I before this final book, turning around it, probing it, crossing it, circling it and simultaneously plunging into it, into its heart, through multiple, distinctive approaches. I would like—how I would like!—to find the straight path that points toward the author, him, the living man" (*Ces voix* 226). The Camusian text is especially enticing to the reader who comes to this writing from every possible angle in her deep desire to know the person who penned it. She underscores that a different Camus can be seen in this final book, a Camus that the reader caught glimpses of in earlier works, but who emerges here with qualities that are less "compressed," as Djebar puts it: "Indeed a 'first Camus,' perceived in the past in the texts of youth, comes back to us in this *Premier Homme*, with mastery and suffering barely compressed, with the inner battles that accompany the forties" (*Ces voix* 231).

Djebar cannot speak of Algeria without emphasizing that Saint Augustine was also from this North African region. She sees him as a predecessor whose *Confessions* can be considered an example for Camus's autobiographical expression. By establishing a connection between the writing of these two men, she affirms in parentheses that the personal aspects of Camus's life are intimately tied to the land he grew up in: "His autobiographical project (his life up to the age of forty, his loved ones, his genealogy and, enveloping all of that with a powerful coat, the Algerian land) seems to him to be worthy of these great precursors" (*Ces voix* 231). Djebar herself is inspired by the life and writings of Augustine, as she explains: "Augustine's ardor for his native land—mine too—and this sensuality that he cannot stifle revive my bleeding wound: this light 'suddenly subtracted,' according to him, from generations of women parked, confined, more and more closed in, in the darkness even in the middle of the day, in the name of what rotten tradition can we explain it?" (*Ces voix* 223). The metaphor of light that Djebar employs in this passage recalls the title of the reflections on Camus by Bey, a writer who cannot engage in the act of writing without evoking the condition of women in Algeria for generations: "Must I add that to be a woman, and, moreover, an Algerian—the object of so many reductive clichés—makes it even more difficult for me to intrude in what another woman writer from the Maghreb designates as 'the speakers' circle'" (*L'ombre* 33).

Maïssa Bey is showing much more than a humble attitude when she expresses her reticence to penetrate the circle where each one has the right to speak. She reveals the long-standing reality in her country that women do not have the possibility of taking the floor, much less the pen. As a woman who still lives in Algeria today, she must fight against the stereotypes and expectations that surround her; as a writer, Bey draws attention to the present challenges women in Algeria inevitably face; as a reader, she concentrates especially on the women who appear in the work of other writers: "women who, discreetly, too discreetly perhaps, make their way through Albert Camus's oeuvre" (43). It is the mother who emerges with the greatest strength in this oeuvre, if we study Bey's analysis closely. This mother is naturally the first to be named: "First, the mother. As Camus specifies, 'Every man is the first man, that's why he throws himself at the feet of his mother.' A phrase that resonates strangely in our ears, like a distant echo to this sentence taken from a verse of the Qur'an: 'Paradise is at the feet of mothers'" (44). If the mother provides an explanation and justification for the autobiographical book, she deserves a parallel title in Bey's point of view: "The first woman. *Desperately loved*" (44). This mother is not only appreciated, she is not simply admired, she is adored, indeed *"venerated, made sacred"* (45).

Bey notes that in *L'envers et l'endroit* (*The Wrong Side and the Right Side*), Camus paints the portrait of a mother that critics qualify as quiet and immobile: "Silent, frozen, like a statue, constantly expecting" (*L'ombre* 45). There is a resemblance between this mother and the mother in the writer's last work: "It is this mother who we find in *Le premier homme*, always walled in the same silence, indecipherable" (45). Like Bey, Djebar seems fascinated with the silence, the voicelessness of this mother, especially because the absence of speech reminds her of the women closest to her: "First, Camus's mother, silent; her silence, even before the genius of her son, seems to me to be white as well, as heavy as the veil worn by the women in my family" (*Ces voix* 219). Similar to the silenced women of her mother's tribe whose unheard stories serve as an inspiration to Djebar's written work, Camus's mother is perceived to be shut up in a sort of hushed environment: "And then I improvise: on Camus's maternal non-language. His mother, almost dumb, remains seated eternally by the window (like my maternal aunt, so sweet, residing in Belcourt, who at this very moment is intoning, in sorrow or patience, scraps of verses of the Koran)" (*Le blanc de l'Algérie* 28).

In her study of "the legacy of Albert Camus and the work of textual memory," Debra Kelly indicates that this recent tendency of focusing on Camus's writing is far more prevalent among Algerian women writers than it is among men, and she speculates on why certain similarities might have spurred women writers to more readily make reference to Camus: "They are more ready to collapse the colonizer-colonized opposition and identify with a man who would have been excluded from full participation in the Algeria constructed by nationalist discourse after independence, just as women have been, and who has been perceived in an ambiguous position ever since with regard to the country of his birth" (228). These women writers can indeed identify with Camus's "ambiguous position" when it comes to Algeria, and they certainly know from personal experience and sharing with others that multiple forms of exclusion exist in their native land, but it may be Camus's depictions of the mother in *Le premier homme* that has served as the greatest impetus for women writers' newfound, sustained attention to his writing. This last work opens up a new perspective on the writer, one that places him *in relation* to this cherished woman.

When Djebar asks herself why this particular work by Camus intrigues her so greatly, she arrives at this surprising conclusion: "Hours later, going to bed in the same room, those last nights, deserted by my shadows, I had a vague understanding of why I had been attracted to the last written words of a writer, at a moment when he was running towards his death. To his mother, who died six months after him in Belcourt, and yet still waiting at her window" (*Le blanc de l'Algérie* 28). This immobile, cloistered woman who is nonetheless looking outside, this woman who is totally turned toward her departed son who has promised to return, seems to capture Djebar's attention and pique her interest. This woman who is frozen in an expectant position will never again meet up with her son, and remains apart from him even in the end: "Six months later, Albert's mother was to be buried right beside her own mother, dead three years earlier: two ladies, the old and awesome Spanish woman and her gentle, nearly mute daughter. . . . Albert Camus lies almost opposite them, in Lourmarin, on the other side of the sea" (*Le blanc de l'Algérie* 105). This definitive separation between mother and son is all the more poignant because he had invited her to come with him to the other side of the Mediterranean, according to the narrative of *Le premier homme*: "It was he who could not bear that pinched look of a dying person he had suddenly seen on her face. 'Come with me to France,' he said to her, but she shook her head with resolute sorrow: 'Oh no, it's cold over there. I'm too old now. I want to stay home'" (77).

The use of the term *chez nous* in *Le premier homme* is striking because the character who pronounces the words is the mother, she who is not from the country she inhabits, as Chaulet-Achour reminds us when she addresses Albert Camus's situation: "Quick birth of a child of emigrants" (205). There is a complex relationship between the immigrant mother and the Algerian land that is "home" to her, because she suffers from a geographical ignorance that the narrative voice in *Le premier homme* elaborates on:

> . . . his mother, who had no idea what history and geography might be, who knew only that she lived on land near the sea, that France was on the other side of that sea which she too had never traveled, France in any case being an obscure place lost in a dim night which one reached through a port named Marseilles, which she pictured like the port of Algiers, where there was a shining city they said was very beautiful and that was called Paris, where there was also a region named Alsace that her husband's family came from—it was a long time ago, they were fleeing enemies called Germans to settle in Algeria, and now that same region had to be taken back from those same enemies who were always evil and cruel, especially with the French, and for no reason at all. (67)[1]

Having never set foot in France where her son resides, the mother cannot call this far-off country "chez nous," nor can she call it "chez toi," for the Algerian land—the place where she gave birth to Albert Camus—is the only dwelling place imaginable for her. She conceives of this country in simple terms: It is a question of *la terre* and *la mer* and the relationship between these two entities. She does not have a global understanding of geography and history; all of that remains obscure for this illiterate individual. It is the erudite son who explains his love for his mother in terms that are comprehensible to him, choosing to highlight the land and the sea, as Maïssa Bey's analysis makes clear: "But Camus is a writer. He will say these words, or at least he will write them, hiding behind a 'geological anonymity. Land and sea,' and he will dedicate them to the one 'who will never be able to read this book,' to the woman who will never be able to hear them" (*L'ombre* 47).

Camus's geographical and familial itinerary is summarized as follows in Djebar's *Ces voix qui m'assiègent:* "Albert Camus, born in Belcourt to a Spanish mother, in such poverty that he is scratched with tuberculosis; then, like those of my race, he early becomes orphaned by his father, and blinded by the sun. He exhausts his youth there, retaining somber lucidity and insolence, leaving in turn, for good, for the north" (221). It is significant that the sun is present in Djebar's remarks, for what we might call "luminosity" is pertinent to Camus's life and work on several levels. Djebar underscores the definitive departure for the north undoubtedly in part for personal reasons, for this movement resembles her own journey from her homeland. In-depth studies such as Jane Hiddleston's *Assia Djebar: Out of Algeria* evoke this displacement as a crucial element of Djebar's theoretical and novelistic work. While Algeria arguably never leaves the woman writer, a certain distance from this native country is necessary to her writing project, in Djebar's own opinion: "I have been far from Algeria in order to write for seventeen years now. To be able to write, I have to come in complete freedom, at ease and with the happiness of space" (Rieck). Bey points out that, in spite of the distance that separates Albert Camus from his native land, this place remains with the writer. According to her critique, the country of birth is not only an inspiration for, but it serves also as the content itself of all that Camus writes: "There is, and this is considered to be *the very substance of his oeuvre, the celebration of a mother-land* [*terre-mère*], *of a land drowning in this sunlight that often, in 'an obscure dazzle,' blinds and shapes men who can be simultaneously austere and outrageous*" (*L'ombre* 42; my emphasis).

Le premier homme is a text that contains an entire lexicon associated with the sea and the native land, as well as with the blinding Algerian sun, as we see in the following passage: "But he had escaped, he could breathe, on the giant back of the sea he was breathing in waves, rocked by the great sun, at last he could sleep and he could come back to the childhood from which he had never recovered, to the secret of the light, of the warm poverty that had enabled him to survive and to overcome everything" (41). Not only has the principal protagonist never healed from childhood, but the return to the native country is a joyful event recounted in terms that recall his childhood: "Jacques was half asleep, and he was filled with a kind of happy anxiety at the prospect of returning to Algiers and the small poor home in the old neighborhood. So it was every time he left Paris for Africa, his heart swelling with a secret exultation, with the satisfaction of one who has made good his escape and is laughing at the thought of the look on the guards' faces" (40).

The person toward whom Jacques Cormery heads when he arrives on the African continent is the mother. Loved and adored, she is always young in spite of the passing years: "She was there, her hair still abundant but turned white long ago, still erect despite her seventy-two years; she looked ten years younger because she was so slender and her strength was still evident—they were all like that in the family, a clan of lean people with a nonchalant manner whose energy was inexhaustible; old age did not seem to have any hold on them" (54–55). The affection and admiration the maturing man feels for his mother is evident even in this physical description, so it should be of little surprise that the scene of reunion between son and mother overflows with emotion and tenderness:

> When he arrived on the doorstep, his mother opened the door and threw herself in his arms. And there, as she did every time they were reunited, she kissed him two or three times, holding him against her with all her strength; and in his arms he felt her ribs, the hard jutting bones of her shoulders, trembling a bit, while he breathed the soft smell of her skin that made him remember the spot, under her larynx, between the two jugular tendons, that he no longer dared to kiss, but that as a child he had loved to nuzzle and fondle on those infrequent occasions when she took him on her knees and he pretended to sleep, his nose in the little hollow that to him had the scent of a tenderness all too rare in his young life. (55)

The body of the mother is like a country, opening up to the son who comes back to find himself gain. He seems to explore the maternal body in this passage like an adventurer discovers a new corner of the planet or like a geographer examines the earth. As if he were a lover in the arms of his beloved, the man contemplates each aspect of the flesh he holds tightly to him, this skin too little felt when he was little and helpless, without a father in a country that was not really "his." This depiction of intimate reunion recalls the desired physical closeness that both Cixous and Djebar expressed for another mother, for a figure that each perceived as possessing more maternal traits than their own biological mothers, in the autobiographical texts under examination in the last chapter. What emerges in these retrospective works is that these writers were in need of more tangible, tender expressions of love and affection when they were young.

In her study of Camus and Algeria, Chaulet-Achour cites the spoken words of Maria Casarès as they are transcribed in an interview published in the journal *Lire* in June 1996: "What I have in common with Marguerite Duras is an upbringing in the colonies, in the dissimulation of the indigenous condition. But I have more affinities with Albert Camus. Reading his unfinished novel, *Le premier homme,* moved me deeply. When the little Jacques, born in Algeria, asks his mother: 'Maman, what is a fatherland?' and she responds: 'I don't know. No,' he expresses the obligation he felt to create himself on his own [*se faire par soi-même*], to be his first man, one who constructs his own conscience" (195). This is the oral account of yet another reader of Camus who expresses the great emotion that fills her when she opens the writer's final work. The mother's inability to answer her child is touching, especially when the question he asks is heavy with meaning, due to the country in question and the unique family situation. Chaulet-Achour underscores the complexity of defining this *patrie* by examining the fact that, in *Le premier homme,* people are described in terms of ethnicity, not their place of origin: "The characters evoked are all designated by their ethnic origin, not by their names.... This choice shows the ethnic diversity of Algeria and the way origins are obscured: the son of the anonymous is born, furtively, in a lost corner of the Maghrebian land" (204–5). The mother, who has little understanding of the geopolitical situation in this land where she gave birth to the future writer, is dumbfounded when it comes to defining the fatherland. Without a doubt, it is easier to celebrate the *terre-mère,* in harmony with the title of this chapter, than to sing the praises of a *patrie.*

In the passage of *Le premier homme* quoted above that describes the reunion of the son and the mother after a significant separation, the mother serves as a metaphor for the country. Indeed, Djebar reminds us that the country is always conjugated in the feminine: "Why always Algeria 'my mother,' my sister, my mistress, my concubine, my slave?" (*Le blanc de l'Algérie* 103). The woman writer who poses this rhetorical question would like it to be possible to conceive of the country differently: "Camus, an old man: it seems almost as unimaginable as the metaphor of Algeria herself, as a wise adult, calm at last, at last turned toward life, ordinary life.... In the same way, is it possible to think of Algeria as peace-loving, with her dignity restored?" (103).

Djebar affirms that, even if the writer had finished this book, many things would remain unclear, both to him and to us, "and Camus, well, Camus the Algerian would have finished his novel, *The First Man*. And other mysteries, for him as for us, would be more obscure..." (*Le blanc de l'Algérie* 122; se seraient obscurcis).[2] It may be fitting that this book is incomplete, for it reflects the native land, unfinished and unsteady, in Chaulet-Achour's opinion: "Unfinished autobiography in a country that continues to be born and to seek itself, oscillating—with equal obstination—between life and death" (204). Camus's book has so deeply touched, so profoundly impressed women writers from Algeria because it constitutes with such éclat *une célébration d'une terre-mère,* a "motherland" they cherish in their heart and their creative and theoretical work. Bey and Djebar, each in her own way, have dedicated their lives to the textual expression of this native country—and the mother. For each, these themes remain present and pertinent, located at the very center of their profession and their faith.

These central themes are inextricably linked to another manifestation of Camus's importance in women writers' work, according to Debra Kelly: "The legacy of Camus is also apparent in the need of later novelists to bear witness to the suffering of others" (225). Bearing witness in textual form to the struggles and successes—the trials and triumphs—of others is at the heart of the testimonial writing that makes up *Polygraphies*. The takeoff points that Algeria has provided serve as an autobiographical springboard for written works by women writers that take others into account, as illustrated by Brigitte Weltman-Aron's analysis of Cixous's fictional writing: "In *Reveries of the Wild Woman,* Cixous pursues her reflection on admission as expulsion as a 'form of relationship to the world,' positing an ethical stance stemming from dispossession, indeed embracing it as a way of fostering an unexpected chance to interpret and act in the world, without nostalgia, and with a sharpened attention to the disenfranchised" ("Book Review" 199). The "ethical stance" mentioned above, with its "sharpened attention to the disenfranchised" is reminiscent of Ronnie Scharfman's formulation of Cixous's "un-belonging for/in Algeria" that has inspired the writer to reiterate in her work "an ethics of dialogue, established as early as 'Le Rire de la méduse'" ("Narratives" 97). When Scharfman places the relatively recent *Les rêveries de la femme sauvage* (2000) alongside Cixous's essay originally published in 1975, she creates a critical continuity that is not only necessary for understanding the primary place of Algeria throughout Cixous's corpus, but is also crucial for realizing the importance of Algeria as a point of departure for reading—and writing—the body, a concept that Cixous championed in some of her earlier texts. The next section of *Polygraphies* is devoted to textual representations of the body, and it begins with a chapter devoted to Cixous's evolving corporeal representations, showing how the body is celebrated differently as the author ages. All the while remaining attentive to the body's joys and pleasures, the writer is ever more attentive in later texts to the ills and sufferings of the body—both of one's own and of bodies belonging to others.

PART III Embodiments

CHAPTER 5 | Écrire les maux | Hélène Cixous and Writing the Body over Time

> *So for each text, another body. But in each the same vibration: the something in me that marks all my books is a reminder that my flesh signs the book, it is rhythm. Medium my body, rhythmic my writing.*—Hélène Cixous, "La venue à l'écriture" ("Coming to Writing")

> *The always singular body of the other: every time a history, a memory, sensations, scars, ways of perceiving—in short, reading with your body* [son corps] *the book of the world.*—Hélène Cixous, Photos de racines (Rootprints)

Hélène Cixous is known in many critical circles for one remarkable text: "Le rire de la Méduse." In this renowned essay, she incites women to "write their bodies" in an exhortation of what has become a key concept for women's studies in the years to follow. The *écriture féminine* championed by Cixous in the mid-1970s continues to be evoked and critiqued as a useful yet problematic notion for contemplating writing by women and its possible differences from writing by men.[1] A glance at the entry under this term in *The New Oxford Companion to Literature in French* reveals the positive potential of this writing practice: "According to [its] proponents . . . 'écriture féminine' at least disturbs the tranquil surface of discourse, both by writing in other ways and writing about other things" (271). In style and in substance, therefore, this writing carries with it the possibility of breaking free from established forms of literary production. It opens up the option of writing differently about different things in suggestive—rather than descriptive or prescriptive—prose.[2] While a clear definition of "feminine writing" remains elusive, it is evident that its creativity capacity is related to the body in its multiple and varied rhythms, drives, cycles, and sexuality.[3]

This chapter explores Cixous's treatment, over time, of the body, beginning with some of her first publications and continuing up to the present. In her recent essays and works of fiction, Cixous still upholds the writing of the body, but her emphasis is less on the feminine jouissance of her early texts than on the pleasures *and pains* of corporal existence. Writing the body often parallels the activity of *reading* the body in these later works, and the image one sees upon close (self-)observation bears visible traces of suffering, and of aging. It is the mise-en-scène of the body in the written text, the specific staging of the self, the other, and the mother that changes gradually over the years in Cixous's written representations.

JOUISSANCE: PLEASURE (IN) WRITING

In her 1981 essay on conceptions of women's writing in France, Ann Rosalind Jones rightly identifies the feminine "libidinal economy" as a crucial driving force behind Cixous's textual compositions (373). "La venue à l'écriture" is a work that affirms this assertion when its author creatively translates desire and pleasure into rhythmic writing: "There are sources. That's the enigma. One morning, it all explodes. My body experiences, deep down inside, one of its panicky cosmic adventures. I have volcanoes on my lands. But no lava: what wants to flow is breath" (10). The explosive flow described in these lines can be self-generated, as a later portion of the same textual reflection reveals: "With one hand she holds her animale pressed between her thighs, she caresses it briskly" (34). The results are poetic, and prolific: "She opens up the earth to me and I throw myself in [*je m'élance*]. She opens my body and writing is thrown in [*s'élance*]" (43). In these two short sentences, the connection between physical pleasure and writing is established. Opening up the body simultaneously opens up to writing, but this act was—and, to her mind, remains—subversive, and voices carrying the threat of corporeal punishment echo in the text: "Don't touch yourself. Run away from yourself. He will cut off your hand! He will chill your marrow. He will make you wear mitts" (35). It is undeniably the prospect of losing a hand that frightens the writer most, as evidenced by its primary position in this passage, and this early anxiety over losing bodily parts connected with the writing process does not leave her with the passing of years, as shown by the contents of a more recent essay titled "Obstétriques cruelles." The writer is still far from serene when it comes to taking (pleasurable) risks in writing: "Rapture for rapture, I want to take pleasure in the ignorance of limits and roles, ravish it from whoever forbids me.... I want to play with fire, like other do. But I prefer not to die from it, although I have no choice.... I am afraid of losing my eyesight and my right hand. I prefer not to be decapitated. I am afraid for my head, for my neck, for my wrist, for my writing materials" (108). This quotation on the dangers inherent in writing contains the verb *jouir,* pointing to the enjoyment of literary composition in the context of transgressing established rules and pushing restrictive limits. But the emphasis on the possible negative consequences of written transgression is notably greater than in Cixous's earlier work, and is indicative of a fresh trend in the writer's treatment of literary delights.

The 2001 work of fiction *Benjamin à Montaigne: Il ne faut pas le dire* revisits the masturbatory scenes mentioned cryptically in Cixous's 1970s theoretical texts to focus this time more explicitly on the *guilt* that accompanies these experiences of ecstasy. The direct treatment of impulse and indulgence in this publication is new and noteworthy, as the narrator evokes these irresistible adventures: "I loved The Stupid Thing [*La Bêtise*] as if it were my cat I mean my pussy [*ma chatte*] the being I could not deny any party" (83). She identifies four occupations as requiring inviolable solitude, "reading, reveries, tears, and voluptuousness" (82), the fourth of which is found at the apex of all solitary activity, making up the climax toward which all other occupations mount.[4] These stolen moments of solitary pleasure eventually wreak havoc on the body, affecting corporeal rhythms in manifest manner: "At night I worked at the speed of a pilot in an automobile race, I had to make up for my delay and fulfill my other duties. I lost weight. I had a tachycardia. According to my mother, this is already a result of *The Stupid Thing*" (96). Mention of the mother comes as a bit of a surprise in the midst of this private passage on the destabilizing results of stolen moments of pleasure. The fact that the mother was in on her most intimate secrets hints that, in the writer's own life (if we make the leap from text to *hors-texte*), the private became "public" at an early age. If such a passage can be taken autobiographically, the open nature of secret moments may have paved the way for the publication of deeply personal compositions; it may also have contributed to the writer's sensitivity to bodily matters that extend beyond her self.

In *Bodies That Matter,* Judith Butler focuses on the "scenography and topography of construction," thereby distancing discourse on "women" from a debate that seeks to pit against each other "materiality" and "constructedness" (of sex and gender) as "necessarily oppositional notions" (28). In both theoretical and fictional works, Cixous often highlights the "constructed" nature of the scenes she depicts, to the point that these texts often have much in common with plays, with theatrical compositions, from dialogues to *didascalies*. Blurring the lines between various literary genres in this way mirrors a similar disruption of oppositional categories, especially those of sex, in Cixous's work. Her writing constantly reminds us that language is not innocent, that words communicate concepts that— consciously or unconsciously—come to bear on our conceptions of the world. The neologism *animâle*, quoted earlier, is indicative of an ongoing tendency in this writing to play with and expand standard understandings of sexual difference(s). Recent work of an autobiographical bent reveals that questions on what it means to be a woman may have arisen early in the writer's mind, during her childhood in Algeria.

ALGÉRIANCE: WOMEN AND BODIES

While reflections on motherhood and the maternal are present throughout Cixous's corpus, the mother figure distinguishes herself in a central role in many of Cixous's recent writings. The first-person narrative voice evokes the mother in "La venue à l'écriture," but the reference to her is rather brief and elliptical in this early text: "My mother wasn't a 'woman.' She was my mother, she was the smile; she was the voice of my mother tongue, which wasn't French; to me she seemed rather like a young man, or like a young girl; besides, she was foreign" (28–29). It is not clear in this passage if resembling "a young man" is a positive or negative trait; the description of the mother is generally affirming, since this progenitor is associated with a smile and a voice, and—most strikingly—with the foreign. She does not fit the category of "woman," but this lack of belonging can be interpreted in a favorable light, particularly given Cixous's rather fierce critique of this sexual assignation from the outset of her writing career.

Souffles, a 1975 work of fiction appearing as the first in a long series of texts to be published by Éditions Des femmes,[5] contains a rather volatile passage that refers in the first person to belonging to the category of woman with respect to the body: "I don't become a woman without difficulty, but too bad. . . . Becoming a woman is child's play to me, after all. So I don't care. Will I enclose your breath that I am in the vulgar matchbox of a seductress?" (27; boîte d'allumeuse). The ironic anger of this passage seems to indicate that possessing a womanly figure requires a bit of a transformation, but that it is not entirely out of reach. What is questionable is whether it is really desirable to boast voluptuous corporality when it will only serve the heterosexual mate (for) breakfast: "I metamorphose as well as one can, men nibble . . . on my small salty kissable thighs" (27; bisecuisses).

The changing first-person depiction of the body in Cixous's textual representations begins with her parents, and especially her mother. A conflicting desire to be like *and* unlike this progenitor permeates the first-person narrator's evocations of her own distinctive traits throughout Cixous's oeuvre. Attempts at self-definition must pass (by) the initial point of comparison, the mother's body. An early reference to the writer's own personal appearance in "La venue à l'écriture" resembles aforementioned descriptions of the mother as lacking "feminine" attributes, with the addition here of an "animal" touch: "my body... is elastic, nervous, skinny and lively, not without charm, firm muscles, a pointed nose always wet and trembling and vibrating paws" (19). But a later publication, the 1999 *Osnabrück*, contains a passage in which the daughter is described in her father's words, and all similarity with the mother dissipates in his description: "She had a pyramidal body he said, calling my mother as a witness, an Egyptian body, nothing round of the German, flat buttocks, wide shoulders" (174). These words, written so long after her father passed away, obviously had a lasting impact on the writing subject: "My body took shape according to his word... he said and I was, this very ancient classic form that wasn't recognized then" (174). It is significant that the mother is present at this scene of divine re-creation, that she is called to witness this event.

In book after book, Cixous bears witness to the extraordinary and ordinary moments in her mother's life. She revisits her words, her habits, and even her body, in texts leading up to the powerful 2009 *Éve s'évade*.[6] Perhaps part of Cixous's ongoing fascination with the eponymous Eve is tied to the fact that her mother remains a foreigner to her, in her physical makeup as well as her behavior and attitudes. This is very clear in the autobiographical account of her childhood in Algeria, where, contrary to her mother, she was quite literally *marked* by her desire to know this country. The mother is portrayed as untouched by the land to which she has immigrated, while the narrator indicates that she has completely internalized the country of her birth: "My mother forever virginal, untouched, me printed once and for all, I grasp the evil I see, I've got Algeria in my lungs in my throat I don't find it strange that it should turn me hot and cold and bruise my nervous system with its toxic overflow. I attribute the scars of my marked body to the malgerian force of my imagination" (*Les rêveries* 64). There are recognizable benefits to what the writer has termed a *"maladie algérie"* (16), for it permits the afflicted to perceive hurts and wrongs that escape the untrained, "naked" eye, as we saw in chapter 3. But this malady penetrates to the depths of one's being, and the narrative voice relates its toll in corporeal language: "It was this same anguish that was driving me crazy... and which starts to take over, to invade me, invest my lungs, my ears, my head, saturating me with its absence, its withdrawal, which turns my whole body into a searing pain" (*Les rêveries* 7). The fact that her lungs are mentioned in this passage, as in the quotation above and numerous other passages in Cixous's writing, is significant.[7] As revealed in the very title of *Souffles,* breath has always been crucial to Cixous's understanding of writing; the rhythm of her work is influenced by the tempo of the inhalation and exhalation that propels it. The body is behind the text, and when the body is affected by illness, this alters the content and the form of the writing.

The *maux* of this chapter's title refers, of course, to the physical ailments that can be found in Cixous's more recent writing, but the term also stands for evils or injustices often committed, paradoxically, in the interest of "social health." The racism that reigned in the Algeria of the writer's childhood was barely hidden under this antiseptic veneer, as the narrative voice explains in *Les rêveries de la femme sauvage:* "This 'health' of the social body I experienced as illness, all those defenses, rejections, doors I turned into a personal malady" (70). As a Jew growing up in Algeria, Cixous was attentive to racism from early on. Considered "French" by the Arab and Berber populations of her native land, Cixous was inexorably taken for the "other," mistakenly associated with a country that revoked her citizenship under Vichy's 1940 *statut des Juifs.* This law had results official and unofficial, as she was barred entry not only into the schools of the French colonizers, but also their homes.[8] A victim of anti-Semitism,[9] Cixous quickly became attuned to other forms of victimization, and has dedicated much of her writing to denouncing wrongs in their myriad forms. Her ongoing struggle against misogyny, exemplified by the founding of the Centre de Recherches en Études Féminines at the University of Paris VIII Vincennes, began with an exposure to hostility toward women in the colonial environment of her childhood and adolescence, as she explains in an interview: "I had met sexual hostility before, it was a daily event in Algeria, it was open. I couldn't take a bus without being harassed" (Phoca 11). The harassment in public transportation was verbal and physical, as revealed in uncensored reminiscences between sister and brother in fictional conversation: "Those who claim they have never felt the fat conductors rubbing up against their asses. . . . Take out *ass* says my brother, take ass out of the book. . . . So I'm just leaving the girls' asses in I say and I remove my brother's. On the K one would have liked to have no ass" (*Les rêveries* 68). When she calls attention in this metatextual commentary within the fictional work to the shameful touching to which young boys and girls were subjected, she is also highlighting the selectivity of the writing process, showing how the autobiographical work is constructed according to memory that is either evoked or suppressed, and multiple truths may be revealed or repressed to varying degrees in the final written product. Full exposure of past injustice may not always be the result—or the goal—of the autobiographical text, but the disclosure of truths in their multiple possibilities of expression is inevitably the objective.

Cixous explains in an interview that the violation and humiliation of inappropriate touching was something she learned to expect in her native land: "I thought Algeria primitive . . . Algeria was a colony. As in all colonies violence is rampant and of course it takes sexual shapes and it will attack the weak first, women, etc." (Phoca 11). What was surprising to Cixous upon leaving Algeria was that sexual hostility was not unique to the "colony," that it was just as present in France in "less aggressive" form, as "phallocracy": "In France misogyny is veiled and it is much more insidious and perfidious than anywhere else in Europe. It's awful because it doesn't say its name" (Phoca 11). Cixous has decided to call its bluff, to call it "in the buff" so to speak, to "say the name" of injustice—sexual, racial, and other—in writing, but not without pain.

SOUFFRANCE: AGING AND AILING

It is significant that the mother should be described as a "virgin" in *Les rêveries de la femme sauvage* (110), for her very status as "mother" logically contradicts the assumption of sexual inexperience bound up in this term. In the context of the passage cited above, it is clear that this expression refers to the mother's lack of involvement with Algeria, with its troubles and struggles; in spite of the very hands-on activity of midwifery, the mother has remained unbothered by this territory in which she has come to live; she has not been penetrated and bears none of the physical signs of the "events" around her. This term therefore points toward the ideas of youth and purity that often accompany the status of virginity, indicating that the mother has a remarkable knack for remaining healthy and vivacious in spite of the ills that surround her, and while this could be considered a criticism of the mother's distanced stance, it could also be read as an embrace of the promise of eternal energy. As a virgin, she remains unaffected by the passing of days, months, and years.[10] This optimism with respect to the mother changes, however, when a later text reveals that this figure is not forever untouched by external forces. Eventually, suddenly, the mother in Cixous's text succumbs to the ravages of time:

> I noticed at that moment, upon these words, that she had just aged. It was a cruel and intolerable phenomenon before one's eyes, but undenia-

ble. Deep wrinkles had opened on her cheeks that had been ironed just before her departure, her neck had given up the fight. I trembled before the incredible brutality of time. I was afraid, and of everything, of these alterations, these features that had been cherished for decades, and also the transfers of physical strengths and physical weaknesses that had taken place on the whole first floor. (*Benjamin à Montaigne* 13–14)

This sobering observation is taken from an innovative work of fiction, a textual whirlwind predicated on a trip taken by two elderly women—the narrator's mother and maternal aunt—to their native town in Germany. This journey gives the narrator occasion to reflect on the failings of the body, not just her mother's but her own. She expresses at moments a deep fatigue that becomes so intense that it provokes her to remove her body, to separate herself from it if only for a short while: "I was so tired that I took off my body and placed it naked next to me on the desk. It was the color of the moon, it lost a bit of blood and sweat, I dried it off, that stopped it and reassured me" (55). Physical displacement necessitates corporal structures, of course, and she quickly dons her body to go downstairs so as not to miss the goings-on in the kitchen.

In Cixous's writing, the most remarkable expressions of suffering stem from sympathy. When those the writer loves and cares for find themselves down or in pain, she cannot help but feel for them, in very physical ways, as her texts reveal: "If my friend suffers from a spiritual hemorrhage . . . I quickly start to lose blood as if I had my period, but I don't tell him. I scold myself for my excessive sympathy. . . . If my friend is suddenly hit with the beginnings of an ear infection I am immediately struck with a sore throat" (*Benjamin à Montaigne* 75). This passage, like others, seems to communicate that in the case of Cixous, psychological suffering makes itself *literally* manifest. Identifying with others, or simply interacting with them in intense ways, leads to visible, tangible transformations in health and appearance, according to the writer's reflections. In fact, it is because of her *mother's* aging that the daughter's hair begins to change color: "Each year each year nothing changes and yet. I still had black hair. My mother makes me older: it is her age that poisons me, it changes, it occupies a place among us" (106). But perhaps nothing can equal the torments that come from within, as in this timeless, tense passage in which the first-person voice shares her childhood torment, unlocking the pain of her solitary struggles: "My breath stuck in my lungs . . . I lived an arrest of four days . . . the vital coil suspended, my body crushed in a spasmic fixity . . . I couldn't find what was wrong... my brain in my heart, collected in a fistful of ever tightening muscles" (78–79). *Benjamin à Montaigne* is not an easy book, with its tortuous, torturous turns and its contemplation of failure, of depression, of suicide, of illness in mental and physical forms: "The foreign body that cannot be expelled, the stone from which one suffers atrociously is the thought of death" (59).[11] But it is nonetheless a beautiful book in substance and style, grappling with the ills of existence.

The most striking example of writing the body in Cixous's recent work is the raw depiction of the body as ailing, as aging, as a site of illness and fatigue. Instead of highlighting pleasure and flight, the words to write the sickly body are brought "down to earth," in a lamentation of limitations: "The soul is nonetheless a body I say to my brother, I enumerate my ills, abdominal pains in the soul, curtailed breath, temporal sweats sensation of dark void and vertiginous, dizzy spells" (74–75). The dizzying sensation conveyed in Cixous's recent autobiographical fiction accompanies a significant departure from her earlier understanding of writing the body. Diverting from the "canonical" text that she has come to consider a "curse" in Anglo-American academic settings,[12] she still has recourse to the body, but in different ways, to convey the multiple "constitutions" of the woman writer.

In the analysis of Roland Barthes, the two extremes of bodily sensation may not be as contradictory as we might at first assume: "migraine... and sensual pleasure are merely coenesthesias, whose function is to individuate my own body, without its being able to glorify itself with any danger: my body is theatrical to itself" (60). Staging it appropriately, giving it a "proper" place in the literary work, may be one of the greatest difficulties for the contemporary thinker who seeks to represent the body in writing, a challenge to which Cixous has measured up by depicting her own body as—to use her words from the second epigraph to this chapter—the "body of the other," with its own "history," "memory," "sensations," "scars," and "ways of perceiving" (*Photos de racines* 64). The specificity of her background as a Jewish girl in Algeria and a woman in a Parisian intellectual environment dominated by men has shaped Cixous, literally and metaphorically, into the internationally renowned writer she is today, whose work bears the trace in substance and style of what Barthes might refer to as the "individuation" of something as basic and central as her body. If we apply Cixous's own words to her work, she has learned to "read with the body"—her own and those of others—"the book of the world" (*Photos de racines* 64), and to *write* the book of the world *into* the body. This textual movement has served as an inspiration, whether conscious or not, for a handful of Algerian-born women writers who have taken the risk to depict the body, in all of its sensuality, in written form. The next chapter will focus on corporeal configurations in the written work of Bey, Djebar, Mokeddem, and Sebbar, all of whom have made important strides toward reclaiming and restoring women's bodily desires and drives from a potentially restrictive and repressive patriarchal culture. Their efforts have resulted in respectful, sensitive literary texts that write the body years after Cixous first encouraged women to do so.

CHAPTER 6 | Sexualités et sensualités | Corporeal Configurations in the Work of Maïssa Bey, Assia Djebar, Malika Mokeddem, and Leïla Sebbar

> *... to take the risks of a dangerous truth of which little by little we form the alphabet, or rather the idiom that would allow the enunciation of our mobile location between what is personal and collective, what singularizes and pluralizes our experience, our taste for change and all viable edification, from day to day.*
> —Abdelkébir Khatibi, Le scribe et son ombre *(The scribe and his shadow)*

If Hélène Cixous encourages women to write their bodies with such fervor in "Le rire de la Méduse," her passion is related to her early experience in Algeria. She states in *La Jeune Née* (*The Newly Born Woman*), published in the same year (1975), that what she witnessed in her homeland set the stage for her attitudes to come: "I am three or four years old, and the first thing I see in the street is that the world is divided in two, hierarchized; and that it maintains this distribution through violence" (85). In this divided society, as we have already seen, she was located neither on the side of the "masters," nor on the side of the "slaves" (85), and this position of non-belonging made her especially attentive to others who were "invisible," such as immigrant workers, minorities, and women (84). If her birthplace is a lucky accident (87), since it translated into personal survival while other Jews perished in concentration camps in Europe, Algeria is also a land where she became particularly attentive to the ways in which women have been taught to shun their bodies: "We turned away from our bodies, which we were shamefully taught to ignore, to strike with foolish prudishness" ("Le rire de la Méduse" 55). After her departure from Algeria, Cixous realized that this attitude is not unique to this land and that her texts speak to women everywhere, not just to those who come from conservative places. It is important to see in recent texts how francophone women writers who also hail from Algeria infuse their works of fiction with autobiographical details that often revolve around the body. These writers have found that focusing on the physical enables them to effectively frame the "hybridities" that make them up as individuals who, in ways similar and dissimilar to Cixous, are located *between* continents, languages, and cultures.

In Homi Bhabha's estimation, it is this "inter," this "in-betweenness," that characterizes postcolonial beings who attempt to translate their hybridity in the literary text:

> The theoretical recognition of the split-space of enunciation may open the way to conceptualizing an international culture, based not on the exoticism or multi-culturalism of the diversity of cultures, but on the inscription and articulation of culture's hybridity. To that end we should remember that it is the "inter"—the cutting edge of translation and negotiation, the in-between, the space of the *entre* that Derrida has opened up in writing itself—that carries the burden of the meaning of culture. It makes it possible to begin envisaging nation, anti-nationalist, histories of the "people." It is in this space that we will find those words with which we can speak of Ourselves and Others. And by exploring this hybridity, this "Third Space," we may elude the politics of polarity and emerge as the others of our selves. ("Cultural Diversity" 157)

The four women I focus on in this chapter make personal textual explorations into geographic, linguistic, and corporal hybridities, opening up in their literary "translations" and "negotiations" a "third space" that allows them to escape strict hierarchical categorizations. The novelistic worlds they create successfully show that these authors are influenced by hybridities in the plural, for these women are not always in an *entre-deux*, between *two* well-defined entities, but rather in an *entre* that is situated in a movement among *several* countries, idioms, and ways of life.

The notion of hybridity is neither simple nor uniform, and a precise definition for the term is hard to find. Robert Young points out its positive connotations in the following manner: "There is no single, or correct, concept of hybridity: it changes as it repeats, but it also repeats as it changes. It shows that we are still locked into parts of the ideological network of a culture that we think and presume that we have surpassed.... Hybridity here is a key term in that wherever it emerges it suggests the impossibility of essentialism" (159). In their writing, Bey, Djebar, Mokeddem, and Sebbar avoid essentialism altogether by bringing out the singular hybridities that define them, and that define the heroines of their works of fiction. Each touches on the theme of sensuality in her own fashion, making textual gestures that could be considered transgressive in their common country of origin. They stage the female body in their novels, valorizing the woman in her flesh-and-blood existence without reducing her to the physical aspect of her being. When they broach the subject of sexuality in diverse passages of the literary text, these writers accomplish important work that transforms a "colonial" economy into a "postcolonial" exchange filled with possibilities for relations from the self to the self as well as from the self to the other.

SEXUALITIES AND POSTCOLONIALITIES

Robert Young reminds us to what extent "sexual exchange" is at the very foundation of colonial relations:

> For it is clear that the forms of sexual exchange brought about by colonialism were themselves both mirrors and consequences of the modes of economic exchange that constituted the basis of colonial relations; the extended exchange of property which began with small trading-posts and the visiting slave ships originated, indeed, as much as an exchange of bodies as of goods, or rather of bodies as goods: as in that paradigm of respectability, marriage, economic and sexual exchange were intimately bound up, coupled with each other, from the very first. The history of the meanings of the word "commerce" includes the exchange both of merchandise and of bodies in sexual intercourse. It was therefore wholly appropriate that sexual exchange, and its miscegenated product, which captures the violent, antagonistic power relations of sexual and cultural diffusion, should become the dominant paradigm through which the passionate economic and political trafficking of colonialism was conceived. Perhaps this begins to explain why our own forms of racism remain so intimately bound up with sexuality and desire. (161–62)

Contemporary writers like Djebar and Mokeddem describe sexuality and desire in texts that show the value of these terms, showing that women are sexual and desiring beings, possessing a healthy sensuality that allows for love relationships that express themselves in several languages.[1]

In *Ces voix qui m'assiègent*, Assia Djebar establishes a connection between writing and love, between words and the body: "For my principal theme, treated in fiction, is which language accompanies, follows, envelops beings, during lovemaking: dialogues or monologues, or soliloquies, words that slip out, avowals of abandonment during the instants of intimacy" (237). In *L'amour, la fantasia,* a novel inspired especially by a desire to know why words of love elude her in French, Assia Djebar evokes the four languages available to Algerian women. The first three are Arabic, Berber, and French. The fourth is the body, and the author stages this language in its relationship to physical love: "The fourth language, for all females, young or old, cloistered or half-emancipated, remains that of the body: the body which male neighbours' and cousins' eyes require to be deaf and blind, since they cannot completely incarcerate it; the body which, in trances, dances or vociferations, in fits of hope or despair, rebels, and unable to read or write, seeks some unknown shore as destination for its message of love" (180). Young's comments on "the cultural politics of hybridity" and the relationship between commerce and sexuality, between exchange and the body, are pertinent to the representation of the female body in the work of such authors as Djebar. Young's insights into the racialized nature of sexuality and desire constitute a crucial contribution to reflections on relations. When they describe the singular body in its different states, women writers elude the racist labels that seek to pigeonhole individuals according to their appearance. The drives and emotions that influence the women characters in these writers' texts reveal the complexity of hybrid beings whose bodies are a rich and complex terrain for thinking through the possibilities for loving and giving, as well as for creating places and forms of exchange that extend far beyond the pocketbook.

Djebar is certainly influenced by Cixous's writings on the body, and by her call to women to write their bodies, as Sauheila Ghaussy argues in her essay titled "A Stepmother Tongue: 'Feminine Writing' in Assia Djebar's *Fantasia: An Algerian Cavalcade.*" As Ghaussy articulates, "Djebar's specific employment of language as connected with the (female) body inevitably leads to questions concerning constructions of the female body by and within discourse as well as the construction of discourse by the body, and it leads to questions about difference, sexuality, and about what French feminists have called *écriture féminine*" (457). Though Ghaussy points out an awareness that "Irigaray and Cixous have been criticized for essentializing woman in their theories of écriture féminine" (457), she argues against this interpretation, focusing instead on the objective of "open[ing] up new discourses on 'femininity' and the body" "in order to promote feminist politics" (458). What I find particularly compelling in Ghaussy's article are her insights into how language is at work in Djebar's text. Ghaussy ascertains that "by deliberately blending fiction and experience, fictionality and language," and playing with conventional gendered distinctions between writing and gender, Djebar "undoes the male/female binary" (458). Disrupting preconceived notions with respect to gender, language, and writing may begin with the portrayal of the individual who is responsible for so much in her own "coming to writing," as in that of other women from Algeria: the father figure.

THE FATHER FIGURE

Maïssa Bey's novel *Surtout ne te retourne pas* (*Above All, Don't Look Back*) creates a parallel between the Algerian land and the body of the principal protagonist; both suffer from a trembling that shakes them profoundly and painfully: "The earth is moving. The ground trembles and I am unsteady on my feet" (41). Following the natural disaster of the earthquake, the young woman loses her memory. Her amnesia is not only intellectual but corporeal as well, and she must become reacquainted with her body when she sees herself in the mirror. The desire that is born when she (re)discovers herself in her reflection is related to an unknown history: "Could it be that other hands have caressed me, have passed along my body? That they have brought to life in me a similar, similar trembling?" (147). Her attempt to read her body does not yield any precise answers to these questions: "I don't read any imprint or mark on this body of mine which has appeared strange and foreign to me ever since the day when the earth expelled its entrails" (147). This character is fleeing, and the rhythm of her hurried steps appears to be in harmony with the ground she covers:

> I walk through the streets of the city.
> I walk forward, behind or ahead of—I don't know, I'm not sure, but what does it matter—ahead of or behind a dense cloud of intermingled dust and ashes....
> I walk on and everything in front of me abruptly cuts off my breath, my gaze—penetrates my flesh. (7)

The trip she undertakes with such courage is forbidden by both her family and the customs of her country: the narrative voice informs us that a woman is not supposed to walk alone outside the home in Algeria, that she must be accompanied if she ventures out. The fact that her flight is prohibited makes it all the more difficult.

Djebar's *L'amour, la fantasia* opens with a depiction of the young protagonist accompanied by her father on the road that leads to the school: "A little Arab girl going to school for the first time, one autumn morning, walking hand in hand with her father. A tall erect figure in a fez and a European suit, carrying a bag of school books. He is a teacher at the French primary school" (3). This oft-cited scene is remarkable for the hybridity it contains. The character of the father is dressed in a way that reflects his double inheritance, Western and "Oriental," for he wears both a European suit and a fez. He is a teacher of French, but he is Arab. This inheritance is the gift he gives to his daughter, who heads toward the French school where she will receive an education that will bestow her with a wardrobe and a vocabulary far removed from those reserved to the other young Arab girls in Algeria.

The author underscores the importance of this opening scene when she returns to the same image at a different point in the novel: "My father, a tall erect figure in a fez, walks along the village street; he pulls me by the hand and I, who for so long was so proud of myself—the first girl in the family to have French dolls bought for her, the one who had permanently escaped cloistering and never had to stamp and protest at being forced to wear the veil . . . I walk down the street, holding my father's hand" (*L'amour* 213). It is here, in the precisions of this later passage, that Djebar calls attention to the unprecedented movement of the girl who has access to the outside world while others are confined to the indoors when they reach puberty. She benefits from a privilege normally reserved to the French girls who are completely unaware of what is happening with their Algerian counterpart: "At the age when I should be veiled already, I can still move about freely thanks to the French school. . . . The French girls whirl around me; they do not suspect that my body is caught in invisible snares" (179). The French school is not the only place of study for the girl; she also frequents Qur'anic school, where knowledge is not unrelated to the body: "This Quranic learning, as it is progressively acquired, is linked to the body" (183). In a similar manner, her body is caught up in the act of learning French: "As soon as I learned the foreign script, my body began to move as if by instinct" (181). The fact that she learns both languages and their respective traditions destabilizes the preconceived idea that one is more natural than the other. The notion of hybridity effectively does away with prejudice tied to the ideas of cleanliness because it emphasizes the fact that no race or culture is "pure."

The protagonist of *L'amour, la fantasia* is faced with a choice that unfolds naturally between the two trainings she receives as a young girl: "As I approach a marriageable age, these two different apprenticeships, undertaken simultaneously, land me in a dichotomy of location. My father's preference will decide for me: light rather than darkness. I do not realize that an irrevocable choice is being made: the outdoors and the risk, instead of the prison of my peers" (184). The outdoors and risk are elements that distinguish and inspire Djebar's oeuvre, as the essays collected under the title *Ces voix qui m'assiègent* attest: "The source . . . of *l'écriture féminine* must be preserved. For it is anchored in the body, the woman's body that has become mobile and, because it is found in Arab territory, has from that moment entered into rebellion" (86). When she affirms that the source of *écriture féminine* should be preserved, the writer is making reference to the important place that she accords to the voices of women from Arabic and Berber languages that are translated in the French text. Her maternal heritage finds its way into her written work: "Therefore my word, which can be double, and perhaps triple, participates in several cultures, while I only have one writing: French" (42). The initial movement in space, outside the harem, that led to this literary translation took place thanks to the father and his hybrid status between two cultures as a French instructor in Algeria. It is not an accident that other women writers from the Maghreb, like Maïssa Bey and Leïla Sebbar, have this personal detail in common. Coming to writing in French during their childhoods is something all three of these individuals owe to having an Arab father who was an instructor of French in Algeria.

Je ne parle pas la langue de mon père (I don't speak my father's language) is a beautiful work, lyrical and fragmentary and repetitive, in which Sebbar evokes memories of her Arab father. He is a dignified, admirable man who is often silent and whose secrets the author is eager to uncover. The narrative voice recounts autobiographical moments from early years spent in a country that she should be able to embrace as her homeland, but where she is nonetheless considered a foreigner: "We, his children and his wife, foreigners in the popular, 'indigenous,' Muslim quarter, where he was the absolute master of the school and the benefactor of all the inhabitants, men, women, children, his people, fathers, mothers, sons and daughters of his people, of his language, of his land. And we? Shut up in the citadelle of the French language, of the colonial republic" (31). Sebbar stands out from the other women writers in this study because she has a French mother and an Arab father; she embodies a certain hybridity in her person that complicates the already ambiguous status of the young girl who grows up in a bifurcated colonial Algeria. According to a female character who expresses herself in the book, the difference between French and Algerian girls is clear: "The little French girls wore short dresses and skirts. They dressed this way and no one in the European homes thought that it was necessary to lengthen them by several centimeters in order to cover their thighs, at least down to their knees" (61). The young principal protagonist may be in the country of her father, but it is the morals of the mother's country that prevail in her experience: "He couldn't keep his daughters sequestered, like other fathers who had forbidden them from school, from the Qur'anic and French schools" (33).

As the title of her work indicates, Sebbar did not have the opportunity to attend the Qur'anic school, unlike Assia Djebar who benefited, at least for a short while, from this dual education that carried linguistic, cultural, and religious implications. On the contrary, it is the lack of Arabic, her ignorance of this language of the father, that inspires the author's quest throughout her oeuvre: "To hear the voice of the beloved stranger, the voice of the land and the body of my father that I write in the language of my mother" (125). Since she doesn't know her father's language, the daughter is forever distanced from him in a metaphorical sense, even after the family leaves Algeria for France: "That's what he thinks and, since his children were born body and language divided, it is that way, it has to be that way, until the next generation of children, strangers beyond the seas, far from him, to whom he spoke in the language of exile, the only one from then on, with the accent and the voice and the laughter or the anger of his absent, abandoned land" (23). The narrator underscores the silence that characterizes this being whose history remains unknown and thus, for the most part, presumed or imagined: "My father doesn't answer my questions" (23). If he keeps silent about certain elements of his past, the narrator does the same. The father is unaware of the way his daughters are treated when they walk in the street.

According to Sebbar's autobiographical account, it was beyond the walls of the house that she became aware of sexual difference and the status of girls and women who ventured outside in this country: "Thus my father, the commander of the fragile fortress of the colonial language, was unaware that his daughters were not sheltered from the sexual rage of boys.... The school teacher of the Republic, my father would never know that the silence of his language, in the house of the Frenchwoman, was transformed into words from hell, once the girls were out the door. They were asphyxiated, stunned by the repeated violence of the Arab speech, the language of sex" (28). The father is spared the reality of the verbal aggressions his daughters suffer from. His ignorance is a question of language, in part, for the girl can hardly recount what she understands without understanding. With what words, and in what language can she relate what regularly happens to her when she finds herself outside the home? But the father's ignorance stems also from modesty, and this publication by Sebbar reveals a truth that is typical in these works by women from Algeria. The writing of sexuality, as well as the writing of desire and sensual pleasure, necessitates a certain distance from the father. Writing in French is thus *both* a gift from the father *and* something that must be reappropriated by the daughter who makes it her own by writing the female body, by writing *herself*. This is why the relationship that is simultaneously tense and liberating between the body and language is at the very center of French-language writing by women from Algeria.

In *L'amour, la fantasia*, Assia Djebar discreetly describes a wedding night that takes place far from her native country. On this determinative day, the young bride wishes to get in touch with her father and tell him what she is feeling: "As we prepared to celebrate the wedding in our temporary Paris abode, ... thoughts of my father filled my mind: I decided to send him a telegram, assuring him formally of my love" (105). The expression of love for her father is made in the tongue he teaches, the language of the other that has become her only language of writing: "Perhaps I needed to make this public gratuitous declaration: 'I-love-you-in-French'" (105). When she declares her love openly, the daughter follows the example of the father, who had the courage to go against the taboos of his tradition and address letters directly to his wife: "The postcard was, in fact, a most daring manifestation of affection" (38). In Djebar's work, sensuality is as much a question of language as it is a matter of the body. The lovemaking she suggests in the text is generally not embellished, because the carnal union as she depicts it often bathes in silence.

The awakening of the female body in this particular autobiographical novel is anything but silent, for the virgin reacts vocally to the pain of penetration: "And I tiptoe up to the cry uttered on deflowering.... The sharp cry of relief and sudden liberation then abruptly checked. Long, infinite, first cry of the live body" (106). But the couple does not exchange a single word during this event that unites their bodies for the first time: "How can this blood be transformed into a ray of hope, without the two bodies being soiled? A well nigh mystical approach. In this Parisian wedding permeated with nostalgia for the native soil, no sooner has the bridegroom set foot in the room with its brand-new bed, and pink-shaded lamp placed on the floor, than he hurries to the waiting woman, he gazes down at her and forgets all else" (*L'amour* 106). The absence of words between husband and wife echoes the absence of discussion on this subject among women, as the first-person narrative voice explains: "Travelling in the Métro during the next few days, I stare closely at all the women I see around me. I am devoured with curiosity as if I were some primitive creature: 'Why do they not say, why will not one of them say, why does each one hide this fact: love is the cry, the persistent pain which feeds upon itself, while only a glimpse is vouchsafed of the horizon of happiness?'"

(107). The affirmative ending of this passage, this glimpse of possible happiness, indicates that a woman may find fulfillment in an amorous relationship if she and her partner find the appropriate words to accompany gestures of affection.

As we saw in chapter 2, Djebar refers to autobiographical writing as a *"mise à nu,"* a sensual, physical act that resembles the act of lovemaking. It is this act that also necessarily recalls colonization: "But this stripping naked, when expressed in the language of the former conqueror (who for more than a century could lay his hands on everything save women's bodies), this stripping naked takes us back oddly enough to the plundering of the preceding century" (*L'amour* 157). Even if she avows elsewhere that French was once the language of rape, of sexual violations perpetrated by the French invaders in her country, Djebar maintains that the former conqueror has not succeeded in "possessing" women's bodies. Despite his strength and domination, the body is something that eludes him. She who writes in the language of the former colonizers does it with her body, through her body, in a movement that demands the participation of her body: "To write is to return to the body, at the very least to the moving hand" (*Ces voix* 138).

GRAFTS AND GRAFFITI

Malika Mokeddem alternates chapters written by a man and a woman in her novel *L'Interdite* (*The Forbidden Woman*). Vincent and Sultana are the names of the central characters who narrate, in turn, revealing their feelings and experiences in the first person. Sultana resembles the author, having spent part of her life in her native Algeria and a later portion in France, where she currently resides. A doctor, Sultana practices a profession little known to women from her country of origin; she returns to the desert of her childhood when she learns of the death of a friend, or rather, of a lover, dear to her heart. This is the land where she spent the critical formative years of her life, but she is not "home": "The desert. Oran. Paris. Montpellier. A division of lands and a division of my interior countryside. Land that is dear to you, and that you're forced to leave, keeps you forever. By leaving, you become unused to yourself, you no longer live in yourself. You're nothing but a stranger everywhere. An impossible halt and an even more impossible return" (87). The position of permanent foreigner is uncomfortable for Sultana, who remains faithful to her vocation when she describes her pain as an exiled woman in medical terms: "I had a heart attack over my Algeria. Such a long time ago. Now my heart is again pounding without pain. But an aftereffect of necrosis remains: the bucket of abandonment at the never-sealed source of blood. I'm half paralyzed over my France. Little by little, half of my body has again found its automatic functioning, recuperated its sensations. Yet a zone of my brain remains mute to me, as if not lived in" (67). It wasn't a desire to find healing that motivated Sultana to return to her country of origin, but Vincent has made this trip to Algeria for the first time precisely because of the illness he is seeking to overcome.

Vincent, as his name suggests, is French, and had no connection to Algeria until now, when he learns the identity of the woman who saved his life by donating an organ. To his great surprise, the patient discovers that he owes his new kidney to an Algerian:

> A mutual assimilation and truce. "Excellent tolerance of the transplant. It was your kidney we transplanted!" reveled the doctors. But this tolerance couldn't keep me from thinking that with this organ, surgery had implanted in me two seeds of strangeness, of difference: the other sex and another "race." And the feeling of this double *métissage* of my flesh became deeply rooted in my thoughts and pushed me uncontrollably toward women and toward this other culture, which until then I had haughtily disregarded. (21)

Vincent marvels continuously at the double alterity he carries within him, at this other who carries him, who lives in him and makes him live. Like Sultana, but in a completely different way, Vincent has come to Algeria looking for a deceased person, for someone who is no longer there but whose presence is nonetheless undeniable and whose body lives on in memories.

The quests that Vincent and Sultana carry out in Algeria in Mokeddem's novel recall Djebar's insight in *Ces voix qui m'assiègent:* "It seems to me that it is through the bodies of mothers that the words of uprooted children begin to work, to be silent [*se taire*], and to hide [*se terrer*], in order to conduct research about the loss of the place of origin. . . . That is the future of an inevitable graft" (201). The recipient of a graft from an Algerian woman, Vincent has come to Algeria to somehow seek the loss he carries, an original loss that made of him an original being, a *hybrid*. He is not disappointed with this ambiguous status; to the contrary, he is ecstatic about it: "What a feeling to know that I had the same tissue identity as a woman and, moreover, a woman from elsewhere! Those who tell lies about the races would do well to take a glance at genetics!" (91). When he denounces racism in these exclamations, Vincent affirms on a genetic level what Homi Bhabha maintains with respect to culture, that purity is a myth, that hybridity defines us as human beings, and we only have to look to history (as the historian Assia Djebar does in her work) to find confirmation of this: "It is only when we understand that all cultural statements and systems are constructed in this contradictory and ambivalent space of enunciation, that we begin to understand why hierarchical claims to the inherent originality or 'purity' of cultures are untenable, even before we resort to empirical historical instances that demonstrate their hybridity" (156–57).

We have already noted that Sebbar is the fruit of a "mixed" union, to take up the cliché term; she is the daughter of an Algerian father and a French mother. In *Je ne parle pas la langue de mon père,* the author puts into question all notions of purity, not with respect to her own identity, but by turning to the appearance of her father's side of the family. In this autobiographical account, her French mother is surprised when she sees the light-colored eyes of her husband's relatives, a sentiment that inspires her father to revisit the history of his people: "That's why many from Tenes have light-colored eyes. One day, a boat collapsed at Cape Tenes. It was in 1802, I believe. The men from the tribes fought with the French sailors, there were deaths on both sides. Five women escaped the massacre ... In Tenes they held onto the virtuous women, even if they were Christian. They preferred nuns as ancestors. These shipwrecked Frenchwomen all had light-colored eyes. The five of them were naturally beautiful, pale and blond. That's how it was. We are the descendants of these women" (114–15). The father's words reveal that miscegenation has existed in Algeria for a very long time; there were "Franco-Algerian" unions even before the French conquest of Algeria in 1830. But, significantly, these mixed marriages are nonetheless connected to colonization. According to the father's story, the boat in question was heading toward Haiti, a land that was trying to liberate itself from the colonial rule of the French.

L'Interdite by Mokeddem calls attention to the audacious aspect of sexual relations between races when Sultana returns to her country. Just as the boys yelled insults at the young girls in Sebbar's aforementioned book, so the men shout injurious remarks at the accomplished woman in this novel. One man in particular makes very rude reproaches, bringing up the female protagonist's past in the following manner: "There's no point in making idiots of us! You're none other than Sultana Medjahed. Sultana, Sultana, ha, ha! Sultana from what? Like mother, like daughter! You, you make a fuss with me, but you sleep with the Kabyle and the roumi. When you were younger you were already sleeping with the roumis. Who was the first one to have you?" (100). The private act of lovemaking is made public in this passage where a man's voice rings out, mocking a woman. The use of the pejorative term *roumi,* in italics in the French text, underscores the foreign provenance of the men with whom it is alleged that Sultana made love. Not only did she dare to sleep with someone of another race, but she also deigned to do it with someone whose race was that of the former enemy.

The woman who is referenced in the title of *L'Interdite* is exposed to the judgments of others everywhere she goes in her country. She is denounced not only for her private life but also for her public life when the women she treats in an Algerian hospital interrogates her about her progeny: "I'm not totally a monster. In spite of my functions and my appearance, my body belongs to the league of candidates to the swollen body, to the faithful of the cult of the womb" (72). Men scrutinize her when she returns from the hospital on foot: "Leaving the hospital, I stroll aimlessly. Not for very long. Very quickly, feverish eyes overcome my indifference, interrogate me, interrupt me. Crowd full of eyes, black wind, lightning and thunder. I stroll no longer. I cut through a crowd of eyes. I walk against eyes, between their fires. En sortant de l'hôpital, je flâne sans but. Pas longtemps. And yet I no longer have a body. I am nothing but tension losing my way between the past and the present, a haggard memory that recognizes no reference" (68). This passage affirms that things have not changed in Algeria since the times of the childhoods described in the works of Djebar and Sebbar. An adult woman who returns to the country is subjected to condemnation if she walks in the streets. Her body is the center of attention, even if she contends that she no longer has one.

Sultana may say that she doesn't have a body anymore, but sensuality continues to play a considerable role in her existence, whether it is a question of her lived experience or her dream life. Her sexuality comes through in strong, moving passages like the following: "His hand, trembling a little, moves across my face as if it were a sculpture. I give in to it entirely. The wet yellow of his eyes causes exciting agitation. Out of our bodies glued to each other, from our looks that scrutinize each other, a dizziness arises" (39). The whirlwind of emotions felt in this textual moment is rendered through short, staccato sentences that leave the readers breathless, like the female protagonist. The positive potential of such moments of physical love is evoked in a single sentence by Vincent, who reflects on how his feelings for Sultana are good for him: "A woman, a love, are saving me from myself, healing me from my transplant and from the paradoxical feeling of a remedy derived from mutilation" (116–17). When these two beings unite, the relationship between the Frenchman hybridized by the graft from an Algerian woman and the Algerian woman hybridized by her life as a "Western" woman in France makes all sorts of things possible. According to Djebar, "The unavoidable *métissage* that nourishes every creative act takes the form of [*se vit dès lors*] an interior dichotomy, a painful amputation, a denial or a forgetting of its genealogical diversity" (*Ces voix* 56).

NEGOTIATIONS AND IDENTITIES

When Boniface Mongo-Mboussa asks literary critic Jean-Marc Moura about the concept of hybridity, the respondent draws from Bhabha's writings to explain that an understanding of the flexible nature of identities goes along with this "postcolonial" notion: "The hybrid world is a site of negotiation between two parties. It is understood that each party arrives at this site of negotiation with an identity that is not clearly defined, with a position that is ready for compromise, to ally itself with the other in order to try to realize something together. . . . Hybridity is therefore not a confrontation between two fixed identities, but rather the meeting of two identities that are in the process of becoming and who, through this negotiation, are going to become and 'become of'" (301–2; advenir). In *L'Interdite,* Sultana's return to Algeria brings her face-to-face with an identity that is unclear with respect to her past and fluctuating when it comes to the present. Vincent, in Algeria for the first time, is adjusting to a new, fragile identity that comes from the presence of another within him. Their love relationship, far from being a "confrontation between two fixed identities," is instead the reunion of several identities in flux.

Djebar's writing often illuminates the changing nature of every identity. In her novels, sexual relations can serve as catalysts for the multiple transformations that individuals experience. The diverse, unexpected "mixed" couples of various backgrounds that appear especially in *Les nuits de Strasbourg* show to what extent hybridities are the manifestations of a vivid hope in the future when they give place to exchanges filled with sensuality that is linguistic and corporeal.[2]

The female characters in contemporary writings by women born in Algeria must negotiate in order to make advances in their lives and reach their various goals. In *Vaste est la prison* (*So Vast the Prison*), Djebar presents the figure of an Arab mother who appears European: "She spoke now with no accent; her light chestnut-colored hair and her clothing from the most elegant shop in Algiers made people think not so much that she was a Frenchwoman (at forty, she seemed at least ten years younger, looking chic and a little tense) but rather a bourgeois from northern Italy or a frenchified Spaniard" (194). She takes advantage of her appearance and her knowledge of the French language to arrive at the prison in France where her son is incarcerated. She uses her intelligence and her allure to negotiate with the men who are detaining her beloved child, and she finally convinces them: they yield to her desire to see Salim, *"exceptionnellement"* (191). It is clear in this poignant passage that women often have to employ their intelligence along with all of their sensuality to achieve the desired ends. Successful negotiations are sensitive to sexual differences without entering into violent relations of physical force.

Maïssa Bey turns to her deceased father in *Entendez-vous dans les montagnes...* (Do you hear in the mountains...). The personal and emotional reflections in this book are evoked in the context of a train ride across France. The principal protagonist has fled Algeria for this country, where she is astonished at the ways in which sensuality is proclaimed in public: "Billboards, everywhere, nude bodies, offered, intertwined, brazen. And all of these couples tightly hugging, the need they have to touch each other, caress each other, kiss each other, everywhere, anywhere" (20). It seems contradictory to the Algerian woman that, while the bodies of passionate women are visible at every turn in France, nobody seems to see *her*, even the man who is seated across from her in the train compartment: "He doesn't look at her. Since she has been in this country, she has had a hard time getting used to not existing in the eyes of others" (10). He who shares this à huis clos with her does eventually look at her and tell her that he knows her country. She is disoriented: is it that obvious that she comes from elsewhere? Then she remembers that her jewelry from Kabylia announces her place of origin and reinforces her status of foreigner here (28). The foreigner that is Maïssa Bey seeks to learn in this particular work what happened to her father, who disappeared during the Algerian War.

Entendez-vous dans les montagnes is a hybrid publication containing transcribed dialogues of words exchanged that give way to poetic passages in italics. The appendices at the end of the text consist of documents belonging to the father, and the very first page displays a photograph whose caption indicates that this image is the only one that remains of this man. According to Jean-Marc Moura, postcolonial texts possess qualities that literary critics must learn how to read: "This amounts to treating works as hybrid oeuvres where two cultures coexist in a constant negotiation. What is interesting about a work is precisely this plural negotiation that takes place within each chapter" (Mongo-Mboussa 302). Like Sebbar's *Je ne parle pas la langue de mon père,* Bey's hybrid work asks questions without providing answers, exploring the different, often painful possibilities of the past. The script of the Frenchman and the Algerian woman on the train opens up the floor to a conversation between the two sides in the former conflict in Algeria.[3] In this narrative, the last words, pronounced by this other who was among the torturers, point to the physical resemblance between this lost father and the daughter who seeks to know the circumstances of his passing: "I wanted to tell you ... it seems to me that ... yes ... you have the same eyes ... the same look as ... as your father. You look a lot like him" (72). The hesitant speech of the man discloses a considerable depth of emotion. Years after this war was lost, he feels a loss of control, an acute regret for having hurt the other who was the father of this charming woman, and a desire to shed light on a situation that hurts both of them. Rather than run away from a difficult truth, Maïssa Bey does not shy away from trouble in this text, bringing to the forefront a woman who is searching for her multiple identities in the country of the other, confronting the absolute other in order to do so. This protagonist is not afraid to exchange words that wound, thanks to an overriding concern to lay claim to the past, to find oneself and to advance toward a more peaceful future. Such negotiations are not simple, but they lead to a realization of the plurality of each hybrid being in a postcolonial world.

Writing the body has unique meaning for women from Algeria, who have often been the victims of painful exclusion—whether racial or sexual—because of their appearance. Bringing up the body in the text is already a courageous move for many of those who were raised conservatively, but going so far as to celebrate the body in textual terms is an undeniably daring and meaningful gesture with particular significance for those intimately aware of the restrictive roles reserved for many women in their homeland. In their representation of the body, as in other ways, literary texts by francophone women writers are inevitably influenced by their authors' particular *histoires* in a particular place. The formative moment their authors spent in colonized Algeria is more than a backdrop for these literary texts; it is a lens from which to see the world. It has created within them a sensitivity to the multiple layers of meaning that are more than skin-deep, and it is this important experience in their native land that has driven these resolute, determined women to compose texts that adhere to the definition of *Polygraphies:* rich, innovative autobiographical works with an orientation that extends far beyond the individual self.

The next section turns to interpersonal relationships, to interactions between the individual and others that cannot be understood apart from the themes explored in the three preceding sections. When women writers engage in literary depictions of relationships, this place of departure that is Algeria and an understanding of the body that stems from this place inevitably emerge. Testimonial composition—this understanding of life and text as connected to others, as communicating to and for others—is by definition *in relation,* fluctuating and evolving in its portrayal of stories and narrations belonging to others as they interact with the self. In the section that follows, titled "Reverberations," I will examine the ways in which the autobiographical text opens up to others in compelling ways when individuals are shown to be acting and reacting, conversing and exchanging, both in Algeria and elsewhere, in the literary text.

PART IV   Reverberations

CHAPTER 7 | **Ruptures intimes** | Sentimental Splitting in the Work of Assia Djebar

> *How then does the text, as it escapes you on its way toward the other (male or female readers, those who await you or who are there by accident), yes, how does this writing—of you and about you—tear you apart, ripping out pieces of yourself*
> —Assia Djebar, Ces voix qui m'assiègent *(These voices that besiege me)*

Much has been written about Assia Djebar's multiple cultural and linguistic affiliations, and the various separations that have occasioned her many belongings. In this chapter, I explore another aspect of her oeuvre, one that has not yet been examined in detail: the portrayal of love relationships in recent novels. In a number of works by Djebar, long-lasting relations between heterosexual couples prove scarce. Breakups recur frequently in Djebar's literary production, a fact that Beïda Chikhi addresses in the following general terms: "These love stories, often problematic from the point of view of the Muslim morale, were experienced in silence, in hiding, and now, suddenly, have been revealed to the public. This public delivery sometimes becomes tragic in the novel, as it does in reality, and seeks to make people sensitive to what should not be considered a challenge to the law, but rather a quest for happiness" (46). An examination of various textual representations of what I call *ruptures intimes* will help us to decipher the multiple meanings of these "finished" relationships. I contend that the end of a love affair in Djebar's various writings is inevitably portrayed as a positive occurrence, opening up to movement and possibility and resisting the trap of settling down in the form of establishing roots and embracing predictability. While separation is painful and trying, it makes the individual stronger and freer in Djebar's texts, wherein sentimental splitting ultimately presents the only solution to continued creativity in art and life.

L'amour, la fantasia, Djebar's first openly autobiographical publication, depicts a wedding that falls outside the borders of the participants' native country, an event that we examined briefly in the last chapter for what it revealed about the relationship between the bride and bridegroom. Since the matrimonial event is set in Paris, as we saw, the traditional gestures accompanying this rite of passage in Algeria do not take place. Not only is the community absent, but the father is missing as well, and the reader is presented with a mother out of context, deprived of the mourning that usually follows the symbolic crossing of the threshold in Djebar's religious and cultural tradition: "But tradition demanded that when the women in the bridal retinue are ready to escort the ride, the father wraps his burnous around her and leads her over the threshold in his arms. At this moment of separation, the mother weeps copiously, sometimes noisily—you'd think it was a wake without the liturgy" (*L'amour* 104). The narrative voice moves from the general trend to her own particular case, slipping from the third to the first person to evoke her mother's reaction in this poignant phrase: "My mother, for her part, found herself in a wintry Paris and had no cause to weep" (105). The fact that the mother does not shed any tears on this occasion prefigures the dry eyes to come; this particular expression of emotion is not found in the writer's treatment of separation in her written work. Instead, a different form of communication is privileged: the cry.[1]

From the outset, marriage means breaking with the past for the first-person narrator of *L'amour, la fantasia:* "What marriage meant to me first and foremost was departure" (122). This initial rupture—geographic and affective—serves as a portent for other separations. The eventual dissolution of the marital contract is present in the very description of the newlyweds' first night together. The tearing of the hymen, with all its pain and promise, fails to produce a fusion between the two united bodies, resulting in rigid silence, rather than open verbal exchange, as we noticed in the previous chapter. The bride's only means of verbal communication on this momentous evening is a scream, and her outburst marks yet another departure from tradition: "Normally the bride neither cries out nor weeps: she lies an open-eyed victim on the couch, after the male has departed, fleeing from the smell of sperm and the idol's perfume; and the closed thighs prevent any cry from escaping" (*L'amour* 108). It is remarkable that the bride is not customarily allowed any means of expression on this occasion; instead, she is described as a "victim" who is abandoned by her mate as soon as intercourse is complete.

In a matter of pages, the marriage has come to an end after a long, sinuous, faltering fifteen years: "A long history of convulsive love; too long. Fifteen years pass, what happened is of little account" (*L'amour* 114). The duration of the relationship hardly seems anecdotal, but the time spent together is not integrated into the text; it is as if this past is only important as prelude. Once again, the narrative voice alternates between the first and the third person to tell of a solitary nocturnal promenade in the streets of

Paris at the final hour of this relationship, a walk intended to bring closure and perspective to the principal protagonist. Coming full circle, she finds herself screaming once again, as she did on her wedding night, yet she is so absorbed in her thoughts that she is unaware of the sound she is producing: "this outlandish voice, this lamento which I involuntarily sing.... The wailing stops short" (116). The man who is privy to this accidental solo, the attentive stranger mentioned in chapter 1, plays an important role in helping the distraught woman move beyond this marital relationship at its end: "Hearing the man implore me, like a friend, like a lover, I regained soon afterwards my zest for life. I threw off the shackles of love, ridding myself of the canker that consumed me" (116).

In a later autobiographical volume by Djebar, *Vaste est la prison,* the specter of divorce hovers over the unconsummated adulterous love story of the novel's first section, until the split between husband and wife becomes final. The details of the text reveal that bringing the marital relationship to a decisive end is not unproblematic. Enamored with a younger man and dissatisfied with her marriage, the first-person narrator recounts her impulse to confess her feelings to her spouse: "I asked him to listen to me, that we be willing to say 'everything' in one night" (83). It is significant that the confession that takes place does not lead to a positive outcome. Indeed, breaking with the code of silence and revealing her deepest desires leads to battering: "First he insulted. Then he struck.... 'Adulteress,' he muttered" (85). Even this violent behavior is not enough to make the wife leave the relationship for good; she returns to her role in the home after a brief separation: "In fact two or three weeks after this breakup, I agreed, yes, agreed to return to my life as wife . . . I accepted, yes. I see once again the sequence of my return unfolding and—now that it is all over, now that all connections are broken, my passion evaporated—disintegrating" (97). Coming back to the husband after a brutal beating seems illogical in retrospect, but the word *passion* in this quotation serves as a key to understanding the reason(ing) behind such a return.

Vaste est la prison contains a heartrending passage that sets up a contrast between a passionate love unto death and a fleeting pleasure that lasts but a moment. The former is what the narrator seeks, and finally locates, in a forever-removed Western literary institution; she determines that the latter is all she can hope for in Islamic tradition. Trying to reconcile the desired passion that extends up to (and beyond) the grave and her religious and cultural background therefore proves to be unfruitful: "This final love, this passion to the point of death that I seek. Because there is no Isolde in

Ruptures intimes 131

Islam, because there is only sexual ecstasy in the instant, in the ephemeral present . . . as for myself, I want still to be loving with my last sigh; yes, I want to feel, even when borne off on the shoulders of funerary bearers, on that plank, I want to feel myself going toward the other, I want still to love the other in my decay and my ashes" (108). This desire to love until her last breath and even after her physical demise is incompatible with the reality of her situation. Later in the text, it becomes clear that her idealization of the love affair stems from an intoxication with poetry, "a secret exaltation of sentiment. . . . As a result soon afterward, and too quickly, I fell into love for the first time, absolutely" (302). The exalted sentiments expressed in poetry are not in step with everyday existence and with ordinary communication in her native Algeria. On the contrary, the very language of her husband's community bears witness to relationships that are doomed from their inception: even women in "harmonious" marriages refer to their husbands as "the enemy" in Arabic (109).

The narrator in *Vaste est la prison* appears to conclude that, while passion is ephemeral, the absence of passion can be permanent, and she decides to terminate her marriage rather than settle for this disappointment: "Put up a door between the husband and myself. Now. Forever!" (109). What lasts forever is therefore not love, in this case, but the end of love. No more returns are possible after this final farewell. It is not within the specific context of her marriage, but rather with respect to a long, unspoken and unrealized love affair—the unconsummated relationship of the first section—that the word *adieu* emerges in this novel. This word follows (after several pages) the textual reflection on the impossibility of passion, seeming to affirm the difference between this "immortal" emotion and its more "earthly" counterpart, an ordinary love affair. In a significant narrative twist, the "adieu" becomes the moment that defines the relationship that precedes it as belonging to "true" love or its simple imitation: "So, frequently, in what is ordinarily called a love story (often only a story of abduction where it is never really decided who is the thief and who is the one taken), the ending is settled by exhaustion, or asphyxiation. There is never the disinterested elegance of an explicit goodbye, or a goodbye blown like a kiss, sent like mercy or a gift" (111). The depth of the emotional ties between her and the younger man necessitates a proper goodbye and leads the narrator to elucidate the importance of this closing note: "There is always a goodbye in a true love story" (111). The elegance of their final encounter, its grace and its gift, is contained in the certainty that their paths will never cross again.

In her analysis of this "intimate story" from the opening section of *Vaste est la prison,* Debra Kelly concludes that Djebar wrote it out of a "need to know herself better, to be as close to self as possible" (*Autobiography and Independence* 301). Kelly concludes that for Djebar, telling this story is tantamount to coming to "self-knowledge," to "full possession of selfhood," since the "narrator steps out of one life and into another" as a writer (302). It is important that the dissolution of this initial relationship is connected to writing in this examination, and that the specific type of writing that these breakups stimulate is self-oriented, providing the writer with the opportunity to "find herself" and to define herself outside of a particular marital status. The experience of this first "adieu" paves the way for a series of farewells, according to the narration. The relationships that follow are not mentioned by name. They are briefly referred to in collective form as shorter and denser than the drawn-out story of the first section of this novel. If they are not characterized by "passion," these later affairs are marked nonetheless by attraction, even if they more often resemble friendships tinged with tenderness than purely physical encounters marked by uncontrollable desire; whatever their particular flavor, these couplings are by nature temporary, and they all carry with them an ending: "there were other goodbyes" (113). What is significant is that even as they increase in number, and even though they all meet with an end, the narrative voice admits that despite their irrevocable halt, these experiences will carry resonance for years to come: "Pauses in an inner music, never to be forgotten" (113). It is noteworthy that the final chord of the relationship, the very point of parting, remains most vividly memorable afterward. Perhaps this is why the narrator delineates the details of her divorce in novel form.

During the time of separation prior to her formal divorce, the principal protagonist of *Vaste est la prison* plunges into her maternal heritage and finds a precedent for her flight from what has become an unfulfilling marriage. Just as her grandmother held firm and insisted on her legal rights on the occasion of her own divorce decades earlier, so the protagonist does not back down when it comes to this split. Her aunt's questions during this period of transition make clear the obscure nature of the rights of women in their Algerian homeland, and underscore the importance of being familiar with and insisting on the implementation of the law: "You are leaving the man, you flee, you abandon the unlocked house to him? Is that the law, are you at least retaining your rights? . . . Alas, where are our rights, whether we are illiterate or educated, all of us, all women? It is as bad as yesterday" (217). Literate and educated, the main character is familiar with the law but refrains from using it to her advantage before the judge: her silence and a hint of a smile lead to "a verdict of separation, ruling that the 'fault was mine'" (315). She is unconcerned with material gain; for her what matters in the divorce is that she has exercised her right to repudiate her husband, and has in this way had the last word in their conjugal life. In a similar manner, Djebar is also indifferent to the possibility of exonerating herself, and putting the blame on another, both in her personal life and in her work. What matters in her written testimony is not a desire to set the record straight in a futile effort to make up for the past but a desire to move on, to step forward with an understanding of the past that will be fruitful for the future.

In *Vaste est la prison,* the mother jumps with surprise when she learns that it is her daughter, rather than her son-in-law, who has pronounced three times the performative utterance that terminates the relationship in Islamic tradition: "She was startled by the Arab word, *repudiation,* that I had used! 'Irrevocable,' I added, 'because it was pronounced three times! I know. I am the one who made the vow!'" (313). Telling her mother of her divorce is important, for bringing her marital relationship to a formal finish does not solely affect a woman's relationship to a man. It also comes to bear on her rapport with other women in the community. The most obvious example of this is to be found in the main character's attachment to her mother-in-law, whom she meets in an airport two or three years after the divorce: "Here in this chaotic airport I discovered how much this one loss from the breakup of my marriage hurt me, the loss of this woman alone, her, the mother of my first husband" (335). The loss of this cherished woman is perhaps the most painful aspect of this breakup, and it is not the only example of its kind. The narrative voice admits that it is the rupture with mothers and sisters of significant others that proves to be most difficult to overcome: "When I leave a man, I have a hard time getting over the absence of his mother, or sometimes his sisters" (337). Choosing a lifestyle that defies commitment to any one man over a long period of time precludes a steady, familial-like relationship with other women.

Recalling an evening out with her husband shortly before the disintegration of their marriage, the first-person narrator of *Vaste est la prison* describes an episode in which she distanced herself from the group of women, her relatives, by dancing alone: "I think that the important thing was the challenge my engulfed body made by expecting to improvise the movements. The important thing was to distance myself as much as possible from the collective frenzy of those women" (61). Even if this private dance causes the women around her to feel betrayed, she who is finding her own improvisational movement cannot turn back. Separation from the women of her homeland is the price she must pay for her "solitary dance, fleeting, 'modern'" (61).

Djebar's autobiographical texts illustrate the fact that rifts in male-female relationships are not the sole impetus for her separation from the women of her native land. Sentimental splits between her and her lovers mirror in significant ways the departures—real and metaphoric, and especially linguistic—that characterize the writer's life path.[2] The act of "translating" her compatriots' words into French is not only fraught with historical and technical difficulty for Djebar, it is also an undertaking that creates a gap between her and those whose stories she represents on paper.[3] If it is a challenge to accurately render the words of others in her work, but it is perhaps an even greater trial to write of oneself; metatextual commentary on the autobiographical genre in *L'amour, la fantasia* contains remarkably vivid, visceral words that address in corporeal terms the linguistic break this textual enterprise entails: "To attempt an autobiography using French words alone is to lend oneself to the vivisector's scalpel, revealing what lies beneath the skin. The flesh flakes off and with it, seemingly, the last shreds of the unwritten language of my childhood. Wounds are reopened, veins weep, one's own blood flows and that of others, which has never dried" (156).

Even in this painful passage, recourse to the French tongue can be interpreted as a mixed blessing, for it carries connotations that are positive.[4] First, speaking autobiographically is possible in French, but it is not an acceptable form of speech in the dialectical Arabic of Djebar's homeland. Speaking of themselves in the first person is not a possibility for women in Algeria: "The 'I' of the first person is never used; the time-honoured phraseology discharges the burden of rancour and râles that rasp the throat" (154); "How could she say 'I,' since that would be to scorn the blanket-formulae which ensure that each individual journeys through life in a collective resignation?" (156).[5] It is not the collectivity that poses a problem here, but rather the resignation that characterizes it, as exemplified in the absence of any idiosyncratic form of expression or creative formulation. Secondly, a French educational system in her town permitted the future writer to "escape" from the harem and "avoid" the veil in her adolescence; her cousins and friends did not enjoy the same privileges. Writing in French has given Djebar freedom of position and possibilities for movement that many women in Algeria do not possess. This is why, in her 2006 acceptance speech at the Académie Française, Djebar embraced

Ruptures intimes 135

French as her own, in an important passage of affirmation, indicating that the language has now become a part of her very body, as intimate as a heartbeat: "For decades, this language is no longer for me the language of the Other. It is almost a second skin, or a language that is infiltrated in yourself, its beating against your pulse, or right next to your aortic artery . . . providing the rhythm for your walk." Finally, the separation from the tongue(s) of her homeland is not final (in contrast to the divorce depicted in her texts). The narrative voice in *L'amour, la fantasia* demonstrates the capacity of the Arabic "mother tongue" to overcome distance between man and woman, to (re)create intimacy between two remote individuals: "I finally recover my power of speech, using the same understatements, interlace the allusiveness of tone and accent, letting inflexions, whispers, sounds and pronunciation be a promise of embraces. . . . At last, voice answers to voice and body can approach body" (129).

In Djebar's recent texts, even when the "miracle" of love does emerge between a man and a woman who are willing to take the risk of getting to know each other, a rupture of the budding relationship is inevitable. This is not the case for all of the couples represented in these texts, fortunately, but it is certainly the situation for the principal protagonist and his or her significant other. The term *significant other* is particularly appropriate to describe the partners Thelja and François, who come together—in spite of their different ages and contrasting backgrounds—for nine nights of lovemaking in *Les nuits de Strasbourg*. A strong, intelligent young woman from Algeria, Thelja is in charge of these nine romantic encounters with the older Frenchman. She dictates the conditions of these interludes from the outset and thereby eliminates in advance any hope for a long-term relationship. The sharing that takes place between these two individuals over the course of their nights together is free from the constraints that accompany the very prospect of a lasting arrangement.

Thelja, having broken free from the bonds of marital responsibility and maternal duty in her native country, has no intentions of settling down in Strasbourg, nor does she entertain thoughts of prolonging her liaison with François beyond the projected nine nights. This arbitrary period will be enough to convince him to adopt a nomadic lifestyle that resembles hers: "I insist on changing hotels every night. . . . Why? Maybe it is my way of making him feel that he should become a nomad! Without attachments, like me, but in his own town, the place of his past, the place where he works!" (*Nuits* 109). What is crucial in this quotation is the message of the final three phrases; Thelja has not managed to free herself from attachments within the geographical space of her own country. For her to make a clean break, a change in location—a crossing of borders both real and symbolic—was necessary. But she is right to assume that such a radical rupture is not needed in order for her lover to sever long-established ties. The narrative reveals that François's apprenticeship under the direction of "this nomadic brunette" is effective: "he will never settle down again" (297).

While François's words are occasionally present in the form of spoken dialogue in *Les nuits de Strasbourg,* the reader seldom has access to this male character's thoughts and reactions. Such is not the case in *La disparition de la langue française,* a 2003 novel in which the first-person narrative voice belongs to a man rather than a woman. The narrator provides us with the perspective of a man who falls in love with a woman who, in a remarkably similar way to other women in Djebar's corpus, embraces movement and appears to shun attachments that can quickly transform themselves into obligations. The narrator asks the following rhetorical question about his new love in an attempt to "pin her down," to "get a read on her": "She is close to forty now: a mature woman, anchored, but where?" (*Disparition* 132). As in the earlier publication, *Les nuits de Strasbourg,* the nights the two lovers share are limited: "I promise to speak to her, in turn, to seek myself, to let myself go during our next night: the last" (*Disparition* 151). It is clear in this instance that the man is not content with the brevity of this romantic encounter. He puts off the thought of their parting and dreams of the possibility of a whole life together: "I liked this interlude. It gave me the illusion that the two of us could spend a whole life together still" (152). The rupture that will soon separate them is a very literal break, a "tearing," in the narrator's view, that is part of a painful reality: "Everything became lighthearted voluptuousness, and I could no longer perceive the prosaic reality that was going to tear us apart!" (167; nous déchirer).

The choice of the adjective *prosaic* is critical to this exclamation and the message it conveys, for this term recalls the aforementioned passage from *Vaste est la prison* in which the first-person narrator indicates that it was the intoxicating effect of poetry that provoked her first love: "An intoxication with poetry . . . made me fall in love for the first time, absolutely. That lasted seventeen years" (302).[6] This autobiographical account reveals the ending of this "absolute" experience of first love, which is portrayed in curious terms in *L'amour, la fantasia.* Instead of focusing on details of misery and mistreatment, the narrator indicates that it is the happiness of this marital situation that becomes unbearable in retrospect: "a happy life is compact, uneventful. Satiety lasts long; too long" (114). While the words *boredom* and *routine* are not employed in this laconic treatment of the end of the relationship, they certainly are contained within the striking link to death in this work: "I freed myself from voracious love and its necrosis," declares the narrator, who has been "exhumed" from her burial place as a married woman (*L'amour* 132). A return to the prosaic is what marks the later texts by Assia Djebar. These works contain no "poetic" aspirations of an eternal love that is forever burning in its intensity and fulfillment; instead, they communicate an understanding that love is best when—like life—it is treasured in its unique time, when it is appreciated as a fleeting night, when it is taken as an ephemeral moment to be savored.

The outdoors is a metaphor that continually recurs in the work of Assia Djebar. Often communicated through such terms as *soleil* or *espace* or *rue*, the urban settings for this francophone writer's novels are presented as joyful places to be discovered. Following the dissolution of her first marriage, as depicted in *Vaste est la prison*, the daily existence of this unattached woman is marked by an awareness of the elements: "As for myself, when I left this *mahakma* at midday, all I saw outside was the sun. And a second later I felt its actual heat, its vibration almost exploding against me, right in the chest" (315).[7] While the sun is often present, its occasional absence is not a source of deep chagrin after her "liberation," as we learn in *L'amour, la fantasia:* "Spending every day laughing, dancing, walking. The only thing I long for is the sun" (116; Seul le soleil peut me manquer). What is most valued in this portrayal of existence after the undoing of marital ties is—without a doubt—movement.

Just as the principal protagonist of *Vaste est la prison* improvises on the dance floor in a decisive gesture of individualization among her countrywomen prior to her divorce, so the writer benefits from freedom to come and go as she chooses after this decisive rupture. Her connection to space brings her a "simple joy" that stands out in sharp contrast to the sentiments of her female compatriots who have bent their own wills in order to live harmoniously: "I felt I could not accept for myself the almost funereal joy of their bodies, verging on a fettered despair" (*Vaste* 61). Indeed, her joy is completely different: "Simple joy, thick of course and slow, joy in space each time it opens up, unscathed joy" (*Vaste* 302). Thelja of *Les nuits de Strasbourg* describes a love for space that struck her when she was but eighteen years old: "an irresistible urge for space. Space attracted me!" (315). The autobiographical voice of *Vaste est la prison* concurs: "So, intoxicated with space and motion, I dreamed my life; I danced my little life of an odalisque who has left the frame for good, at least until I turned forty. . . . And ever since? Between shadow and sunlight, between my vulnerable freedom and the fetters imposed on the women of 'my home,' I zigzag along the frontier of a bitter, voracious land" (321–22). The very zigzag movement of this quotation reveals Assia Djebar's own reticence with respect to the nomadic lifestyle she frequently depicts as idyllic. The liberty of continual displacement, the freedom of constant rupture, carries with it a real sense of vulnerability. It is significant that the character Isma in another autobiographical work, *Ombre Sultane* (*A Sister to Scheherazade*), returns to her home after years of travel and considers donning the veil and moving back in with her community; such a reparation of a breach may represent a deep human desire to reconnect with tradition and to reestablish a sense of stability in a world that may be just as "voracious" as the bonds of marital commitment.[8]

Breaking with her land and her language has left painful traces in the writing of Assia Djebar, as have the terminations of various amorous relationships. Always moving on may not ultimately be satisfying, but it is, as presented in this oeuvre, the best solution. Splitting up gives way to "sunshine," to employ Djebar's term, and it is this source of light and energy that puts things (including the writer's pen) in motion. If no returns are possible, if separations are definitive, then literature is nonetheless the place of revisiting the past and reconnecting with the other, with a multitude of others, as Thelja reminds us in *Les nuits de Strasbourg:* "It is not yet the end of the trip, I am not sleeping in the train on the way back, there is no return yet, there are never any returns, François, I am calling you now, I am hailing you . . ." (348). The forlorn lover of *La disparition de la langue française* echoes Thelja from afar: "I write, haunted by Nadjia, and I hope that she will recognize my voice, reading me one day, even at the other end of the earth! . . . I write in her shadow and despite the separation" (180). Literature is the place of the call, and the cry; it is the location of rupture and reparation, of infinite possibility. It is the "space"—and the only steady, ongoing "relationship"—chosen by a liberated, ever-moving Assia Djebar, the place from which she will never return.

CHAPTER 8 | Lourds retours | Coming Back to Algeria in Malika Mokeddem's *L'Interdite*

> *My unexpected sisters and I give each other Algeria and for the past we have the future without violence of which we dream together.*
> —Hélène Cixous, "My Algeriance"

The depiction of male-female love relationships, and their eventual, inevitable endings in Assia Djebar's recent writings, finds an echo in a recent text by Malika Mokeddem titled *Mes hommes* (*My Men*). In this autobiographical work, Mokeddem revisits her relationships with various men in her life, and the final chapter reveals that like Djebar, this Algerian-born novelist has not found a passionate love to last her lifetime, though she remains optimistically open to the possibility. In light of this lack of continuity in her love life, Mokeddem states her awareness of the importance of returning to her childhood in order to find herself again: "After all the rebellions, ruptures, departures, and exiles, only our childhood can reconcile us to ourselves" (169). The numerous breaks that make up her life story necessitate textual returns from her adopted country, France, to her homeland, like the one that takes place in *L'Interdite*. This suggestive work of fiction, published in 1993, was the focus of some of our explorations of sensuality and the body in chapter 6, but it merits further examination as a text that straddles the boundaries between fiction and autobiography in a gesture that imitates the vacillating movement of impossible return that the text embodies.

While *L'Interdite* is not strictly "autobiographical," it is nonetheless infused with important personal elements: "Malika Mokeddem certainly put a great deal of herself in *L'Interdite* when she declares with respect to her novel: 'My story must revisit its wounded past in order to heal from destructive nostalgia while preserving itself from the dead-ends of the present; exile is survival'" (Bénayoun-Szmidt 117). These words attributed to Mokeddem are taken from a quotation in an article by Christiane Chaulet-Achour, appropriately titled "Autobiographie d'Algériennes sur l'autre rive: Se définir entre mémoire et rupture" (Autobiography by Algerian women on the other shore: Defining Oneself between memory and rupture). The autobiographical element that runs throughout Mokeddem's oeuvre is engaged in exploring the relationship between memory and forgetting, between making reparations with the past and breaking with it definitively. A statement on the back cover of the author's ninth book, *Je dois tout à ton oubli* (I owe everything to forgetting you), brings to the forefront the ambiguous nature of autobiographical labels when it comes to these works of fiction: "After two autobiographical texts, *La Transe des insoumis* and *Mes hommes*, Malika Mokeddem adopts the path of the novel here, to explore a painful part of her memory that involves her relationship with her mother." We might understand this sentence to mean that Mokeddem feels more at ease in a work considered to be strictly fictional to explore the painful aspects of her memory than she does in a text that is declared to be autobiographical. The implication that more personal truth may be communicated in a novel that does not bear the qualifying adjective *autobiographical* than in one that does is in line with our understanding of the testimonial nature of the intimate writing under consideration in *Polygraphies*. I would like to propose a close reading of *L'Interdite* with this understanding in mind, focusing more on the multiple truths that may be revealed in the novel than on a detailed search for textual reflectivity that might allow us to draw connections between the work and the life of the writer.

Principal protagonist Sultana is a doctor in Montpellier, an exiled woman who believes that she has put fears, threats, and confinement behind her by leaving her place of birth. But when a former flame writes to her and she goes back to Algeria, this strong and supposedly detached woman discovers that she is haunted by her country, that she has not left her past behind in definitive ways. Indeed, this impromptu return reveals that the daughter of illiterate nomads remains tied to her homeland despite her present life and work in France. Her education and professional activities may have provided a certain distance from home, but they have not replaced the ghosts of an indelible past. At the same time, her country has moved on, it has changed to such an extent that she is not at home there, that she is a veritable anachronism, a vestige of a period and a place that no longer exist. This powerful work proves that emigrant writing that seeks to represent home always finds itself in the middle of past and present, caught between the memories of what once was and the incongruities of what the place of origin has become.

PHYSICAL AND METAPHYSICAL RETURNS

L'Interdite is dedicated to two entities that have suffered from interdicts: the Algerian francophone writer Tahar Djaout, "forbidden to live because of his writings," and a women's group named Aïcha, "my Algerian women friends who refuse to be forbidden." The author calls attention from the outset to the controls and dangers that writers and women must constantly face in Algeria, as well as to gender differences. The book takes the form of alternating chapters bearing the names of their narrators: Sultana and Vincent. The obvious advantage of this structure is that two different perspectives are represented throughout the text, that the voice of an Algerian woman is valorized alongside that of a French man. But as it turns out, we cannot categorize in such simple terms these two individuals whose paths cross in Algeria under unusual circumstances. Each of these narrator-protagonists is a hybrid being in various senses, as we have already seen, characterized by connections to Algeria and France. Vincent is the most obvious embodiment of this hybridity, since, as we saw in chapter 6, he has received an organ transplant from an Algerian woman. Following this operation, he has taken time off from his professional engagements as a university mathematics professor and has embarked on a journey to Algeria, a "return" of sorts, to the place of origin of "this foreign woman with the same identity," as he puts it (22). Recall that Vincent is fascinated by the otherness of the person whose "tissue identity" is an exact match to his own. Not only is this person of another ethnicity, but she is also of the opposite sex, and his complex identity is further complicated by her vital presence within him: "Gascon, Christian, and atheist by my father; Jewish by my mother, Polish and practicing out of solidarity; North African through my transplant and with no borders, through a 'tissue identity,' I nevertheless have gregarious and stubborn habits. My identity gathers nectar according to its own will, makes its honey, and crosses one old tannin with another. It mixes, accommodates" (49). Vincent's trip to Algeria is a journey to a place he has never been, but this movement nonetheless constitutes a return, at once figurative and real.

Sultana indicates from the novel's outset that she never imagined a return to her homeland was possible: "I would never have believed it possible to return to this place. And yet I've never really left it. All I have done is incorporate the desert and the inconsolable into my displaced body. The have split me in two" (3). This brief paragraph from the book's opening page reveals the intensity of Sultana's relationship to the country she has never completely left behind, since the desert has become a part of her displaced body. She evokes the tearing that has split her in two, as she describes again elsewhere: "I carefully envelop myself in my dissident and different Sultanas. One is nothing but emotions, exaggerated sensuality....

The other Sultana is sheer will" (6). The splitting comes up again much later in the text, when she refers to "My Sultanas, antagonists, find themselves disjointed, dislocated. . . . My two parts feed off of each other. Separated, they are both deactivated, defused. And I, who lived in their narrow junction, tumultuous and torn between . . . I find myself, in the name of their scission, drifting in a calm, detached from everything, frozen" (67). As the latter part of this quotation suggests, her identity cannot be cleanly bifurcated, and in later passages she admits to "several dispersed me's" (86) and explains as follows: "I've been many-faceted and torn apart since childhood. That's only been aggravated with age and exile" (111–12).

Multiple movements, numerous flights have contributed to the accompanying diverse identities that Sultana describes in textual moments of reminiscing and soul-searching, inspired by this unforeseen return to the place of her birth, a village called Aïn Nekhla: "I see myself again as an adolescent girl leaving the region for Oran's boarding school. I remember the painful circumstances of that departure. As flight becomes rupture, as absence becomes exile, time itself shatters. What remains? A rosary of fears, the inevitable baggage of exodus" (3). Even the man for whom she has returned, the deceased Yacine Meziane, is someone whose love she fled and now that she has come back, too late, Sultana realizes that she is revisiting distant shadows, an endeavor she never should have undertaken: "Our love has never been anything but that: flight. What did I come here to find? I have the unpleasant sensation of having yielded to something whose origin was decency, to a sort of desire for voyeurism. I should never have revisited these places from my past. The little girl that I was is still there among the shadows of other children who had a similar fate" (17). Sultana cannot help but wonder why she was moved to return *now*, why this precise moment is the one that inspired her to take the trip she never thought she would: "Why this sudden desire to reestablish contact? Is it because I was sick of the world? A nausea resurfacing from other things forgotten, through disenchantment with somewhere else and other places, in the harsh light of lucidity?" (4).

This book is in many ways about the body, about physical displacement and its consequences. As Winifred Woodhull reminds us in *Transfigurations of the Maghreb*, "In the case of Ben Jelloun and other Maghrebian writers such as Khatibi and Rachid Boudjedra, textual nomadism stands in relation to real changes in the writers' geographical location—their movement between France and the Maghreb" (89). It is perhaps no accident that Sultana, who is a physician, has recourse to corporeal metaphors when describing her relation to the two countries that make up her itinerary: "I had a heart attack over my Algeria. . . . I'm half paralyzed over my France" (*L'Interdite* 67). When she meets Vincent, she is able to converse with him about the biological and anatomical details of his transplant and, again, to make an important metaphorical statement about the incorporation of foreign bodies: "The same goes for the transplant as with any integration of a 'foreigner.' The work of reciprocal acceptance is necessary: chemical work exerted by pharmaceutical remedies on patients' bodies, for one, pedagogical remedies on the social body, for the other" (118). Sultana speaks with authority on the question of physical remedies, but she also speaks with authority on the question of social remedies, for she is a foreigner in France, a place that has hardly incorporated her effectively: "In France now, I'm neither Algerian nor even North African. I'm an Arab. That's as much as to say nothing. Arab, this word dissolves you in the grayness of a nebula" (112).

What becomes clear to Sultana as time passes in Algeria is that while a return may be possible in body, it is hardly possible in spirit. She is forced to admit that this is a return that isn't one: "A return that isn't a return" (67). This startling revelation makes her reconsider the past, indicating that time has cast a shadow on everything that "ruined my images of years past, destroyed my childhood vistas" (102). She is estranged from and forever a stranger to the places she haunted as a child: "You believe you're returning and it's a foreigner in you who discovers and is surprised. You don't even find yourself in what this foreigner sees" (138). Sultana, who immigrated to France years ago, hopes that she can sort out all that she is observing and experiencing in Algeria from the safe distance of her new home and another self, once she has gone back: "I'll see this from Montpellier, from the perspective of another, more distant and wise self" (138).

Given the emphasis on the body in this text, it is particularly striking that Sultana should describe her return to Algeria as an exercise in *disembodiment:* "As if this realization of the impossibility of a true return had consumed my other desires, had disembodied me. My punctual body evaporated. The others, dispersed in my varied strangeness, are no longer anything but far-off dreams, as if unfulfilled. It is insidious, this feeling of an impossible return, in spite of the return. The inability to find this 'lost space' expels you from the present and from yourself" (113). The fact that Sultana cannot locate what should be clearly and easily situated compounds her sense of foreignness in the place that arguably should be the most familiar to her. This experience is not all that unusual for migrants, as illustrated by Susan Stanford Friedman's comments on "imaginary homelands," drawing from Salman Rushdie's text of that title: "Many migrants and diasporics associate home not with a particular location but with an 'imaginary homeland,' with the experience of being perpetually in between cultures, or with an affiliation based on a communal identification that crosses national boundaries (e.g., religion, gender, queerness, indigeneity). The writing of home has become in a variety of ways, from the literal to the metaphoric, increasingly deterritorialized" (262).

The deterritorialization of the homeland, as portrayed in *L'Interdite*, seems to go hand in hand with disembodiment, even as attention is paradoxically called to the body, and in particular the female body, in Algerian society: "And yet, I no longer have a body. I am nothing but tension between the past and the present, a haggard memory that recognizes no reference point in herself" (68). This statement comes in the midst of Sultana's self-depiction as a woman walking on the street in Algeria, making her way through a crowd of eyes riveted on her. The contrast between the embodied subject whom everyone examines and the disembodied individual who is free from the constraints of time, suspended between the past and the present, points again to the indescribable complexity of return, especially for someone who may never have truly fit in to her "native" surroundings. Sultana brings up the doubt that she ever perfectly matched those around her: "I haven't found my native reflexes yet, if I ever had any" (63).

METROPOLITAN MIGRATIONS

Sultana intimates that she had particular difficulty adapting to the environment while growing up in her homeland because of the way women are treated here. *L'Interdite* repeatedly addresses the situation of women in Algeria and delineates the many places and activities that are forbidden to them. The street itself is a location of segregation: "It shamelessly inflicts its masculine plurality and its feminine apartheid" (7); it is a place where women can hardly be found: "almost total absence of women in the street" (22). Funerals are off-limits as well, as Sultana is informed even as she seeks to attend the ceremony for her departed lover. Sultana, like another woman named Samia, is not in line with societal expectations when she seeks to elude these restrictions, as the words spoken by a young girl named Dalila indicate: "My brothers say that Samia is a whore. It's not true! Samia, she just wants to study and walk in the street when she wants to and be left alone" (27).[1]

Vincent, who is seeing Algeria for the first time, and with an eye particularly attuned to the plight of women, cannot get over the way they are forced to the sidelines and are practically absent from the landscape. When he goes out in the evening, he discovers that they are not to be found at all: "a night of pain, deprived of women. The total absence of women creates a feeling of unreality. I'll never get used to it! In a hurry, busy, they go through the day, the time to cross a street, the time for some courage, between two markers of the forbidden" (51). His point of view sheds new light on the unseen heroism that characterizes the smallest of acts in the everyday existence of Algerian women: "I would not want to be a woman in this country. I would not want to have to permanently carry the burden of these looks, their many forms of violence, sharpened by frustration. For the first time, I realize that an Algerian woman's most ordinary act is, from the beginning, charged with symbols and heroism, because masculine animosity is so great, so pathological" (53). This understanding of the heroic actions of women in Algeria permeates the text. Those who live in this country are out of necessity heroines, individuals whose very existence is the result of a constant struggle. They have learned how to navigate an unfriendly system and gained autonomy one small step at a time, as Salah, Yacine's best friend argues: "The women here are all in the resistance. They know that they can't attack head-on an almost totally unjust and monstrous society. So they have taken to the underground of knowledge, of work, and of financial autonomy. They're persevering in the shadow of men who stagnate and despair" (111). Salah makes these laudatory statements about women's modes of survival all while giving Sultana a lesson: "They don't lapse into useless and dangerous provocation, like you" (111). As in many other points in the novel, Sultana stands out in contrast to the women of Algeria, for her personality and her actions do not coincide with theirs. Rather than make subtle advances underneath a submissive cover, Sultana chose to leave this society early on: "Little by little, Algeria's threats and restrictions became so frightening to me. So I fled from everything" (35). She is not a true Algerian, in the assessment of her male interlocutor, who doesn't understand when she takes offense with his choice of adjective. In Sultana's view, there is no qualifier more false than that one! What would it mean to be *une vraie Algérienne* after all?

Sultana's initial flight led to many subsequent departures, taking her from one urban location to another. These multiple displacements make her even more aware of the loss that takes place each time she picks up and moves on. The series of exits that make up her life have made of her a definitive foreigner, wherever she may be. Her self-portrayal as a body in motion, as a foreign body in perpetual movement, with no opportunity for rest or return, frees Sultana from any delusions about national belonging. She sees the faults of both Algeria and France, and concludes that what truly matters is the individual: "Yes what do countries, nations matter, what do institutions and all the abstract ideas matter when it's in the individual himself that the worm is immortal" (66). While she is certainly an individual, and this text constantly emphasizes her uniqueness, it is ultimately a sense of community that Sultana finds herself turning toward in the end, as we will see in a moment.

HAUNTINGS: PLACE AND MEMORY

In his article on Malika Mokeddem's *L'Interdite,* Mustapha Hamil declares that "the abandoned home country seems to haunt the exile wherever she goes" (56). Sultana is indeed haunted by her country, but she is also haunted by many memories, repressed and suppressed, from her past in this country. It is no wonder that in the chapters that bear her name, Sultana reflects on the workings of memory. There is no doubt that revisiting her old haunts helps to fill in some of the gaps in her recollection: "This house . . . in its grip, my memory panics between past and present. Time undergoes a contraction, a condensing" (32). She indicates that putting this past in order was something she desired, a difficult task after so many years of flight: "During my entire trip I waited for this instant. I was waiting to be able to enter this place and close the door again behind me, to attempt to reconstruct a scattered past: a few small islands of happiness gnawed away by years of autism and aphasia and the cracks caused by absences and departures" (32). These words are located close to the beginning of the novel. It isn't until near the end that we learn the unthinkable details of Sultana's past, in a chapter composed by Vincent. He quotes her as she recounts a murderous moment from her early childhood, when her father and mother exchanged blows and their battle became so violent that her mother fell to her death. The five-year-old Sultana witnessed this horror, as well as the subsequent death of her little sister, who was buried just two days later.

The haunting loss of her mother and sister is something Sultana has not gotten over. It is the deep impetus for her continual desire to depart, for the sense of lack she carries within her, for her denial of all inheritance. Sultana stifled a significant part of herself when her mother and sister passed away: "The other part of me, the part who had disappeared with my mother and my sister, I couldn't picture her. I had banished her. Or maybe it was she who didn't want me. I don't know. Yet I always felt her in my shadow, a silent noise attached to my thoughts and whose invisible thread I didn't succeed in cutting" (131). This personal haunting, this sense of ghostly self-transformation, is the greatest exile Sultana knows. Not only have the two females to whom she was closest been removed from her, but she has also been removed from herself as a consequence. It is not anecdotal that she refuses to eat after this incident, that she should deny her body and become nothing but a skeleton, practically a spirit. It is not an accident that she should refuse motherhood and focus instead on a career as a doctor. The profession of physician allows her to apply her mind over matter, so to speak, to control the body as much as human knowledge will allow.

CREATING NEW SPACES: FEMINIST COLLABORATION ACROSS BORDERS

Despite her deliberate departure from her native country, Sultana admits that the country nonetheless took on some positive hues from the vantage point of France. She had grown nostalgic for her homeland on some levels during her years away, but the trip back changed these feelings: "I feel the fire of nostalgia only at a distance. Returning has killed my nostalgia and left me only with naked exile. I myself have become this exile, cut off from any attachment" (66). Any connections that she might have sought to establish with the passing time, any desires for filiation and affiliation with her homeland, are stifled once she sets foot on Algerian soil: "absurd Algeria, its self-mutilation and its schizophrenia; the Algeria who commits suicide every day" (66).

The return to Algeria illuminates Sultana about her situation as a migrant. According to Susan Stanford Friedman, "Migration has been a powerful stimulant to literary expressions of identity in motion and the self-fashioning that new homelands require" (264). The critic argues that migration can be understood in a metaphorical sense as "a way of unmooring the subject from illusory certainties of language, representation, and being" (268). Sultana insists that her return has helped her realize just that: "My return here will have at least served that purpose, to destroy my last illusions of being anchored" (137). It is return that makes her realize that she could never settle down, never feel settled, in a single location: "How can I make them understand that my survival is only in moving around, migrating?" (137). She is like the aforementioned Samia, a woman who, because of her movement, no longer has spaces she can call her own: "Nomads are like my sister Samia, they've lost their space" (81).

Sultana cannot stay in Algeria, despite the fact that some women ask her to in the name of solidarity (141–43). She knows that France is not a perfect location, but she settles for this solution, since leaving this country for yet another would be an unrealistic move:

> Leave again? Leave both France and Algeria? Carry to some other place the hypertrophied memory of exile? Try to find somewhere else without roots, with neither racism nor xenophobia, without warmongers? Without a doubt, this phantasmagorical country exists only in the hopes of utopians. Any refuge is precarious, as soon as one has left for the first time. Elsewhere cannot be a remedy. The differences in geography can do nothing against the constant similarity of men.... My only real community is the community of ideas. I've never had any affection except for bastards, lost souls, the tormented and Wandering Jews like myself. (67)

Sultana's departure from Algeria at the close of this novel is not a flight in the way her first trip to France was. When she left to build a career and establish herself, she did so all by herself, with no sense of community with others. In contrast, this return to Montpellier is a movement that is not the equivalent of the cutting off of ties but rather one that carries the hope of creating a lasting sense of community with the women of Algeria. Though she cannot stay with them in person, she will remain with them in spirit, as the writing of this book attests.[2] The written word constitutes a gesture toward the production of new communal identities for Algerian women, one that stems from the belief that women should seek out movement, in whatever possible manner, that will allow for the development of *new spaces,* in concert with the ideas expressed by Friedman: "Not a static essence, space in these terms is a location for the production of communal and individual identities" (263). These spaces transcend borders; they are not limited to any precise place. Sultana opens up the possibility of transnational community when she pronounces the following words, the final statement of the book: "Khaled, I'm leaving again tomorrow. Tell the women that even from afar, I am with them" (154).[3]

The new spaces for women's solidarity explored in this text are inextricably linked to the possibilities of language. In *Migrancy, Culture, Identity,* Iain Chambers calls attention to the ways in which language is necessarily transformed through movement: "For the nomadic experience of language, wandering without a fixed home, dwelling at the crossroads of the world, bearing our sense of being and difference, is no longer the expression of a unique tradition or history. . . . Thought wanders. It migrates, requires translation. . . . This inevitably implies another sense of 'home,' of being in the world. It means to conceive of dwelling as a mobile habitat" (4). Mireille Rosello devotes a chapter of *France and the Maghreb: Performative Encounters* to the concept of the ghostly encounter, in which she argues that if such an encounter "is performative, it makes us conscious not that we have dealt with loss once and for all but that the acute sense of an irreparable loss is what must be written with the appropriate *qalam*" (163). It is crucial that the empty dwellings once filled with loved ones that Sultana comes across during her return to Algeria are the spaces that trigger her desire for connection. She is struck by the rootlessness, indeed the homelessness, of those who have perished: "The dead women of my family have no more shelter. They've been lost among the diaspora of shadows that haunt masses of fallen rocks and debris" (102). The impossible return, this "fatal pilgrimage" (67), inspires Sultana to find the proper equipment to write of irreparable loss, to gather bits of the past to make movements and create connections, to carve out new spaces in the present.

This is also the textual enterprise that Zahia Rahmani engages in when she addresses the tragic loss of her father, beginning with her first autobiographical novel, *Moze*. The words from the title of Susan Ireland's article on this text, "Facing the Ghosts of the Past," point to the importance of Rahmani's effort to grapple with the haunting presence of her father's ghost and to redress in textual terms the troubling, overlooked aspects of history that brought this silent man—and others like him—to dire desperation. While this Algerian-born woman's writing does raise "the question of how to bear witness to the injustices of the past" and the "narrative process" contributes "to putting an end to collective amnesia," as Ireland convincingly argues (309), Rahmani's autobiographical novels—especially *"Musulman" roman,* the central focus of the next chapter—also testify to the pain of loss that is truly irreparable, even if these inspired and inspiring written works finally do lead to a greater recognition of the suffering that is the result of wrongdoing on a grand scale.

CHAPTER 9 | Fille de harki | Relating to the Father, Country, and Religion in the Writing of Zahia Rahmani

> *I want to testify, but I don't know how—Zahia Rahmani,* Moze
>
> *My nieces sigh over all of the low blows they are dealt, "Arabs," "Muslims"... They close themselves off to the violent effects of the shock that teaches them that, even if they were born in this country, of a blood that believed in a future for its children, they will never have a homeland.—Zahia Rahmani,* France, récit d'une enfance *(France, narrative of a childhood)*

Zahia Rahmani's literary work stems in many senses from a need to testify to a torment that is intense, immense, and inevitably extends beyond expression. It is no accident that she often has recourse to the terminology of the trial in her writing, for she has repeatedly felt a need to defend herself against a slew of accusations directed at her person. But as Anna Kemp has pointed out with respect to Rahmani's first novel, "The narrator may not be able to fully bear witness to her father's life and acknowledges that her attempts to do so inevitably constitute a form of betrayal" (109). The writer is aware that her words will never completely represent—or make reparations for—wrongs committed on both sides of the war that officially came to an end the year she was born but whose repercussions continue to be felt. This awareness means that Rahmani can never totally do justice to the past, but she can nonetheless stage it in innovative literary terms that cry out for reconsideration, for renewed understandings of the multiple factors that make up contemporary identities, and for new ways of naming herself and others.

In the very title of her 2005 publication *"Musulman" roman*, Rahmani calls attention to the complexity of Muslim identities. Placing "Muslim" in quotation marks—and in the masculine form—and juxtaposing it to the generic classification of novel are movements that establish a distance between the female narrative voice and the labels applied to Rahmani. The autobiographical text draws from various crucial moments from her past to point to the reasons why the writer is compelled to address her linguistic, national, and especially religious belongings in the present. While international current events and political tensions are only evoked in metaphorical terms, it is nonetheless clear that the post-9/11 global climate, and specifically the treatment of Arab prisoners during the war in Iraq, have prompted this work. Defining herself in the light of recent historical developments, Rahmani answers to the name "Muslim," but with an informed hesitancy. Her innovative prose draws from sources as diverse as the Qur'an, oral tales from her native Berber tongue, and children's books in French, in order to present a composite image of an idiosyncratic heritage that cannot be fully encapsulated in the designation *Musulman*.

The author's resistance to labels is an underlying theme running throughout the book. The inclusion of the word *novel* in the title is just the first in a series of gestures that are meant to challenge—and disrupt—the reader's expectations. For, unlike a novel, *"Musulman" roman* is divided into five acts preceded by a prologue. These divisions seem to imply a play, and the possibility of performance arguably changes the reader's approach to the work. But, while dialogue plays a crucial role in this text, it is clear that this is not a typical theatrical piece of writing. What seems to be highlighted by these unusual chapter divisions is instead their dramatic content: the work revisits striking episodes that date from an ancient and recent past and that range from religious roots to personal struggles, from the epic to the intimate. The author has chosen to evoke these episodes in an elliptical style, with a syntax and a rhythm that do not belong to the typical structure of the French language in which she writes. She has also opted to include a variety of names that make the reader question who is who and what a name—proper or otherwise—really signifies in the end.

The book opens with a return to origins: the first-person narrative voice admits that she has become "Muslim" again. The identity she had fled as a five-year-old child just arrived in France is one she has been forced to re-adopt as an adult because of a polarized international atmosphere that has developed in the aftermath of the U.S. terrorist attacks of September 2001. As a prisoner of this term, the narrator is captive to the connotations it has taken on in recent times: "We are, they said, evil. Thus did they decide" (17). This subtle reference to the discourse of U.S. president George Bush and the words pronounced following the attacks is not solely meaningful with respect to the United States; it carries significance for France as well. The narrator makes it clear that she has known compartmentalization and exclusion from early on. In fact, this novel can be seen as a continuation of the reflections found in the author's first publication, *Moze,* in which the tragic story of her father's life—and death—is revealed with poignancy.

Forced to leave their Algerian homeland in 1967 because of her father's status as a *harki,* or an Algerian serving as an auxiliary with the French army during the Algerian War of Independence from 1954 to 1962, the Rahmani family had no choice after the French loss but to take up residence in the country for which her father had fought. But France did not make them feel welcome; to the contrary, they were given a cold reception marked by suspicion and deep-seated mistrust. The situation was so humiliating and her father's shame so great that he finally committed suicide on a meaningful date: the eleventh of November, the day when France commemorates the end of the First World War with fanfares, parades, and celebrations marked by great military flair.

As she grapples with this tragic familial event while writing this first work, Rahmani has occasion to revisit a brief history of the mistreatment of Muslims in North Africa:

> Muslims have always been scorned. They were killed in such large numbers and so freely throughout the preceding decades that really they were only good for exploitation and domestication for present necessities. Those from North Africa were looked down on, first through skirmishes, thefts, and sequestrations. Then, they were disdained through deprivations, epidemics, and famines. Some were even shown off in fairs. They were sent to the gallows or executed if they fled the draft, if they refused to serve the French flag. There were those in the front lines in 1914 and those who, after this war, recruited as a labor force were already finished men. (94–95)

This text reminds us that the Algerian War was not by any means the first time Muslims from Algeria were called to the battlefield to risk their lives on behalf of France. The poetic lines composed by this woman writer call attention to the fact that an important precedent can be found in the First World War, and that forced participation in this monumental combat was only one example of a series of abuses committed against Muslims from her place of origin.

The circumstances of her father's engagement in the Algerian War were particularly complicated, however, since fighting on behalf of the French in this conflict necessarily meant fighting against fellow Algerians who sought liberation from long-standing French domination on their soil. The dilemmas that result from Moze's conscription are multiple, and his loss is unspeakable. The daughter revisits the father's history in a manner reminiscent of the earlier summary of Muslim mistreatment:

> Moze was an Algerian. A Muslim of Algerian origin according to the terms in use. France, the conqueror and the indebted, appreciating his land, his ancestors and his power, made him a French Muslim from Algeria. That's what he became. When the war came, this Frenchman was requisitioned. Moze was a soldier of a war. That is what distinguishes him from others. It is not as a refugee belonging to a people that he left. It is not as a repatriated individual or someone who has voluntarily left his country. It is as a military man that he longer has a country. (112)

Like in the earlier passage, the sentences in this quotation are short, staccato phrases that follow each other quickly. The rhythm of the text is precipitous, as one idea leads to the next without much development or explanation. One event follows upon another, in a succession of incidents that ultimately deprive Rahmani's father—and thus her whole family—of a country. This profoundly creative text therefore delves into the multiple problematic identities that clash in her father's experience. Rahmani underscores in this particular passage the fact that Moze has been batted about and redefined by a national entity that used him and no longer has any use for him. Since the French have lost the war, he is forced to leave his native country, Algeria, but France can never become his country because the French do not see him as a Frenchman. The ironies of this situation abound, marked perhaps most noticeably by Moze's mastery of French: "Are we speaking of a Frenchman? He spoke very correct French, as is proper for an indigenous person educated in the colonies. Moze did not have any accent. He used this language with the elegance of the handsome Frenchman he was" (123). The fact that Moze has no accent whatsoever is significant, because it indicates to what extent he has mastered the language of the former master. In this short passage, his linguistic competence enables him to make a smooth transition from "indigenous" to "French," even though those around him do not perceive him as the latter.

Moze is a book that paints a well-rounded portrait of a man who embodies the ambiguity of the twentieth century, as the writer puts it. In a striking passage replete with exclamations, the cost of this embodiment becomes quite clear: "My father carried the ambiguity of this century: ignominious humanity. The ignominious humanity of this century! We were sacrificed because we were nothing! Arabs, Muslims. We were used to cover up the flight of an army! A carpet of dead bodies to serve as memory. This cowardice is abject! We have paid the price! Now make it so that I can reunite my family in one place! Do it! We must bring this to an end!" (128).

The plight of the harki is well expressed in passages like this one, in which intense suffering and alienation are brought to the forefront in a plea for rectification. These short sentences followed by exclamation points punctuate a text that cries out for an end. They also testify to the fact that the pain the father has known is not dissimilar to that the daughter has experienced, she who inherits a similar status without any choice: "I am the daughter of the numbered *harki*" (120).

The daughter is like the father in more ways than one, as the first-person narrative voice affirms when she declares that she now has the same writing as Moze: "I write like he does, down to my signature, which is his. I inherited his writing. I could have rewritten all his letters, falsified them, changed his life, drawn up false documents, continued to make him live, harassed his superiors, his masters, written to his jailers. Become a phantom. A phantom who understood what must be done. A deadsoldier come back from the dead!" (77). The daughter who has taken up the pen with her father's own handwriting is on a striking mission. It may not be that of falsifying documents, but it is undoubtedly that of continuing his life, in the sense that writing revives the personal story in potentially permanent ways. In literary form, the daughter uses her signature that is the father's in order to call attention to the injustices he suffered and to harass his superiors by exposing the faults that have been committed against an individual and, by extension, his family. It is worthy of note that critics who have turned their attention to this particular text have often made the mistaken assumption that the book's title is synonymous with the father's first name. As Anna Kemp states: "Published in 2003, *Moze* is offered as a testimony to the life and death of the author's father, Moze, who killed himself on Remembrance Day 1991, after visiting the local war memorial" (91). In fact, the title *Moze* is a contraction of two first names, that of her father and that of the author: Mohammad and Zahia come together to form "Moze";[1] in a similar manner, the father figure and the writer unite to tell a collective story, one that has implications for their whole family, as well as for other families like theirs who have taken up residence in France but cannot call this land their "*homeland*," as the second of this chapter's two epigraphs so effectively reveals.

The "deadsoldier" in Zahia Rahmani's neologistic juxtaposition is not forgotten because she has brought his plight to the forefront of her work. Highlighting the metaphorical death that preceded his literal passing, the daughter wields a mighty weapon that makes use of this inheritance to bring attention to the ills that a forced participation in the other's war has brought to the victim, and to an entire country. The harki, Algerians who had suffered from French domination for so long and then became soldiers for this dominator, were thus forever unable to rid themselves of the colonial yoke.[2] Rahmani signs her father's story with a hand that has merged with his, recounting his experience in poignant terms so that the ambiguity of his "betrayal" of his native country comes out against the backdrop of the monstrous betrayal he suffered at the hands of the French, a betrayal that continues to this day, if we follow Rahmani's logic.

The daughter, effectively stripped of father, fatherland (*la patrie*), and her father's faith, as she describes it in *"Musulman" roman*, hoped that the latter's death might help her "justify" and "guarantee" her life on the "European continent" (38). This second novel is the desperate, disparate account of her disappointment upon discovering that her father's death changed nothing with respect to her own belonging in France. As soon as the slightest thing went wrong, in her words, "I was suspected. I was designated. I was once again given a father, a religion and a vocation; a Name. "Muslim," I know it is endless" (38). Rather than fight this title, the narrator affirms it in the text, claiming to "flee ahead" of the name she foresees assigned to her. Anticipating the label does not necessarily make it easier to bear, but it does allow a moment to reflect on it and to redefine it according to her personal history, study, and understanding.

Coming back to her "Muslim" beginnings entails a revisiting of the beginnings of Islam, and *"Musulman" roman* contains a playful yet precise account of the early history of the three monotheistic religions. Rahmani places Islam in context alongside Christianity and Judaism as she evokes the Qur'an. She immediately situates the Muslim holy book linguistically, indicating that Arabic is the language of Islam but also calling attention to the Qur'an's borrowings and adaptations from other, foreign languages, those of the Old and New Testaments (29). Rahmani asserts that transmission of the Muslim faith took place not only in written, but also in oral terms: "At night, until very recently, mothers educated only in the spoken word continued to rock their children to the beautiful flavor of words" (30). Islam is tied to the Arabic tongue, but not exclusively, and the narrator recounts that she was introduced to this faith as a young child, thanks to the female voices of Berber speakers; this mother tongue she had once squelched has recently come back to her, much like her early religious designation, and her ties to Algeria.

Grappling with her "Muslim" heritage reminds the first-person narrator of her childhood experience, of the geographic dislocation and the European education that brought her so far from her roots. *"Musulman" roman* contains a powerful rendering of the mental acrobatics that accompanied the unrelenting linguistic apprenticeship its author received as a young girl. Learning to read the French language found in the children's book *Le petit Poucet*, the girl left behind her Berber language for a full ten years; between the ages of five and fifteen she did not pronounce a single word in this tongue, not even with her mother. She maintains that the French were unaware that she even knew another language, and that she left behind the "minor language" into which she was born in order to fully enter the "living" tongue of her new place of residence (73). If the French language was not beyond her grasp, the country unfortunately was, and this was mostly because of a complex personal history and its intersections with an unacknowledged larger history.

Zahia Rahmani's third novel, published just one year after her second publication, boasts a title that hints at its autobiographical content: *France, récit d'une enfance*. The author began life in Algeria at a crucial moment in history, 1962, for this year marked the loss of the last of France's colonies. But as a child growing up in France, she discovered that the war that determined the fate of her family and the course of her life was not recognized in her adopted country, either in official or unofficial form. In an essay inserted in italics into this book, Rahmani explains this lack of recognition in what Susan Ireland refers to as a "minimalist, telegraphic style" (308): "The Algerian War didn't take place, the schoolbooks said. It is true that in France, there was no trace to be found of this war. And the silence of soldiers, it's known, doesn't make any noise. This war had taken place elsewhere and I was bringing it into what seemed to me to be a repainted décor. Behind there was a layer that they had been hasty to cover up. Silence, said the French people. I didn't see this war" (109). Rahmani is unable to deny war, unlike the French history books and people who surround her during her childhood. She addresses the subject directly and doesn't hesitate to tackle the contentious topic of the 1990s, a brutal decade of civil war in Algeria that could hardly leave her indifferent: "I know no such thing as a clean war. The decade that followed was an affliction for me. Algeria hit too hard. As soon as I heard about bombs and deaths in Algiers, I fearfully awaited the phone call that would deliver me from my worry" (111). Remaining in touch with family members back in Algeria, she experienced this war with great emotion. From afar, she could not understand how those in the midst of the violence managed: "On the phone I never stopped asking my cousins, How do you do it? How do you do it. Tell me, how do you do it, how do you keep on holding up?" (111–12).

It is significant that these questions are posed to the *female* cousins, to the girls and women who have to put up with war in their country and who must navigate a violent reality on a daily basis. In an unpublished interview I conducted with Rahmani, the writer eloquently addressed the central role women play in wars, indicating that large-scale conflicts could not take place without their contribution: "They are a real presence, if only because the places we come back to for rest and nourishment are women's spaces." Women may be "anonymous," practically "absent" from "histories," but they are essential to the "transmission" of those histories in Rahmani's culture. The specificity of women's suffering and women's challenges emerges at various points in Rahmani's literary work, as do questions of gender equality. As a young student receiving an education in France in the 1970s, the girl naturally began to want things to work differently in the microcosm of her home: "At this moment, I want the house to be a question of everyone and not just that of only women and girls. I want the same rights as my brothers. I will not do anything to relieve them. I say it and I say it to them. This sort of attitude will not allow any compromise. I am still unaware of how to make couscous and all these good things that my sisters regularly make for me today" (93). The narrator brings the consequences of the past into the present when she avows that cooking is something she has always refused to do because of the gender connotations this activity carried for her. This "feminist" revolt finds expression in the same paragraph as a reflection on the physically and verbally violent relations she had with a particular sister, an older sibling whose past would explain why she was prone to outbursts of rage: "I cannot understand her violence, I know nothing of her terrible years in Algeria and her massacred childhood. It isn't until much later that I will learn of it. The horror of what she lived I cannot envision as a child" (93). The incomprehension she experiences as a child who is unaware of the brutality of armed conflict is quickly changed into a deep understanding of war as a daughter of a harki.

The lessons of war have not been easy for Algerian children on French soil, but Rahmani affirms that rejection from both sides of the Mediterranean has taught her that the most important duty of the offspring of this unfortunate conflict is to live: "We had to go beyond the state of lamentation and of permanent requester in which they hoped to keep us on one side and the other. We know how to learn from the condition of our fathers. The question of choice and of fault, of betrayal with our brothers, we have known it from the most tender age. By taking on the experience of our parents, we have known more than any other what war means" (113). Rahmani bravely claims that she and other children of harki are the "legitimate heirs of a war" (112) and thus turns around a situation of shame and judgment, making possible the personal expression of pain when only silence has reigned in the past. The writer suffered especially because her father never spoke of his anguish, never found words for his distress. Her writing project seeks to remedy that silence by giving voice to the complexity of her own experience alongside that of others.

Rahmani's inspiration for her third book stems from a desire to tell her ailing mother how much she owes her. It is in this poignant and profoundly personal text that bears the name of the French nation in its title that the writer pays homage to someone who has refused to assimilate in this adopted country. Unlike the daughter who is a published author of literature in French, the mother does not speak the language of this land, nor does she accept its message that she should be ashamed of her history. The mother has long sought to instill in her daughter a sense of pride in her origins. It seems paradoxical that the erudite writer's mother is illiterate; she will never read with her own eyes the phrases her daughter puts to paper. But this strong female character who has been through so much, who has weathered the war in Algeria and survived her husband in France, is not without wisdom.

In a short story published in 2007, Rahmani allows the mother's knowledge to shed light on the "figure of a man" of the title. It is this informed parent who speaks, informing the daughter of her progenitor's true status in ways the silent man never had: "Your father didn't wear a uniform, my mother tells me" ("Figure d'un homme" 255). The mother goes on to explain that he was a mayor and therefore only put on the scarf sporting the three colors of the French flag when he was alongside soldiers from the French army. The daughter protests, saying that official documents stamped in France in 1973 indicate otherwise, providing him with a military history that the mother insists is fictional. In the latter's solid assessment, harki was the only description they could find for him when he emerged from prison: "Yes but what could he be? A repatriated man? He had spent five years in prison. So, a *harki*? Why not" (255). It is significant that the words "why not" are not followed by a question mark. There is no hypothetical element to this well-used phrase in this instance, for the father had no say in the matter. French officials labeled him a harki in their hasty effort to dismiss his case as efficiently as possible.

The narrator of the short story sees things differently following her mother's illuminating comments. She begins to look in the archives of her familial history and discovers how very unreliable official documents are: "Since that moment I have been wary of archives. So my father who is a *harki* never wore a uniform. This discovery is not a relief, but rather an infamy. I said that I know everything about war. The first lesson, what you must know, is that you have to arm yourself against war documents" (255).[3] Rahmani makes this statement with good cause, for she finds a validated document indicating that her parents and their six children were killed by gunfire in Algeria in July 1962, prior to the author's birth. The strange irony of this obviously erroneous discovery incites the autobiographical narrative voice to restate her intimate knowledge of war: "I know everything about war, since I have come back from one" (255). The author arguably pitches her own battle on the injustices of the past through the written word, thanks to the understanding gained from the mother's spoken words. The mother's perspective provides her with the tools she needs in order to revisit the past and reformulate the present outside the restricted terms that contemporary Western societies have reserved for her.[4] As Anna Kemp has written, "Rather than opt for silence, Rahmani's narrator instead invests hope in the power of testimony to redress the wrongs of the past and their legacy" (109). This testimony is infused with renewed energy, thanks to the mother's insights.

In Rahmani's *France, récit d'une enfance,* religion emerges as a source of trouble in the particular "ghetto" that she inhabits in the French village of her upbringing: "I don't live in a black ghetto in Memphis where everything would be forbidden to me but in a white ghetto where every individuality is refused. The word God is never pronounced in my presence, but they reproach me for the religion of my parents without saying why it is worse than another. Their conviction is that I am a Muslim. For them, it is a measure of barbarity" (133). This statement on the way she has been ostracized due to her family's faith serves as an echo to her earlier work *"Musulman" roman,* in which she explains the thoughtless lumping that has effaced all idiosyncrasy, that has effectively done away with all personality: "All day long, one talked only of them and one saw only them: Muslims. Muslims. Not women, men, and children who were being done the oldest injustice in the world, only Muslims. And by wanting them to be what one wanted, by being afraid of them, they became one: a savage horde" (97). What is so especially aggravating about this unproductive tag that has been applied to all, without distinction, is that it fails to take into account the wonderfully rich nature of each individual and demonstrates a pernicious racist attitude that is nearly impossible to overcome. The repetition of the term *musulmans,* in the masculine plural in the above passage, reveals the repetition with which this term lacking specificity is literally thrown around, in a "round" that inevitably keeps returning, and that eventually creates what it has prescribed, as the rhythm and the force of this quotation demonstrate.

In *"Musulman" roman,* Rahmani laments a personal situation that defies all easy categorization. The Algerian-born girl at the center of this autobiographical work discovers that all of the labels applied to her do not fit: "In France, I had just gone through my revolt. I hated my father. I blamed him for our miserable life as Arab French which we were not. If only we were Arabs, I told him, if only we were, but we weren't. If only we were immigrants, but we weren't. If only we were French, French for decades, but we were still not. . . . I began to hate all these identity marks that attached themselves to me like crap to the ground. Arabs, immigrants, exiles, Muslims, I saw us kept in an infectious universe where even those who led the most miserable lives owed it to themselves to be satisfied with their condition" (84–85). The narrative voice again employs short sentences and a repetitive structure to reveal—in a clever way—truths about identity and the untenable, indefinable position that she has always held in France. This is a situation vaguely reminiscent of the one that characterized Hélène Cixous's early years in an Algeria that had no place for those of Jewish origin; Rahmani has never fit the acceptable list of classifications that define those who inhabit France. However, even though the country may elude her, she is officially a French resident. Upon entering the lycée, the girl is asked about her nationality and finds herself puzzled, unable to respond. She finally produces the proper papers, proving her French citizenship, and *French* is the adjective that fills in the appropriate blank on the form. But years later, the narrative voice tells us that the papers were not enough for her then, or now: "Today I have misplaced this nationality" (86).

In light of the uprisings in France in October and November of 2005 and then again in December of 2007, Zahia Rahmani's text takes on special resonance. The words she has put in print extend far beyond herself: "I would not be only an exiled, immigrant, Arab, Berber, Muslim or foreign woman, but more" (92–93). Those ethnic minorities who flamboyantly manifested their anger and frustration may have felt equally disgruntled with regular identity checks that single them out as visibly different from those who have been French for decades, or even centuries; they may have felt similar contempt for the tags that have quickly been applied to their situation, but that fail to take into account the multiple factors that make up any identity. When it comes to Islam, the personal quest Rahmani describes in *"Musulman" roman* attests to the fact that this religion is varied and complex and that, for her, it is made up of scholarly, familial, and emotional factors. Indeed, her assertion that she is much more than the aforementioned components of her identity is a timely statement that, read in the context of her multifaceted "novel," may serve as an antidote to the contemporary syndrome of hastily classifying members of a faith that is far from uniform by using the word *Muslim* as sole descriptor.

The word *musulmans* in the masculine plural form is what takes over the opening paragraph of the novel's fourth act, as the word *fear* pervades the text for the first time. What instills such fright in the narrator is the omnipresence of "Muslims," an indistinct, nondescript entity that occupied every word and every image. The autobiographical "I" expresses sorrow because she has been grouped together with others under this heading.[5] She has been named this way, accused of this crime. When the government functionary hounds the narrator in the dialogue that makes up the bulk of the fourth act, insisting that she provide her French papers as proof of her identity, she determines to take refuge from such questioning in the desert. But the violence of the civil servant's invasion of her privacy is echoed in the following act, entitled "Desert Storm," when a soldier ruthlessly interrogates a woman prisoner, assailing her with question after question about her birthplace, nationality, progeny, beliefs, occupations, travels, history, and plans. These interpellations inspire the narrator to go to the origins of her name. She locates its roots in a time that preceded Islam, when the God of the Jews *and* the Christians was called Rahman, a word meaning merciful (140). The singularity of this name is what the narrator would like to confer to her child, not a religious belonging to one particular faith rather than another; this name is what she would give, were it possible. In Hebrew, the root of *rahman* is said to refer to the womb (140). She does not have any offspring, but departing from current prisons to give birth to new horizons is what Zahia Rahmani would like to do, in her name. *"Musulman" Roman* is the incarnation of that wish. In the next chapter, as we will see, Maïssa Bey depicts an orphan born in Algeria in 1962—the same year Rahmani was born—who seeks new horizons in her relationships with other women in her homeland, in an exploration of the possibilities of finding self-definition and self-affirmation through community.

CHAPTER 10 | Fabulation et imagination | Women, Nation, and Identification in Maïssa Bey's *Cette fille-là*

I know nothing about my first filiation. I do not know where I am from. I don't have roots. I don't have genealogical points of reference.
—Maïssa Bey, Cette fille-là *(That girl)*

All geography and genealogy have become sterile.—Maïssa Bey, Surtout ne te retourne pas (Above All, Don't Look Back)

Maïssa Bey's 2001 novel *Cette fille-là* is not strictly autobiographical, but its ambiguous status is offset by the clear personal investment of the writer in the text. While a young woman who is not the author serves as the narrator of this creative work, Maïssa Bey is present in undeniable ways, as exemplified in a specific textual "slippage," whereby the words attributed to this narrator within the text are reproduced on the back cover as pertaining to Maïssa Bey.[1] This rich, polyphonic text is illustrative of how fictional renderings of lived experience can become powerful pieces of prose, telling testimonies that seamlessly move from the personal to the plural. The young female protagonist who narrates this text turns to Algerian women and their memories, paying attention to private lives, to focus on what has been excluded from official versions of events, from national archives, and to truly enrich our understanding of the past.

In his book-length study *Experimental Nations: Or, the Invention of the Maghreb*, Réda Bensmaïa calls attention to the immense creativity required to portray the nation in literature. He identifies a "third and final period" (25) of writing in Algeria that participates "in the process of the formation (or narration) of the nation" (22), a postcolonial period in which the writer becomes "increasingly conscious of the status of his or her fabulation" (22), highlighting the role of supposition and imagination in the text. Fabulation is not disconnected from the concept of testimony, as Ranjana Khanna's provocative juxtaposition of the two terms suggests: "To bring the concept of trauma into the study of colonialism also requires a particular concept of forgetting and remembering—at times a repression, and at other times a new and conscious fabulation, or testimony" (97). Assia Djebar, who has devoted much of her textual reflections to both memory and forgetting, is cited by Bensmaïa as an exemplary writer of this third period of writing Algeria, and we can add Maïssa Bey to the list of those who engage in literary "demythification" of the nation, according to Bensmaïa's precisions: "Far from reinforcing any given myths of origins, any given fiction of the eternal nation or of the intact community, literature was transformed into a privileged instrument for the demystification or, rather, the demythification of a country that had been reduced to nothing more than the stooge of a State that would never rise to the task with which its people had entrusted it" (26). In *Cette fille-là,* the demythification of the nation begins with a demystification of the woman who was born from scratch, so to speak, and whose past must be invented in a similar sense to that of the country.

Bey's *Cette fille-là* is in line with works by Algerian writers like Djebar, especially as it engages familial ties and strains to reimagine the relationship between gender and nation. In this chapter, I analyze this work of fiction by exploring the use of the tropes of possession and dispossession to represent the ambivalent desire of the novel's protagonist to belong to a lineage and a nation (and thus possess and be possessed), while simultaneously guarding her agency over her thoughts and movements (to be detached and dispossessed). Proper names are a central theme in *Cette fille-là,* serving as a reminder of past and present inequities in Algeria. In her treatment of names in this novel, Bey exhibits an awareness of the crucial importance of naming and its relation to power. As Jacques Derrida argues in *Le monolinguisme de l'autre,* "Every culture institutes itself through the unilateral imposition of some 'politics' of language. Mastery begins, as we know, through the power of naming, of imposing and legitimating appellations" (39). The politics of language and the power of naming go hand in hand in *Cette fille-là,* a text in which the principal protagonist struggles to give Algerian women the power to name themselves, to reinforce and legitimize their own appellations.

BRINGING UNHEARD CRIES TO WRITTEN HISTORY

Cette fille-là is a work of fiction that brings together the experiences of a variety of Algerian women. The book features a parade of women whose names are used as chapter headings: "Yamina," "Kheïra," "M'a Zahra," and "Houriya" introduce a cast of characters from the outskirts of acceptable Algerian society. Like Malika, the girl to whom the title points, these women of different social, racial, and ethnic backgrounds are gathered together under surveillance in Oran. This location eludes definition, as do its occupants. It is significant that no descriptive word, that no *name* is

Fabulation et imagination

adequate to describe this residence. It is neither an insane asylum nor a house for wayward women; rather, it is a place for those whose presence is disruptive to other members of society: "neither a retirement home, nor an asylum. Not a hospice either. All of these things at once" (14). It is significant that this ill-defined place serves as the locus for a novel in which Bey rethinks the character of national identity and belonging by reinventing the imagination and desire of Algerian women. This is precisely why she situates this written work in a "no-man's land." While men are also present in this dwelling, these residents are rarely mentioned in the novel: the narrative voice focuses instead on women. In an interview with Suzanne Ruta, Bey explains that the novel represents an effort to "liberate captive voices and inaudible screams" and "bring them into written history, because just as they are, they represent the underside of a society that claims, quite hypocritically, that it has freed itself from all forms of oppression." Bey indicates that since most of the women represented in the text are illiterate, and therefore could not relate their personal experiences in writing, they "have no other voice than that of a narrator in search of her own history."[2] This explanation is reminiscent of Algerian francophone writer Kateb Yacine's oft-repeated description of his work as *une autobiographie au pluriel*, a plural autobiography that finds its inspiration in a variety of voices. Bey's attention to the stories of different characters certainly harks back to Kateb's 1956 groundbreaking text, *Nedjma*, but this influence isn't manifest until the final pages of *Cette fille-là*.

Bey has underscored on many occasions her conviction that it is necessary to give women life through voice. In her analysis, many in Algeria have suffered in roles they have not chosen. While the paths of their experience cannot be recovered and reoriented, placing their words in writing can accomplish much; she insists, "We must allow women to speak because they don't have the opportunity to."[3] *Cette fille-là* is particularly effective because the multiple stories that give expression to the heretofore unspoken experiences of a variety of Algerian women intersect and resonate with the life story and principal preoccupations of their young interlocutor. Malika's experience is gradually unraveled in fragmented form among the threads of other life experiences belonging to the women around her. The diverse nature of their disjointed narratives combines to dispel any single prevailing stereotypical image of an "Algerian woman," and it effectively unveils the multiple competing forces that make life challenging for many individuals in post-independence Algeria.

The inclusion of a number of women's voices in the literary text immediately recalls the work of Djebar, who has exerted an undeniable influence on Bey's writing. Bey has paid tribute to Djebar in various publications, demonstrating her familiarity with and admiration for the work of this acclaimed woman writer from her homeland. Djebar's *L'amour, la fantasia* contains a third section in which women's voices intermingle with the autobiographical narrative voice. Jennifer Bernhardt Steadman has shown that in this section "voices are no longer contained in discrete chapters, but stories overlap and interrelate. A collective story begins to emerge as the identity of individual speakers is deemphasized and connections are drawn among women" (175). The alternating chapters in this third section of Djebar's novel are simply titled *Voix,* a word that can be read as singular or plural, and this confusion is undoubtedly intentional on the part of the author. The mixing of voices contributes to the effect of interrelatedness and connection that Steadman identifies. The narrator elucidates the complexity of translating these voices from Arabic and Berber into the French text, highlighting the difficulty of putting to paper the experiences of others, as well as the inherent division and inevitable separation that are involved in this well-intentioned act (161).

L'amour, la fantasia points toward the impossibility of finding a single, definitive version of the past and fully relating any story.[4] In Donald R. Wehrs's analysis, "Djebar's evocation and undermining of diverse ways of telling both the narrator's and Algeria's stories reflects suspicion that all possible beginnings are already ideologically invested, already stamped with patriarchal silencing of women's voices, veiling of women's experiences" (843). Wehrs astutely articulates that "Djebar's narrator comes to locate the beginning of identity and signification in traumatic disruptions of normative speech" (843), a concept that pertains to Bey's *Cette fille-là.* For different reasons, locating the beginnings of the women in this text proves elusive. The narrative demonstrates how Algerian power structures, whether colonial or postcolonial, have excluded many individuals from official records. The writing of the past that takes place in this text necessarily begins with individual accounts that set the record right in crucial ways, starting with intersecting personal stories that point to injustices on a larger scale. This writing is in essence a *rewriting,* in line with Anne Donadey's understanding of the term: "Postcolonial writers feel the necessity of rewriting the past because the dominant versions of history have left blanks, gaps, and misrepresentations" ("Postcolonial Memory" 66). As she delves into her own past in an effort to fill in some of the blanks, even if only with her own imagination, Malika has recourse to the descriptions of others.

Donadey's analysis of Djebar's *La femme sans sépulture* underscores the fact that this work of fiction does not re-create "a totalizing, mythologizing narrative of Zoulikha the heroine, but . . . rewrit[es] her story by paying attention to the parts . . . that remain alive in others' memories" ("Postcolonial Memory" 69). In like manner, the narrator of *Cette fille-là* is not only concerned with recovering her own past; she is also in the process of reconstructing a larger past that takes into account the different experiences of a handful of women in Algeria. What strikes the reader is the role that memory plays in reconstructing a past in the text that is neither "totalizing" nor "mythologizing"; instead, it is uncertain and filled with possibilities.

It is worth noting that neither Djebar nor Bey consistently brings women's expressions to light in formal, recognizable ways. When Bey refers to the transposition of women's "inaudible screams" in the aforementioned quotation, the author is addressing a crucial aspect of her writing project. Inspired by Djebar, Bey allows women to "speak" through screams in the written text, revealing a form of language that may be unconventional but is nonetheless filled with meaning. It is also a form of communication that is frequently suppressed because it is unacceptable in Algerian society. In *L'amour, la fantasia*, Assia Djebar devotes space to a female figure who differs from other women: "the woman who raises her voice" (228; la femme qui crie). The narrator indicates that Algerian women could be condemned for a variety of illicit behaviors, but that the most scandalous among them was speaking out, crying out, making oneself heard outside the walls. The individual whose complaint and protest were not sublimated in prayer or in whispered confidences, but instead were set free to resonate for all to hear, was marginalized from the outset. Letting her expression escape in this way reveals that the silence around her is forced: "To refuse to veil one's voice and to start 'shouting,' that was really indecent, real dissidence. For the silence of all the others suddenly lost its charm and revealed itself for what it was: a prison without reprieve" (204). The narrator of Djebar's novel claims that writing has meant a return to "the cries of women silently rebelling," to what she calls her *"seule origine"* (229). This only origin is not stifled by writing; to the contrary, writing permits true freedom of expression: "Writing does not silence the voice, but awakens it, above all to resurrect so many vanished sisters" (204).

Cette fille-là follows in the footsteps of *L'amour, la fantasia*, allowing women to cry out in the written text in ways that would marginalize them in Algerian society. Malika and the women she meets in confinement have long held inside the cries they long to let out: "As a little girl, I practiced crying out in silence.... It takes training to learn to hold everything back. To keep it all within you, to refuse to let anything slip out" (178). Malika didn't have recourse to the normal names a child instinctively shouts when things go wrong: "mommy" and "daddy" were inaccessible to her because she was abandoned at birth. Instead, she has learned to scream when she is utterly alone, to yell without emitting a sound, to utter a cry that she has positioned at "the other extremity of silence" (178). This text, revealing the humiliations and insults that characterize the experiences of a variety of voices that combine to make up a "chorus of women" (161), arguably situates itself at "the other extremity of silence."

UNDOCUMENTED ROOTS: UNKNOWN IDENTITIES

While Bey's approach to relating multiple stories and histories has a great deal in common with Djebar's method, what sets much of Bey's work apart is her focus on individuals who have no sense of identity rooted in family and community. Djebar's *L'amour, la fantasia* opens with what has become a well-known image among readers: "A little Arab girl going to school for the first time, one autumn morning, walking hand in hand with her father" (3). The young girl going to school later merges with the first-person narrator, a figure who is presented from the outset in a filial relationship that paves the way for a future as a writer. Thanks to the father, an instructor of French, the daughter earns an education. Throughout the novel, the narrative voice makes references to both sides of her family, to ancestors distant and close who have contributed to her life and life story, giving us a fuller understanding of her background, of the voices and the words that make her who she is.

In contrast, the narrator in Bey's *Cette fille-là* is without familial connections. Malika was abandoned as a newborn and has never discovered even the smallest detail about her biological parents.[5] Every aspect of her genealogy is left to her imagination; her lineage remains a mystery. She explains that there is only one word to describe this predicament in Algerian Arabic: *"Farkha"* (bastard): "No other word for us to designate children conceived outside of wedlock. None of these euphemisms that can be found in other languages" (45). She is constantly suspected of a dishonorable conception in this society where roots matter and where offspring of illegitimate couplings are shunned and mocked, as Malika's case illustrates. The narrator contemplates the expression *fille d'amour* (love child) in the French tongue but rejects this softer term as well, because it also carries negative connotations for her, not to mention an entirely different, Western understanding of what constitutes love between a man and a woman. The problem is that, from the outset, her existence poses a problem for those around her. She projects that others call her the "Incarnation of a Fault," "the Material Proof of the Crime of Fornication," as she puts it in a poetic passage (44). Her very existence puts into question the honor of a woman, the honor of a mother, *her* mother, and this is unforgivable: "Nothing is forgiven in our country. Especially not dishonor. It is transmitted, it comes back, as visible as a congenital defect. Without ever burying itself in forgetting, it bounces back, from generation to generation. It is part of inheritance" (45). The inheritance of dishonor is the lot of the parentless child, since the very fact that her parents are absent necessarily means that she was conceived in a dishonorable union. By disappearing from the picture when their daughter was just an infant (and perhaps long before, in the case of the father), the parents failed to give their offspring a name, and this lack is the equivalent of dishonor, Malika's only inheritance. Unlike the narrator of Djebar's autobiographical text, who learns from her maternal grandmother about relatives who make up that branch of her family tree, Malika is at a loss: "No branch to hang onto" (50).

Malika's birth coincides with the end of French colonial rule in Algeria, as she was born shortly before the war came to a close: "It must be said that during this troubled period of my birth, still humbly referred to at the time as the period of the events of Algeria, it was certainly more common to find loaves of plastic bread at the doorways of homes than abandoned children" (44). With humor, the narrative voice underscores the incongruous nature of the sudden appearance of a baby in the midst of violent warfare. In this passage, the interruption of her birth stands out in contrast to the potential interruption of a bomb, but the violence of both interruptions is nonetheless clear.[6] The parallel between her birth and the birth of the nation is established in this single sentence, a crucial parallel for understanding this tragic figure and her country.

Historian Benjamin Stora has focused on questions of memory and forgetting in his publications on Algeria, notably in *La gangrène et l'oubli* (Gangrene and forgetting). In a recent interview, he expressed how the end of the war that led to independence from France was a moment of critical importance for the Algerian nation: "For Algerian society, the 'War of Independence' founded the Algerian nation and, as a repercussion, crystallized national sentiment. The war thus constitutes a rupture of representations. Collective memories, images of the other and the self are broken and recast at this point" (14). Stora's observations provide a sense of the overwhelming task of reconstituting a nation after colonization. They identify the war as the pivotal point, as the moment when images and representations no longer carry the same connotations, and as the moment when the self is reconsidered, when difference is redefined, when collective memories are reformed. But the results of this process, of this "recasting," were unfortunately not always positive. As Réda Bensmaïa points out, "At the time of independence, all means were valid to reach the desired ends, to produce a national entity or identity. Yet it soon became obvious that these ends would not be easily attained" (22). Those who were new to power were eager to provide fresh definitions for the nation and to efface the memories of what came before independence in order to facilitate the construction of a new national identity. *Cette fille-là* is a work that demonstrates the hopelessness of such a project, that illustrates the difficulty of doing away with memory altogether. When the women make their weekly trip to the public bathhouse, Malika listens to the collective memories that predate her birth. The women's accounts are sometimes muddled, precise details such as places and dates are occasionally unclear, and the negative aspects of the earlier period are unduly glorified, but these voices nonetheless share portions of their history that help Malika to understand her own past, and present, in a new light.

RECOVERING WHAT WAS LOST: POSTCOLONIAL TRACES

Malika stands out from other conversationalists who share her abode because of her youth; she can only listen as older women reminisce about the days when Algeria was still a French colony. Despite the time lag between their lives and hers, the women have much in common. Malika's own struggle to find a name and a place in Algerian society echoes the ongoing effort of a new friend, "Aïcha," to correct the error on her identity card. This illiterate woman is adamant that Malika must write a letter on her behalf to the *procureur* insisting that there has been an error, for her first name is not "Jeanne," even if her official papers present it as such.[7] This mistake is flagrantly anachronistic, as no post-Independence child would be given a foreign, "Christian" name, according to Malika's reflections: "Jeanne. For what I know, this first name is not known to the nomenclature established by our supercilious civil servants. The nomenclature presented to all new parents at the town hall before their child is registered in the governmental records. Official list, without any possible deviation. First

Fabulation et imagination 171

names carefully chosen with respect for the Muslim Arab tradition. But maybe in her time things were different..." (27). The narrator, unfamiliar with the previous politics in her homeland, can only speculate about the way newborns were named when the French were in control. Her knowledge of the present gives her suppositions about the past some clout, as those in power can impose their names on others. In *Theories of Africans,* Christopher Miller underscores the fact that "personal names are a reflection of cultural politics, bearing the mark of Christianity, Islam, and local cultures. The order and usage of names varies widely from culture to culture in Africa, even in those places where Islam and Christianity have imposed standardized 'first' names by the millions" (116).

"Aïcha" is reticent about the origin of this misnomer, but persists in keeping it secret; the others in this residence call her by her "true name" of Aïcha and remain unaware of her official appellation. The lack of explanation gives Malika's imagination free reign to reconstruct the pivotal scene in which Aïcha's birth was reported. The fact that the year of her birth, 1930, is uncertain points to the disorder that prevailed when the baby's existence was reported to the proper authorities of the time: "The explanation may be there. There is no doubt that births not declared within the required limit are numerous here, what they call 'presumed' births! The registers from the time of colonization contain more than one" (28). This passage reveals the extent to which the identity of those born in Algeria under French rule was considered unimportant to those in power: significant numbers of individuals were not appropriately registered in the official books, and this oversight was of little consequence to the colonizers.

Indeed, Aïcha is not the only resident whose birth date remains a mystery; Fatima is an ageless woman, victim to the same dismissive categorization: "She is an ageless woman. She too has a 'presumed' birth date. She wasn't declared within the required time. That's how they're called, the 'presumed.' It is a very easy solution that provides a probable year for those who were called indigenous during the period of colonization" (79). Arbitrarily assigning names and titles, calling the colonized by terms that vehicle foreign concepts and classifications, are activities that abound in this novel that rereads the past through the lens of the present. The fact that the narrative voice is often given to speculation and imagination in order to reconstruct the events of the years gone by, in order to revive the unwritten record of a history that is often one-sided in its written form, reveals the lack of materials and the loss of the trace of the period of French domination in Algerian history.

Alice Cherki calls attention in her work to what she terms the "confiscation of memories" in Algeria, an unfortunate reality that prevents "plural identifications," the multiple points of connection that individuals need to find their place in contemporary society. She indicates that the principal concerns today are social inequalities, the aftermath of the violence of the 1990s, and a massive skepticism with respect to power (178). Bey's novel, while published in 2001, is situated in the 1980s, just prior to the decade of civil war that Cherki mentions as a major preoccupation.[8] It nonetheless illustrates inequalities and misuses of power, and it sheds light on a social and political situation that anticipates the violence to come. This situation is the result of a lack of history, and a concomitant lack of recognition. According to Cherki, "Algerians have suffered from a history written from point zero, a history against nature, exclusive, bogged down by non-recognition of conflicts during the war of independence as well as non-recognition of the historical, linguistic, and cultural diversity that make up this country" (178). The need to write national history from scratch, in a sense, poses serious problems for identity construction among all citizens, but especially among young people, whom Cherki refers to as "the descendants" of this and other colonial wars: "The violence of colonial wars and the silences following decolonization put off in the distance, for the generations that came out of these wars and their descendants, symbolic representations necessary for any subjective constitution" (179). Individuals are in dire need of these symbolic representations in order to situate themselves within a larger community; as Cherki explains, "The denial that has hit collective systems (political, social, juridical) has contributed to preventing these 'descendants' from finding points of reference necessary for creating signs that can be elaborated into memories. It impedes their processes of identification and lays on them the heavy task of metaphorical work, of staging what has been 'silenced' in the history of those who came before them. They don't always manage to do this" (179). The narrative voice of *Cette fille-là* is constantly engaged in this "metaphorical work," staging possible episodes from her own early life as well as conjuring up potential pasts for the women around her. Much of their testimony is recorded in writing exactly as they pronounce it to her, but she finds herself filling in the "silenced" blanks on occasion, and thereby creating memories on a national level as well as on a personal one.

It is significant that this novel does not broadcast a woman's name on its cover. Its anonymous designation of the main protagonist stands out in contrast to the careful naming that takes place throughout the work. The title seems to point to the lack of respect it seeks to correct within its pages. Malika not only delves into her own appellation and its unique history; she also investigates the names of women around her. Allowing them to *tell their stories* means finding out how they *call themselves*: "Jeanne" is really Aïcha, and "Messaouda" is M'barka. Giving these women a chance to recall their names is a move that defies the tagging, the labeling act that pins them in place. Like the larger society from which they have been removed, this residence has classified their cases and closed their books. Opening *Cette fille-là* is an exercise in learning just how limited the suitable definitions for an "Algerian woman" are today, and in exploring innovative paths out of inflexible confines, finding new ways to name women in (our) time.

TRANSNATIONAL TRAVELS: SPACES OF EXCHANGE

M'barka is another woman in the residence with a complicated past; born in Algeria of black skin, she marries in her youth a delightful man who takes her to another of the French colonies, an unnamed African territory in which her color is the same as those around her. Despite this visible likeness, differences abound between her and her new neighbors, and blending in proves to be an insurmountable difficulty: "She is the foreigner. She doesn't speak their language. She comes from the country behind the dunes and the mountains. She is part of those who don't even know the name of their ancestors. Her history begins with her. They don't know with what threads they are made" (131). It is clear in passages like this one that the prejudices that reign in Algeria are also present in other places on the African continent. While her appearance may not prove to be a barrier to integration in the country to which she has immigrated,[9] M'barka finds the fact that she doesn't speak their language to be a significant obstacle to acceptance. What proves to be insurmountable is neither a question of looks or linguistics, however; it is a matter of lineage. The fact that she cannot delineate her ancestral origins means that M'barka is excluded from her new surroundings. The accusation, as it is formulated in the passage cited above, resembles the accusations Malika is continually faced with in her homeland, a land in which she has never felt at home.[10]

The country where M'barka has taken up residence with her husband is one in which spirits are powerful, in which spells are cast, and in which possession is a tangible threat. In order to protect her from this ever-present menace, M'barka and her husband come up with a new name: "From now on, she will be called Messaouda. The blessed one. That is what the two of them decided. So that no one would be able to control her"

(131).¹¹ This passage contains an important reminder of the fact that names carry meaning, and that their significance has influence not only on their bearers but also on those with whom they interact; this truth is particularly salient in Algerian society, as evidenced in the emphasis on names throughout this work of fiction.¹²

Her new name is not powerful enough to ward off demon possession, and after a long struggle to regain her health, M'barka leaves her husband in the arms of the woman responsible for M'barka's ailment and embarks on a solitary journey, a long and difficult return trip to the country of her birth. The narrative does not describe in detail the possession that M'barka experiences, but the very word *possession* is meaningful in the context of the specific relationship that a woman often has to her name. A number of feminist critics have remarked on the way in which a woman's name is not her own,¹³ since her last name usually reflects either her connection to her father or to her husband, and her first name, as we have seen, is often not a matter of personal choice either. It is ironic, perhaps, that the name M'barka and her husband invent in order to avoid the spell is powerless to protect the protagonist from danger, but being "possessed" by something outside the patriarchal order is paradoxically liberating. Freed from marital ties, M'barka chooses her own path back to Algeria and regains possession of her self and the power to tell her own story and reclaim her name.

It is significant that during her time spent on the soil of her forgotten ancestors, M'barka gradually gains cultural literacy in a society that was initially completely foreign to her: "She rediscovers far-off sensations that have come back from further than her memory stretches, strangely familiar. . . . The world has become legible once again" (132). This passage suggests that there is an ancestral memory that persists, even when one has been cut off from one's ancestral homeland. M'barka learns rather quickly to navigate the places and weather the seasons of her new location and manages to become accepted, even adopted, by the people around her. Despite this adaptation, M'barka remains childless for years and her sterility poses an insurmountable problem for her husband's family, and ultimately for their relationship. The inability to prolong the family line, the incapacity to produce descendants is the crucial weakness that provides an opening for another woman to cast a curse and slip into M'barka's marital bed.

M'barka is one of several childless women depicted in *Cette fille-là*, and as such she presents an intriguing counterpart to the motherless girl, Malika.¹⁴ Rather than portraying women exclusively in vertical relationships to their parents and offspring, this novel provides an opening for another

Fabulation et imagination 175

conception of women's interaction with others as potentially horizontal in nature, extending out toward others, beyond the family unit, and even beyond ethnic and national borders. It is not just filiation, but also affiliation, that matter. Women who bear little resemblance to each other, like M'barka, or Yamina, whose tattoos and accent reveal that she is from a distant native region, can speak to Malika, and to each other, despite their differences. M'barka is an especially important character, thanks to her travels, because she embodies the possibilities for transnational communication and connection in accordance with Françoise Lionnet and Shuhmei Shih's description: "The transnational . . . can be conceived as a space of exchange and participation wherever processes of hybridization occur and where it is still possible for cultures to be produced and performed without necessary mediation by the center" (5). The ill-defined place in which these women have been confined outside Oran is an unfortunate microcosm of the larger society; it is a location where prejudice and hierarchy exist. But the very narration, with its inclusiveness and interest in the experiences of others and its creation of intersections, indicates that Malika, whether she intends to or not, is indeed carving out a "space of exchange and participation" in this potential prison, managing to "produce" and "perform" "cultures" at the margins.

FIGHTING "FATMA": RECLAIMING SELF-DESIGNATION

The marginalization of women in Algeria marked the period of colonization, as the experience of Badra demonstrates. In the chapter bearing her name, the narrator informs us that Badra is a woman whose entire existence has been devoted to making herself useful. Even now, in the residence where she has for the first time begun to feel old, she makes sense of her life by throwing herself into work. She cooks and cleans with an energy that recalls her former service in a large house belonging to a French family in Algeria. This was her first contact with what she refers to as a "real family," with children named Paul and Jeanne, a father who is present and affectionate, and a mother who is gentle and attentive and patiently oversees the efforts of Badra, whose name has undergone a transformation following her employment: "She must explain everything to Badra. Badra whose name is now Fatma. All maids must be called Fatma" (154). The uniform assignation of the name Fatma to all domestic help in French homes has been addressed in the writing of other women writers who call attention to the injustice of this blanket designation.[15] The industrious Badra is one among many whose names have been exchanged for an anonymous racial designation in the colonial past. The reasons for this "alias" are multiple; one explanation is that the "foreign" resonance of Arabic names poses a challenge to individuals from France, even those who are willing and eager to learn them.

While those who were hired as domestic help, like Badra, do not feel they have the authority to correct those who call them Fatma, the heroine of Djebar's *La femme sans sépulture* is able to fight against this derogatory appellation when it is uttered in the street: "Zoulikha was veiled and on her way to a party when she bumped into a European woman in the street behind the church. The woman shouted, 'Hey, Fatma!' Zoulikha, taking off her veil, replied, 'Hey, Marie?' in a tone that was almost innocent" (22). Her response offended the European woman: "She practically suffocated with indignation: 'You call me Marie? What nerve!' Zoulikha responded gently, like a schoolteacher (removing the veil from her entire face) and gave her a lesson: 'You don't know me. You address me informally, and, what's more, you call me Fatma! You could have said 'Madame,' couldn't you?'" (23). This anecdote, recounted playfully in Djebar's novel, is important because it represents a scene that rectifies a widespread misnomer and exposes its capacity to belittle, and even dehumanize, those to whom it is applied. It is not an accident that Zoulikha removes her veil to insist that her name is not Fatma and that she deserves the same respect as a European woman. Her gesture contests the blind application of the word that fails to recognize the individuality of each Algerian woman with her unique background and own life story. Zoulikha is able to resist effectively because she has a good command of French, a linguistic skill that not all Algerian women possess, although many of Malika's interlocutors have picked up at least some of the language through various means of exposure. The narrator of *Cette fille-là* also subverts the "Fatma effect" when she highlights individual stories and the names of those who tell them.

The narrator's biological origins are not the only part of her past that remains inscrutable; the source of her name also remains obscure, and this crucial aspect of her identity is one she constantly invents as well. As indicated near the beginning of the novel, the name Malika has a specific meaning: "If you believe my name, for every name has a meaning, I am the queen, or she who possesses. The queen of what kingdom?" (17). The first-person narrator goes on to speculate on a slight alteration of her name, one proposed by those at the residence she now inhabits: "The possessed as well, perhaps. That's what they told me when I arrived here. M'laïkia. Just one letter away" (17). The disconnect between possessing and being pos-

Fabulation et imagination   177

sessed thus emerges in the principal protagonist's analysis of her name. The name she has been given unfortunately does not reflect her status in a society where she possesses nothing. But the slight alteration of her name that results in rendering her "possessed" is surprisingly liberating, since the label of "possessed," similar to that of "mad," frees those who bear it from adhering to the strict rules of society. This was the experience of M'barka, who was disappointed to be separated from her husband but who was nonetheless liberated from the burden of being in many senses his possession. Once she broke free from her status as his wife, she was able to return to Algeria on her own.

Malika's desire to be possessed by her adoptive parents comes back to her in a moment of remembrance; still an infant, she responded with passion to the man and woman who may have named her but whose name would never be hers. She learns at the age of six the harsh lesson that in the Islamic tradition of her society, she is denied the last name of those with whom she lives: "In accordance with the religious precepts of the *sharia*, based on the Qur'an, until very recently, adopted children could not be inscribed under the family name of their adoptive parents. A way of carrying, throughout their lives, the mark of the infamy, real or supposed, that presided at their birth" (75). In the classroom, the young Malika is called only by her first name, for she does not possess a family name.

EMBODYING OTHERNESS: MÉTISSAGE AND MULTIPLICITY

In *Strange Encounters: Embodied Others in Post-Coloniality,* Sara Ahmed explains that "when we face others, we seek to recognize who they are, by reading the signs on their body, or by reading their body *as* a sign" (8). Ahmed argues that "such acts of reading constitute 'the subject' in relation to 'the stranger,' who is recognised as 'out of place' in a given place" (8). These encounters do not take place in a temporal vacuum but instead "reopen prior histories of encounter that violate and fix others in regimes of difference" (8). Ahmed's articulation of meetings between people seeks to contextualize them, according to their historical precedent and power differentials. A crucial aspect informing the encounters Malika describes as she tells her story is her physical appearance. She has light hair and blue eyes, attributes that indicate she may be the result of a mixed union, and that set her apart at first glance from others in her country: she is "different. Other" (22). Her difference is visible, and everyone she comes across reads this difference as a sign, even if they are unable to determine its exact meaning.

Malika recounts the experience of another woman, Houriya, as an example of the unwelcome response those from Algeria exhibit when faced with relationships between French men and Algerian women. It is by demonstrating the incompatibility of their names that she points to the overwhelming obstacles that prevent the enamored Houriya and Jean from marrying: "Houriya. Her name is synonymous with freedom. Freedom, a word that is feminine, even in Arabic. She hadn't thought about it before this day. The 'H' from her name is another trial for Jean. He practices for hours. He cannot pronounce it. It is aspirated, and escapes him, like an elusive source of pain. He fights with this letter that obstinately resists him" (173). Despite the linguistic difficulty of calling his beloved by name, Jean frequents Houriya and the two become quite close until their respective communities separate them forever. The Captain Pelletier reprimands Jean and sends him to another zone, closer to the war's center, and Houriya is ordered to hide out of fear for her life after ruining her honor. Such a development was foreseeable, as the narrative reveals, for even their names don't go well together: "Houriya and Jean. There is a dissonance in the joining of these two names. An incongruity" (174).

There are a few passages in the text when Malika speculates about the possible scenarios that brought her biological mother and father together. She seems to be much more interested in exploring various incarnations of her mother than in contemplating the father. In contrast to the tremendous attraction that the Frenchman Jean and the Algerian woman Houriya felt for each other, Malika does not imagine her parents were in love. She proposes instead that her mother was a prostitute, like the women featured on colonial postcards, and that she gave her body for a passing moment to a foreigner: "Their body offered for an instant, a very brief instant to men of another race, foreigners, infidels who believe that in this way they are penetrating the heart of the mystery of this savage earth that tastes of dust and sand" (51). The direct connection between woman and nation established in this passage is shown to be a fantasy of the male colonizer who seeks out "new pleasures," "barbarous pleasures," in Algerian brothels. In a phrase filled with sardonic humor, the narrator asserts that the prostitutes receive "the ejaculatory spasms of civilizing work" (51), alluding to the "civilizing mission" that supposedly motivated French colonization but that hardly explains this rampant sexual behavior. Malika imagines that she is the fruit of such spasms, the bastard child whose father and mother represent two conflicting, irreparably disparate sides. She is an entirely unacceptable entity in postcolonial Algeria because of the *métissage* she embodies. In a metatextual moment in Djebar's *L'amour, la fantasia*, the narrator refers to her writing as follows: "Actually, it is they who are writing to each other, using my hand, since I condone this bastardy, the only crossbreeding that the ancestral beliefs do not condemn: that of language, not that of blood" (142). In this society, where ancestry carries such consequence, there is apparently no place for those of mixed heritage, but the presuppositions of "purity" that such an attitude implies are quite ludicrous, as we are reminded in *Cette fille-là*.

The narrative voice in *Cette fille-là* underscores the irony of the feigned surprise that characterizes contemporary reactions to children who are "too blond" or whose eyes are a "strange, disturbing blue" (78). Such reactions are striking in a land where multiple peoples have mixed for centuries, resulting in a rich mélange of races and origins: "As if we were unaware of all the multiple genetic combinations that have come together to make Algerians what they are" (78).[16] Turning her own lack of family ties into an endless source of imaginative inspiration is an act that reveals this young woman's capacity to adapt and create in the face of discouragement. She realizes that despite the negative connotations of this unknown personal past, her only wealth may paradoxically lie therein: "I am the inheritor of what I must incessantly invent. But that is possibly my wealth. My only wealth" (50). This rich piece of literature bears witness to the potential of writing to express otherwise silenced viewpoints and to reveal the complexities of lived experience in Algeria, particularly among those who are banished because they embody taboos. *Cette fille-là* addresses the cross-breeding that is so unacceptable in Algeria in a text that engages in subtle textual maneuvers that constitute a cross-breeding of a different, more acceptable nature: linguistic.

SELF-POSSESSION: IDENTITY AND RIGHTS

The adjective *possessed*, found frequently in this literary work, takes on new resonance when Malika reaches puberty and her adoptive father's love expresses itself in sexual terms. His physical advances, portrayed in suggestive language, give Malika no choice but to run. The very nature of the father's aggression renders the girl voiceless. As the victim of undesired sexual advances, the girl has much in common with other women who are forced to have intercourse without giving their consent. This episode gives clear evidence of the power differentials that exist on many levels in Algerian society, not only between authorities and civilians but also between adults and children and between men and women. The episode also serves to highlight the difference between the inability to speak and defend oneself in public and the ability to reflect privately and make insightful discernments.

Even though she is unable to defend herself through her own words when her father attempts to rape her, Malika proves to have a profound understanding of language. She sees through the faulty grammatical reasoning others employ to classify her case: "*Multiple and repeated absences. Two adjectives that say the same thing. But it's written in the File. And underlined. File that accuses a habitual offender*" (41; italics in the original). From the dossier at school to the dossier at the residence, her refusal to speak, to respond to precise questions, leads to the following definitive description: "On my file, it is written: SEI. Which means in their language: Strong Emotional Instability. Neither crazy nor retarded. Just a bit deranged. Or rather deranging for the public order" (14). Malika is especially disturbing to the authorities because she doesn't adhere to their way of thinking. After her admittance into this center at the age of eighteen, she leaves one evening and finds an anonymous man with whom she spends a night outdoors making love. Following this incident, she is placed for a short time in a hospital and is interrogated at length, much to her bewilderment: "I still remember the expression of the men in white. Their words. They said rape. They said madness. They said all sorts of words that didn't pertain to me. All of these definitive words that you assign to things you don't understand" (149). In her own understanding, the episode of lovemaking with a stranger was a liberating gesture that carries significance extending beyond the individual to implicate all Algerian women. In a society filled with multiple constraints focusing most often on women's sexuality, Malika's act embraces independence and pleasure, and, most of all, it gives place—and space—to dreams, a prominent theme in this work: "I had broken the published laws that cloistered the dreams of women. That is how I finally came into the world" (149).

Throughout the novel, the narrator calls attention to the fate of women in Algeria, most of whom know little freedom of movement or expression: "She must accept this is obscurity and silence—isn't it inscribed in her destiny as a woman?" (57). Given the lack of opportunity for self-determination among women, it seems natural that Malika should be reluctant to become a woman, as she relates in the book's opening pages: "When I was thirteen, I refused to grow up. . . . I even decided at the age when girls begin to menstruate that I would never be a woman" (11). The blood of menstruation is connected to the blood of the first sexual encounter in a later

Fabulation et imagination 181

passage, in which women's sensuality is stifled, words are forbidden, and sighs are repressed. When the newlywed woman has her first sexual encounter, the only acceptable expression of her experience seems to be the blood shed on the occasion, publicly brandished for all to see the proof of her prized virginity (56).[17] Even though she is hesitant to embrace her womanhood at first, the narrator eventually resigns herself to this inevitability: "I was a woman and I could do nothing against this curse. Curse. Suffering. Shame" (68).

The strong words in this quotation resonate with the forceful language found in the *avertissement,* signed Malika, preceding the first chapter of the book: "Let no one see here an attempt to clasp onto hope in a possible reconciliation with humans and with myself" (9). These words set the tone for the novel, cautioning the reader not to look for a positive outcome. But the deep discontent that is expressed here does not remain constant throughout the novel. Instead, it represents one of a number of textual moments when the narrator expresses a sense of the frustration, or perhaps even hatred, that is characteristic of her generation, according to Mohamed Benrabah, who poses the question: "What happened between independence and today to produce such hatred among the youth who didn't even experience the horrors of colonialism?" (24). Benrabah is particularly critical of the policy of Arabization and its attempt to circumscribe the individual in a system that denies all plurality. Benrabah argues that Algeria does not yet exist as a nation (346), and that in order for it to become one, the totality of the men and women who make up the country must regain all of their rights: "They must finally be able to attain the status of free individuals who benefit from equality and participate in politics" (347). *Cette fille-là* depicts women who do not know from personal experience the meaning of equality and democratic political participation and thereby indicates that Benrabah is correct: a significant number of individuals in post-independence Algeria have not regained their rights. To the contrary, they are controlled by authorities who allow no room for deviation from the declared norms, who accord no place to freedom of expression.

The author possesses firsthand knowledge of intolerance in her native land. Unlike a number of contemporary French-language women writers from Algeria, she has not left her place of origin, and her familiarity with the country as it is evolving in present times is a boon for much of her writing. The close attention she pays to women's names in *Cette fille-là* is at least in part a tribute to her own experience of self-naming and survival in the midst of an ever-present threat. As I mentioned at the outset of chapter 2, Maïssa Bey is a pseudonym. When the high school French professor Samia Benameur began writing in the mid-1990s, motivated by the murder of a fellow teacher, it was necessary for her to hide her legal name because her life was in constant danger. As she explains, "There is no question that by writing, by breaking the silence, by trying to brave the terror that has become a system, I am placing myself at the top of the list of people to eliminate. For myself, for my entire family, I try to preserve my anonymity."[18] The writer came upon her nom de plume by combining a first name that her mother had wanted to give her at birth and the maiden name of her maternal grandmother. She says that it was therefore *through women* that she found the new identity that allows her to speak out and to tell stories without being immediately recognized.

NEDJMA: WOMAN, NATION, AND TEMPORALITY

As Anne Donadey and Françoise Lionnet remind us, "Postcolonial nationalist projects have imagined women as metaphors for a nation" and as a result have often made "women's access to citizenship symbolically more difficult, since it is hard to conceptualize someone as being both the nation and an active agent of the nation" ("Feminisms" 229). The challenge Maïssa Bey has accepted in portraying Malika as symbolic of the nation is to demonstrate how she is also an active agent of the nation, resisting the passivity assigned to "woman" both in a metaphorical sense and a literal sense, with respect to the traditional confining roles of silent, submissive wife and mother that women are expected to occupy in Algerian society.

The older women with whom Malika interacts in *Cette fille-là* are alone and abandoned, and their greatest pleasure consists of revisiting the past, evoking memories of times gone by and often glorifying what used to be. They lament the changes that have accompanied national independence and blame advances in women's rights for some of the current misfortunes in their country. Malika greets much of their nostalgic reminiscing with skepticism, knowing that the past was not as blissful as her elderly friends like to portray it, "these women who are so quick to embellish the darkest of prisons" (161). Malika reflects on the fact that the romanticized past these women describe is characterized by a cloistering, a sedentary lifestyle that impedes enjoyment of the beauty and tenderness of the world, in her opinion. This seclusion meant that every day resembled the next and that women could not expect any variation whatsoever. Malika marvels at the

Fabulation et imagination

powers of amnesia, as these women idealize a period through forgetful reconstruction. Then she realizes that she has also told stories, like these women, in an effort to forget the darkest moments of her own existence.

In his remarks on how time and narrative function with respect to the modern nation, Homi Bhabha points to "complex strategies of cultural identification and discursive address that function in the name of 'the people' or 'the nation' and make them the immanent subjects and objects of a range of social and literary narratives" ("DissemiNation" 292). Passages in which Malika relates the voices that carry collective memories interspersed with her own reactions and reflections effectively stage some of the means by which identifications emerge when subjects are exposed to social narratives. Bhabha chooses to "focus on temporality" because it "provides a perspective on the disjunctive forms of representation that signify a people, a nation, or a national culture" (292). While the women who reminisce aloud together in *Cette fille-là* are not consciously relating stories that "signify a people, a nation, or a national culture," their comments about widespread attitudes and practices during colonial rule, their actions to avoid sending their own male relatives to fight in the Second World War, and other details tell much about national consciousness and belonging. The fact that their travel down memory lane is characterized by a forgetting that is similar to official forgetting of the past in Algeria only reveals the extent to which time and place are tangled in this postcolonial, transnational location, as Lionnet and Shih have asserted: "The national is no longer the site of homogeneous time and territorialized space but is increasingly inflected by the transnationality that suggests the intersection of 'multiple spatiotemporal (dis)orders'" (6).

As the novel comes to a close, Malika discloses a detail about her body: a small birthmark on her left ankle resembles a white star. She speculates about other possible defects that could have explained her mother's abandonment, still seeking an answer to the question of her origins. But the birthmark's attractive shape holds no explanation for why her mother left her. She hopes that it might be a sign, that it could constitute the promise of an extraordinary destiny. She considers the fact that this distinctive design on her body could have exerted an influence on other aspects of her life: "I could have, I should have been called Nedjma" (181). Nedjma, which means "star" in Arabic, is a common first name among Algerian women, but it is also the title of Kateb Yacine's publication, a classic of Algerian fiction that Emily Apter maintains can be "read as a novel about the ill-starred destiny of a postcolonial nation, born of language loss, rape and conquest, illegitimacy and shame, contested paternity and quasi-incestuous love" (304). In his introduction to the English-language version of *Nedjma,* Richard Howard writes that the eponymous character "assumes many a real and symbolic projection: the product of an autobiographical phantasm, she becomes an obscure object of desire in the exclusive perception of the four male characters in the novel, whereas Kateb's own historical vision inevitably infuses her representation with national symbolism" (xxxvi). Howard constructs a convincing argument that Nedjma "embodies the experience of a woman for the first time immune to the successive plundering and abandonment" that are a part of the background of so many mothers in the novel, and as such "her fate suggests a historically paradoxical shift" (xxxvii). This figure points ahead to Kateb's plays, in which he decides to make "use of the ancient declamatory device of the chorus of women" and to compose theatrical works that "reverse the limited portrayal of women so as to usher in a vision of active participation in an ongoing historical process" (xxxvii).

Well-versed in Algerian literary history, Maïssa Bey purposely likens Malika to her textual predecessor, Nedjma, and thus places her novel in relation to this precedent, all while taking the goals of *Nedjma* one step further. What is of crucial importance to Maïssa Bey's *Cette fille-là* is that Malika is the one who is speaking, and that she explores the multiple possibilities for self-representation, seeking out her own points of identification in a society that has unsuccessfully sought to define her and limit her freedom. In the end, she names herself anew, in a move that communicates a reclaiming of her identity as a woman, and therefore as "possessed": "I am the possessed one. My name is M'laïka" (182). The next sentence praises the corporeal implications of this renaming, as she allows her body to release itself from the constraints that surround her and dance to the rhythm of women's songs. Thanks to the affiliations she has created with those around her, she has managed to turn her own filial sterility into flourishing, fertile ground for literary strains that vibrate with new possibilities for women in Algeria today.

Conclusion | Mass in A Minor |
Putting Algeria on the Map

> *The need to bear witness and to have witnesses, that is need itself*
> —Hélène Cixous, "Un effet d'épine rose" (The weight of a thorny rose)
>
> *Nothing shakes her conviction: you have to turn the world into song.*
> *That is her secret, that of all these women*—Zahia Rahmani, Moze

In her autobiographical work of fiction titled *Manhattan: Lettres de la préhistoire* (*Manhattan: Letters from Prehistory*), Hélène Cixous recounts the trip of a French scholar to the United States in 1965, nearly forty years before *Manhattan* appeared in print, in 2002. The young woman who visits various libraries to consult manuscripts is convinced that the people she meets during her travel have no awareness of Algeria. To illustrate the general geographical ignorance she expects to encounter, the first-person narrator relates a conversation that takes place on a small plane heading from Ithaca toward Buffalo, New York. When her interlocutor asks her if she is from the departure city, she responds affirmatively: "I decide vaguely on my American-being. In the end I decide that it is impossible to tell her: I was born in Algeria. In America Algeria doesn't exist" (32). Whereas anyone in France would undoubtedly be able to locate Algeria without hesitation, she assumes that an American would have no knowledge of the existence of this newly independent country, let alone an idea of where it was to be found. The narrative voice goes on to affirm that while she readily divulges many of the intimate elements of her life to those she meets in the United States, she keeps her place of origin a secret: "Soon I found myself confiding the details of my supposed identity to strangers, I never said Algeria, which would have been in vain, but closer more familiar, whatever's most widespread in the world" (32).

When Assia Djebar's *L'amour, la fantasia* first appeared in English translation for an American public in 1993, *Fantasia: An Algerian Cavalcade* boasted a rather extensive paratextual apparatus that wasn't present in the original French text. In addition to a glossary, chronology, and critical introduction, this version contained a map of Algeria, presumably intended to extend a cartographic hand to the unfamiliar reader, providing an indispensable visual aid to navigating the cities and topography mentioned in the novel. The famous term "presumed innocent" from legal parlance might be transformed in this case to presumed ignorant to refer to the support that some publishers appear to assume is necessary for the anglophone reader. Words and expressions from Arabic are not accompanied by a glossary in the French publication; no map is present in the original, either. Whether or not it was a wise move to include these complementary materials in the English version of Djebar's well-known novel, I would argue that such assistance is becoming less pressing, precisely because of the prolific creative work of women writers from Algeria. Maïssa Bey, Marie Cardinal, Malika Mokeddem, Zahia Rahmani, and Leïla Sebbar, along with Cixous and Djebar, have made great strides toward putting Algeria on the map, toward making the land of their birth familiar to others. As I have demonstrated throughout *Polygraphies,* but especially in the chapters of the second section, "Takeoff Points," the French-language writings of women from Algeria have consistently drawn inspiration from and brought attention to Algeria, raising awareness not only of the country's historical past but also of the postcolonial situation of this hotbed for violence relating foremost to religion but also to the inextricably interrelated questions of language, nationality, race, and women.

TRENDS IN TRANSLATION

Both of the aforementioned texts by Cixous and Djebar have been translated into English, as well as into a number of other languages, pointing to the many readers around the world who have been touched by the oeuvres of these women writers from Algeria. Marie Cardinal's work has also had an impact on international readers through translation, as has the writing of Malika Mokeddem and Leïla Sebbar. Maïssa Bey's work is beginning to find a larger readership through translation, with the 2009 publication of the first English edition of one of her novels, *Surtout ne te retourne pas.* Zahia Rahmani's work has yet to meet with translation, though it certainly will. The fact that Bey and Rahmani's novels weren't translated immediately after publication reminds us that it is only relatively recently that the bulk of Cixous's and Djebar's work has been translated into English, for a number of reasons. Perhaps the greatest impediment is the obvious difficulty of adequately translating these rich and unique French-language texts into any other tongue.

Cixous knows all too well how a translated text can take on a life of its own. The 2010 republication of her famous (she might say "infamous") feminist manifesto in the original French gave the author an opportunity to redress some of the wrongs that have been done through and to this work since it first appeared in the journal *L'Arc* in 1975. Indeed, "The Laugh of the Medusa" became *the* essay by which the prolific writer was known on a global scale, obscuring all of her other writings, whether fictional or theatrical, as she explains: "The Medusa went much faster, much farther, much stronger than my works of fiction and then my theatrical writings. Frankly, I was bothered" ("Un effet d'épine rose" 29). In Cixous's analysis, then, this text was seized upon by some as wholly representative of her thought and work; it became immediately and irrevocably associated with her name, to the point that it was all a large number of people outside France knew of her: "I became the author of the Laugh of the Medusa, throughout the universe, which is the same as saying I was its father, or its servant! Wherever I pay attention, wherever I go, it is there: from Japan to Turkey, from Iran to Guatemala, from Argentina to Malaysia, from Lebanon to Korea" (29). What is particularly annoying about this situation may be the dominance of English in this affair. Cixous argues that this text escaped her the moment it was translated into this tongue: "As soon as it was translated into American English, my Medusa took off. And what a trip! Endless, ageless. And, as it were, without me" (29). And universities everywhere accord this essay canonical status, teaching it either in English or—what is even more shocking—in translations *from* the English version (31)!

Cixous's outrage with respect to the celebrated text that she now claims is "foreign" to her is closely tied to her heightened awareness of the fact that, as the adage goes, something has been lost in translation: "It was even able to bring me renown *in English,* and therefore, naturally, with several feathers/pens [*plumes*] and languages lost in translation" (30). The omnipresent English translation is most noticeably insufficient when it comes to Cixous's play on the French homonym that refers to both flight and theft: "The *Vol,* so dear to me, especially thanks to the homonymy from which it benefits in French, is only half-flight in English, where the indecision fades away in translation" (30; et surtout grâce à l'homonymie dont il jouit en français, n'est qu'un demi-vol en anglais, où l'indécision s'éteint en traduction). In her striking comments in "Un effet d'épine rose," a reflective piece that situates "Le rire de la Méduse" chronologically and theoretically with respect to her life and work up to the present republication in the original French, Cixous suggests that many of the grave misunderstandings surrounding this piece stem from inappropriate readings.

In his preface to the republication of Cixous's celebrated essay, Frédéric Regard defends this writing from the misreading that has often been its fate: "We consider the profound error of those who concluded that 'The Laugh of the Medusa' was characterized by biological essentialism" (20). He bolsters his argument against such faulty interpretations by quoting the text itself:

> "We, the women always arriving/happening [*les arrivées de toujours*], from now on, if we say it, who could forbid us?" It is hardly easy to identify here who is on one side and who is on the other of the interdict, the line of demarcation that is nonetheless assumed to found essentialism. The simple test of reading teaches that it is impossible to skim [*survoler*] such a sentence, that in order to steal it [*la voler*], you have to have walked step by step in its prints, panting, retracing your steps, so that, coming back again over the ridgeline, you find the key, and face what is arriving/happening. (20)

Regard insists that readers cannot confiscate the interrogative sentence he quotes in this passage if they have not walked in its steps, if they have not tread in its traces, if they have not lost their footing, circled back, and become breathless in the process. The careful study of this text, the involved reading Regard describes, is reminiscent of the type of reading Serge Margel makes a case for in his study of Rousseau's writing: *reading as testimony.*

Cixous may have been so disappointed with the destiny of "Le rire de la Méduse" because she didn't perceive that international readers had adopted the appropriate stance with respect to her text; indeed, she concludes that they misinterpreted it down to its very classification: "In France *The Laugh of the Medusa* and *Newly Born Woman* were books. Everywhere else in the world, they were acts. Surprise!" ("Un effet d'épine rose" 29). The author indicates that when others take the liberty to apply the label of their choosing to her text: "*The Laugh of the Medusa,* and other *Sorties,* is *un appel.* A telephone call to the world. They said: a manifesto" (28). Her frustration with this categorization arises from her belief in the literary call as intimately related to *others,* to the relationship with others that constitutes the acts of reading and writing, to *testimony:* "The feeling that you can't make progress alone, or take pleasure alone—let's call it *Responsibility*—haunted me. The need to bear witness and to have witnesses, that is need itself: to call is already to be fulfilled" (29).

ALGÉRIANCES, ALLIANCES, DALLIANCES

In "My Algeriance, in other words: to depart, not to arrive from Algeria," Cixous provides an explanation of this title by focusing on the grammatical form of the neologism that is distinctly hers: "I like the progressive form and the words that end in *-ance*. . . . To depart (so as) not to arrive from Algeria is also, incalculably, a way of not having broken with Algeria" (170). This new term she coined to describe her relationship to the country of her birth could be made plural to refer to the many connections women writers from Algeria have with their homeland, whether or not they feel comfortable calling it home. Whatever their particular rapport with Algeria is, they all strive in their lives and work to create bonds with others in various ways that reveal that—like Cixous—they have not broken with Algeria. From the creation of associations promoting literacy among Algerian women to the depiction of the plight of Algerian intellectuals in literary form, French-language women writers from Algeria prove that they are forever affected by their experience there.[1] They repeatedly demonstrate that this background has given them the motivation to move toward alliances, in diverse shapes and on different scales.

Maïssa Bey portrays the pain of a bereaved mother in her 2010 work of fiction, *Puisque mon coeur est mort* (Since my heart is dead), providing a voice, and a musical score, for an individual whose suffering was squelched by unnamed authorities: "They wanted to muzzle my pain. They wanted to reduce me to silence. To oblige me to experience your departure silently, lifelessly, to play my score [*jouer ma partition*] softly" (15). The sorrowful narrator declares her regret that other women have not joined her in her grief, since those who "know how to give voice to the suffering of others" serve a special purpose in the mourning process:

> In spite of it all, how I would have loved to see them open my door, surround me, sit down, rush around me, these women who know how to give voice to the suffering of others, to make it their suffering, to sharpen the blade, to go in search of the point of impact, to plunge their bare hands in, their bare voices in, uproariously, to make the evil come out! It's of little importance that they are considered liars, that they are compared to barkers, dogs crying out! It's of little importance that they are on an ordered mission, that it is as confirmed actresses that they act out the role of the other's suffering. (18)

The others who could have joined her in honoring her son's memory might have been playing a role, as she indicates in this passage, and they might have been exaggerating, or imagining, or even *lying*, as they lent their cries to the expression of unimaginable loss, of unspeakable distress. But none of these accusations are of importance to the mother who speaks in this text.

The possibility that these women might have been participating in a fiction does not make that fiction any less powerful, in her estimation.

This significant passage from Bey's novel can serve as a metaphor for the autobiographical writing examined in the pages of this book. Throughout *Polygraphies,* I have been less concerned with maintaining a distinction between truth and fiction than with exploring and reveling in the multiple truths that can be communicated through fiction, in creative and interesting ways. According to Cixous's point of view, writing does not always take as a starting point what could be considered factual, or *true;* it is by definition made up of the intimate, as well as of magic, and imagination: "This method of investigation is the most private, powerful, economical; it is the most magical, most democratic supplement. Some paper, imagination, and you take off" ("Un effet d'épine rose" 25). Despite its humble beginnings, the written text is nonetheless greatly influential: "Magical efficacity of language: fiction becomes true" (26). Cixous effectively breaks down any presumed barrier between truth and fiction in this affirmation of the way in which fiction has the potential to *become* true. This statement may be taken to mean that fiction has such a hold on our minds that it virtually becomes a reality for us. But it can also mean that, as the theorist asserts, literature may *precede* reality in such a way that it makes things happen, that it calls attention to injustice and brings about change. "In literature things exist that do not yet exist in reality" ("Un effet d'épine rose" 28). This is why she puts out a "call" for writing.

The narrative voice in Bey's novel articulates the positive potential of a chorus of women to make a difference through their cries: "Perhaps, perhaps thanks to this chorus of women whose songs go to the depths of the wound and slash the sore, perhaps this cry—this scream from a beast fatally injured who doesn't stop vibrating in my stomach and bumping against the walls of silence—could have made its way out and erupted in order to shake up the order of time, to disturb the stars before shattering against the indifference of the world" (*Puisque* 18). Even if the indifference of the world wins out at the close of this quotation, Bey's writing in this passage communicates an optimistic message that joint efforts can achieve great things, opening up the possibility that collaborative ventures can go so far as to disrupt time and shake up the stars. Even though the content of this citation is very serious, these claims have a playful resonance, hinting at the fun that can be had in the written text. A little lightheartedness does not lessen the impact of the ideas conveyed in the novel; to the contrary, it often provides them with a particular punch that ultimately makes them memorable. What may appear to be a "dalliance" is actually a strong element in creating alliances between writers and readers, who are drawn to each other through the insertion of humoristic details in the text. There is perhaps no greater advocate for playfulness in the earnest literary text than Cixous, and if we glance at "Le rire de la Méduse," looking at it first in its untranslatable original articulation, we find a salient example: "Ô les zolis zyeux, tiens, zolie petite fille, achète-moi mes lunettes et tu verras la Vérité-Moi-Je te dire tout ce que tu devras croire" (66; Oh the pretty eyes, pretty little girl, buy me my glasses and you will see the Truth-Me-I tell you all that you should believe). All of Cixous's work disturbs the sacred trilogy mentioned in this passage, the "Truth" that is connected to the expression of "Me" in the text written through the eyes of the first person pronoun, "I." The autobiographical elements of her works of fiction—and those of the other women writers in my study—do not force beliefs on readers in an insensitive manner that demands that all others see things through self-focused lenses. Instead, Cixous puts an emphasis in this early text, as in later publications, on writing that is directed outward, on literature that is full of love for others, a love that *is other,* that places the accent on a different beat than we are accustomed to, that shakes up our convictions in order to create space for new and greater truths: *"L'Amour Autre"* ("Le rire de la Méduse" 67).

ALTERNATIVE PRONUNCIATIONS: MUSIC FOR THE MASS(ES)

Focusing on Cixous's italicized term *L'Amour Autre,* Frédéric Regard titles his prefatory comments *"AA!,"* devoting a considerable portion of his analysis to the "jewel" of these two words (20) that he calls the "very signature" of "Le rire de la Méduse" (21). The emphasis on this letter recalls the title of my conclusion, in which the "Mass in A Minor" underscores the *A* in both *"Amour"* and *"Autre,"* as well as in *"Algérie,"* of course. Texts by women writers from Algeria comprise a labor of love for others that may be considered to be composed in a minor key, in the sense that their musical phrases do not always correspond to the sounds our ears are used to hearing. They may also be labeled minor because they bring into the text "lower" tones, those belonging to individuals, particularly women, who are not always treated with the highest respect in Algeria. They do so in order to make music for a unique mass, one conducted in a French tongue that derives from Latin, but that is peppered with words and phrases as well as melodic lines that come from other languages of Algeria: Arabic or Berber.[2]

These texts allow a chorus of voices to chime in, adding their stories to the autobiographical work that is not entirely centered on the writer's singular experience. They are not necessarily written "for the masses," in the sense that they are often complex literary creations that require informed, careful readings, but they are nonetheless composed "for the masses" in that they are on the side of—written on behalf of—"ordinary" others; these texts demonstrate great sensitivity to the situation of those whom political leaders and educated people have often diminished. If the texts I examine throughout *Polygraphies* could be said to contribute to musical pieces composed in A minor, it is because they use minor notes to strike major chords within us, and they therefore make a key contribution to increasing understanding, combating ignorance, and opening up the French text and its readers to other experiences and other expressions.

An excellent illustration of this can be found in Zahia Rahmani's ongoing literary portrait of her mother in various novels, an evolving depiction that underscores the deep intelligence that characterizes this illiterate individual. In *Moze,* the narrative voice explains how she approaches the world: "Moze's wife has a highly valued technique. She is an expert in stories and legends. She does not know how to read or write. The world was conveyed to her through fables" (165). The fables she passes on to her loved ones tell truths that were known to her mother before her, and the techniques of transmission are well designed to make an impression on those who hear them:

> From her mother, she has inherited a different knowledge. One that was taught in the past to isolated young girls: the art of thread and cotton. She knew how to turn a ball into a world of beauty and balance. It was in winter, a propitious and calm period, that she introduced her girls and her boys to this science of harmony that is tapestry. In front of walls of spun wool, they learned to execute the abstract narratives enhanced by erudite geometrical shapes. If you took your eyes off the heart full of rare and happy inscriptions on these warm layers, you could follow along the rolled edges the infinite paths, deep and seductive, along which she asked them to inscribe, through curves and lines, their dreams and their words, their loves and their voices. (157–58)

The "other" knowledge that mothers pass along to their daughters—and sons—in Rahmani's family tradition is much like the art of literary composition, in that it entails a process reminiscent of the interweaving of fiction and testimony that I discussed in this book's introduction. The "harmonies" that are created through this activity are the result of a group effort, of a collective gathering focused on the same goal, one that extends beyond the inscriptions at hand to encompass the imaginary. This work of intermingling reveals that it is not solely lived experience that makes up our reality: dreams are as much a part of us as our loves.

When the autobiographical narrative voice in Rahmani's text speaks of her mother, she often also addresses the larger experience of a multitude of women, especially Algerian women. In her affirmation of her mother's belief in the power of song, she insists that this conviction is not unique to her progenitor: "Moze's wife accepts all explanations. Nothing shakes her conviction: you must make the world a song. That's her secret. That of all these women" (*Moze* 166). The particular music that Rahmani transcribes in her literary work comes from Berber, her mother tongue, and the only tongue of her mother: "Moze's wife speaks a foreign language in this country. A language of which there is a shortage. A language that has been distanced for so long from men's conquests that she has decided to know and speak only it" (159). Years after her arrival in France, the immigrant mother still prefers her native language, refusing to let it go in favor of French. It is Berber that the narrator wants to hang on to as well, even as she composes acclaimed literature in French: "I want to speak of the language of mothers. Everything comes from there, in my view. From this language" (159). Letting this language have a word in the text, allowing it to occupy a significant place on the page, is a gesture of incorporation that moves toward an acceptance of accents, of alternatives, of otherness, and ultimately of difference, not only abroad but also within the borders of contemporary France.

This movement of acceptance must take place in two directions, as Djebar reminds us in *Les nuits de Strasbourg,* her novel set in the eponymous French city. When the voice of one of the text's characters poses a rhetorical question, it is clear that it is not enough for those whose families have resided in France for generations to adjust to the presence of newcomers to their country; it is important that immigrants make an effort to adapt as well: "You, a woman! What is the purpose of emigrating, if you don't expand your mind?" (245). What this novel succeeds in doing with aplomb is reminding readers that one of the most efficient ways to convince people to open themselves up to other mentalities and lifestyles is through linguistic innovation. When languages mix, when new expressions are found, perspectives shift and true exchanges can begin. A touching example of the power of language to bring about change occurs in the midst of a passionate conversation between an Algerian woman named Thelja and her French lover François in *Les nuits de Strasbourg,* when they serendipitously discover a new name for their couple: "*'Alsagérie':* palpate my lips when I reiterate this word that summarizes us" (374). The beauty of this verbal creation is that the word doesn't exist in the language of one or the other, but in both tongues at once, or perhaps in a space outside language: "—Alsace, Algeria... No, instead, *Alsagérie!* ... —*Alsagérie,* this word is in what language? In yours, in mine?" (372). This linguistic *métissage* can be translated into every language, and its crucial combination of sounds can adapt to almost any pronunciation. What is noteworthy in Djebar's novel is that the term is articulated differently, not according to the speaker but according to the addressee of this expression of love:

> In one of my dreams, all that I remember is a sound, at dawn—you, yes you, you were learning my language! So you would have said, if we hadn't invented it—neither your place, nor my place, in both languages at once: *"el za djé rie"*!
>
> —I say the word like you; or no, not entirely: *Al-ssa-gé-rie!* And I take my time on the 's,' I double it because I hear a gentleness in it. Your gentleness!
>
> —And I, a pain. *"Alza-gérie."* I cut it in two this way, so that I can quickly arrive to you.... —The "z" in my childhood alphabet is not a trace of suffering. No. This consonant announces beauty and sparkle: "z" like "zina." Zina, the adjective, means beautiful; as a noun, it designates lovemaking. There is therefore a couple in *"Alsagérie,"* a happy couple, a couple making love. (373)

This neologism, the key to the book, is poetry itself, allowing for accents that come from elsewhere, above all from this specific *ailleurs*—so very close and yet so far—that is *Algeria.*

Thanks to the eye-opening, self-sacrificing autobiographical work of women writers, Algeria has taken on new dimensions and acquired great significance for many readers. The fact that these writers occupy a unique place astride the historical line demarcating the colonial from the postcolonial—proving in both their lives and work that such a division is arbitrary and artificial—gives a particular pull to the messages these writers convey in powerful poetic prose. Their writings demonstrate that a troubled past cannot be forgotten, as in the case of Djebar's Thelja and François, but they also show that it can be transformed through literature into a means of informing the present in crucial ways. They compose literary works in accord with Cixous's understanding of writing as an activity that constitutes a call, as it reaches out to others in an effort to effectively testify and to invite others to do so as well. And their written calls have been heard, I would argue. Perhaps they have not always been heard as the authors originally intended, but that is one of the many rich possibilities of literature: that meaning may be made that eludes the writer, meaning that an attentive reader may nonetheless find in the text. The international interest readers have shown in these writers' work is not the only evidence of their widespread appeal and increasing influence. It is the growing numbers of women writers from outside France that best testify to the impact of the writing examined in *Polygraphies*. Women from around the world are now revealing that they have the ambition and the confidence to compose novels in French, and the women writers in this study have arguably played a role in paving the way for further textual explorations in novel form. Not only have younger women with a connection to Algeria—such as Nina Bouraoui or Leïla Marouane—composed a number of compelling texts in recent years, but writers from such diverse places as Slovenia and South Korea, Iran and Japan, are now contributing to an ever more multicultural and multilingual literary landscape in French, as a result of the courageous groundbreaking work of French-language women writers from Algeria.

NOTES

INTRODUCTION

1 "I am convinced that, in a certain manner, every text is autobiographical" (*Sur parole* 10).
2 In his reflections on forgiveness, Derrida has also pointed out the importance of the presence of a community. He argues that one cannot seek forgiveness in the name of others, whether victims or criminals, but that the apparently personal scene of asking for forgiveness unavoidably involves testimony, and therefore a community: "There is no scene of forgiveness without testimony, without survival, without a duration beyond the experience of trauma and violence; and already in the singularity of the experience, in the coming together [*face-à-face*] of the criminal and the victim, a third party is present and something like a community announces itself. Hence the awkwardness that must be avowed, and the contradiction: forgiveness is an experience of coming together, of 'I' and of 'you,' but at the same time there is already community, generation, testimony; from the moment there is an enunciation, forgiveness granted or not, there is the implication of a community, and therefore of a certain collectivity" (*Sur parole* 139).
3 As Shoshana Felman and Dori Laub make clear in their work, language plays a special role when it comes to testimony. To testify is, in effect, to carry out a speech act that attempts to reach toward truth but does not in itself constitute truth per se: "In the testimony, language is in process and in trial, it does not possess itself as a conclusion, as the constatation of a verdict or the self-transparency of knowledge. Testimony is, in other words, a discursive *practice,* as opposed to a pure *theory.* To testify—to *vow to tell,* to *promise* and *produce* one's own speech as material evidence for truth—is to accomplish a *speech act,* rather than to simply formulate a statement" (5).
4 Derrida insists that literary fiction is precisely this, a text that can be legitimately read as a variety of genres: "One can read the same text—which thus never exists 'in itself'—as a testimony that is said to be serious and authentic, or as an archive, or as a document, or as a symptom—or as a work of literary fiction, indeed the work of a literary fiction that simulates all of the positions that we have just enumerated" (*Demeure* 29).
5 Alison Rice interview with Hélène Cixous, January 2006, Paris.
6 Alison Rice interview with Zahia Rahmani, June 2005, Paris.

1. LE MOI À PLUSIEURS REPRISES

1. In her 2007 novel, *Nulle part dans la maison de mon père,* Djebar refers to the "secularized" nature of autobiography in Western literature, distancing herself from this contemporary tendency: "This is neither a compulsive desire to strip oneself bare, nor a dread of autobiography—this 'secularized' substitute of confession in Western literature" (402).
2. This is my translation from the original.
3. In order to remain as close to the original as possible, this translation from *L'amour, la fantasia,* as well as the one found in the next sentence, is my own.
4. This translation is my own.
5. It is crucial to note that in *L'amour, la fantasia,* a similar shift from the first to the third person occurs following the description of the accident, but it does not take place until *after* a moment of recognition, when the girl opens her eyes and observes the man who saved her.
6. Carine Bourget has also examined Cixous's feeling of "culpability" "for having been on the privileged side" in her analysis of a short story by Cixous titled "Pieds nus" (107). While Bourget asserts that Cixous's guilt is "assuaged by her casting the boy as a would-be murderer" in this short story, I would argue that there is no similar possibility of relief from Cixous's overwhelming sense of responsibility in this scene from *Les rêveries,* since the "murderer" in question has not turned her hostility outward but instead has taken her own life in a movement that recalls Djebar's phrase "a self-murdering gesture" (*Nulle part* 379; un geste auto-meurtrier).
7. Leigh Gilmore establishes a connection between serial autobiography and crime in "Endless Autobiography?" and asks a question with particular pertinence to the crime scene as it is understood in Cixous and Djebar's works: "Like acts in any series, the autobiographical acts of serial autobiographers are always potentially one among an unspecified many. If the name itself suggests a sort of criminality in the form of excess, how is the autobiographical scene structured like a crime scene, one to which the writer may return?" (211)
8. Cixous has expressed a feeling of inadequacy, of illegitimacy, even of having committed a crime, when faced with questions regarding her birthplace. In the following quotation, that feeling of having committed a wrongdoing is connected to autobiography, in intriguing terms: "That I was born in Algeria is a fact which is, from a certain point of view, indisputable. I will never deny having been born-in-Algeria. All the same I just have to say these words: 'I was born in Algeria' to feel a slight ungluing of my being, like a sensation of contraband, and even a hint of novels, something that resembles a genre, as if this sentence were a quotation, the beginning of an autobiography" (*Si près* 45).
9. In an analysis of the functioning of testimony in the context of war crime

tribunals, Ranjana Khanna notes that selective forgetfulness is often at work: "Although it is possible that such testimonies could still be haunted by what cannot be thematized or articulated, by what is not bound by referentiality, or by the bequest from a previous generation, it is likely that such hauntings will be ignored in favor of choosing to forget what is already conscious, or what has been identified as the chosen trauma of a people" (98).

10 The circular nature of Djebar's text as well as its drawn-out, sustained attention to the tramway incident it repeatedly returns to reveals important truths about the temporality of trauma. As Ranjana Khanna notes, "Trauma brings a notion of temporality into justice, which challenges our understanding of the latter term as a simple reparation or restitution for events in the past" (98). Jane Hiddleston draws from the work of Lawrence Langer to make a striking statement on the ways in which experiences of trauma disrupt linear conceptions of the passing of time, as well as the possibility of neatly placing events in the past: "Testimonies prevent us from seeking reassurance in the patterns of progress and chronology, and they force us to confront the unending duration of the traumatic event" (133).

11 Aristotle's comments in *The Poetics* insist on the necessity of arousing both fear and pity in the spectator. The source of these cathartic emotions is the *story line* rather than the decor, the acting, or the setting: "Fear and pity sometimes result from the spectacle and are sometimes aroused by the actual arrangement of the incidents, which is preferable and the mark of a better poet. The plot should be so constructed that even without seeing the play anyone hearing of the incidents happening thrills with fear and pity as a result of what occurs" (49).

12 "Each of us, individually and freely, must do the work that consists of rethinking what is your death and my death, which are inseparable. Writing originates in this relationship. In what is often inadmissible, contrary, terribly dangerous, and risks turning into complacency—which is the worst of all crimes: it originates here. We are the ones who make of death something mortal and negative" (*Three Steps* 13).

13 For Cixous, writing is the privileged medium of expression for the worst aspects of human existence: "It is difficult to write the worst, but it is impossible to say it. Writing exists for the worst" ("Obstétriques" 116). The things that we cannot bring ourselves to say out loud exist in *written* form: "Everything we could never have said, but have read, since at least it's written" (*Three Steps* 49).

14 In a preface to a work by Sade, Blanchot elaborates on the condemning nature of the project of telling all: "To tell all. This single line would have been enough to make this project suspect.... Sade is still pursued because of the same demand: to tell all, you must tell all, freedom is the freedom to tell all, this unlimited movement that is the temptation of reason, its secret wish, its madness" ("L'in-

convenance majeure" 51). Assia Djebar refers to her suicide attempt in *Nulle part dans la maison de mon père* as "an act of solitary madness" (362), but indeed she hasn't shied away from the need to tell all in this text, in a repetitive gesture that revisits this insanity again and again.

2. LA SINGULARITÉ DE L'ALTÉRITÉ

1 Other critics who have focused on the meaning of epigraphs in Djebar's work include Debra Kelly, who asserts that in *Vaste est la prison* the epigraphs "add a dialogic and autobiographical layer" to the text (*Autobiography and Independence* 295) and that they add specifically to our understanding of Djebar's attitude toward the self with relation to the past when they "highlight forms of self-knowledge gained through loss" (296).

2 Leïla Sebbar's father was also a schoolteacher in Algeria, and he happened to attend the same school as Bey's father did, as Sebbar specifies in *Je ne parle pas la langue de mon père:* "From 1932 to 1935, he studies at the *École normale d'instituteurs* in Bouzaréah, in Algiers" (9). It is perhaps not an accident that Sebbar also expresses feelings of being on the outskirts of two worlds, a situation of perpetual nonbelonging due to the fact that her father was an Arab and her mother was French. She refers to this detail as "the first, essential rupture" that explains why she is neither from one side or the other, and her childhood in Algeria is characterized by this exile (*Lettres parisiennes* 199).

3 The figure of the father as the one who gives the language of writing in Bey's case harks back to Djebar's representations of her father, also a schoolteacher of French, who is responsible for her knowledge of the language of the former colonizer. The oft-cited opening line of *L'amour, la fantasia* bears witness to this filial relationship.

3. LA TERRE MATERNELLE

1 "Mother and motherland" converge and intertwine in a number of works by Marie Cardinal, notably *Au pays de mes racines* and *Autrement dit,* with the earlier *Les mots pour le dire* constituting the most prominent example of this tendency. Critics such as Marguerite de Clézio in "Mother and Motherland" have explored the relation between these themes, making it clear that the country and the mother have much in common in this oeuvre. As Colette Hall maintains, "The source, the country of origin . . . takes on maternal characteristics in Cardinal's work" (13).

2 Textual parallels between the mother and Algeria in Cardinal's text include the following: The phrase "L'Algérie française vivait son agonie" (*Les mots pour le dire* 90; French Algeria was in her death throes) is echoed in the mother's experience: "Ma mère vivait son agonie" (257; My mother was in her death throes).

Then, this sentence on Algeria's wounds "l'Algérie déchiquetée montrait au grand jour ses plaies infectées" (92; Mutilated Algeria was openly showing her infected sores) is recalled when the mother displays her own injuries: "[Ma mère] prenait du plaisir à étaler ses plaies" (266; My mother took pleasure in showing off her sores). These translations from the original French text are my own.

3. The trees into which the young Marie repeatedly stumbles suggest a number of interpretations. It is quite possible that they were planted in an orderly manner and that Marie's encounters with them meant that she followed a disorderly path that strayed from the "straight and narrow" course she was instructed to take. As the narrator's reflections reveal, she was propelled by a force that did not always coincide with the path she was supposed to adopt: "I was afraid. I wanted to please my mother. I wanted to live her way, and yet I felt within myself a terrible force pushing me away from the path I was supposed to follow" (134); "Until then, my life had been made up of only a series of efforts to divert myself from the path I made in her direction" (137). The trees she bangs up against in the street could represent the "roots" in the Algerian soil that Marie would like to plant, the belonging to the earth that she so desires.

4. For a study of the importance of hygiene, "whiteness," and women (and the connections among these concepts) in the context of French-Algerian colonial and postcolonial culture, see Kristin Ross's *Fast Cars, Clean Bodies,* especially pages 74–84.

5. One of the most obvious and insidious aspects of the one-sided French educational system in Algeria is language. Singling out French as the only acceptable tongue of communication in school led to a separation between French-speaking children and other children their age. As Leïla Sebbar indicates in *Je ne parle pas la langue de mon père,* Arabic was the forbidden tongue in the school of her childhood: "When the whistle blows, the forbidden language is stifled, turning from a murmur into silence, the boys enter another world" (43). Jacques Derrida provides a thorough analysis of the various linguistic interdicts in the French school system in Algeria in *Le monolinguisme de l'autre, ou la prothèse d'origine.* Those whose education was conducted primarily in French felt as if they had been denied "entry" into the country of their origin, into their place of birth, was in large part related to linguistic separation, to an inability to communicate in the tongue of their native land.

6. Bourdieu quotes from a text by Thomas Bernhard, *Maîtres anciens,* that describes the interrelation of state and school: "The school is the school of the State, where young people are made into creatures of the State, that is to say nothing other than reactionaries. When I entered into school, I entered into the State, and since the State destroyed beings, I entered into the establishment of the destruction of beings.... The State made me enter it by force, as it did of all

the others, and made me docile to it, the State, and made of me a man under State control, a regulated, registered, trained, and educated man, who is also perverted and depressed, like all the others" (34). Bernhard's complaint about the hand in hand operation of state and school rings true in descriptions by Cardinal and Cixous.

7 The recurrent proclamation that certain things "are not done" is most striking in the case of the divorce between Marie's parents. This was a dramatic action that literally made her parents tremble. In the words of her mother, the cause for such physical disturbance was the breaking with tradition: "That is not done in our family" (*Les mots pour le dire* 131; Cela ne se fait pas dans notre famille).

8 In this passage, the narrative voice adopts the words of her mother and reproduces them in the same way her mother swallowed them before her. This move in the narration reveals how completely the language of the mother *entered into* the daughter, affecting her consciousness and structuring her worldview.

9 In her autobiographical *L'amour, la fantasia,* Djebar attests to the fact that she was never allowed to enter a French home in Algeria during her early years: "Throughout my childhood, just before the war which was to bring us independence, I never crossed a single French threshold, I never entered the home of a single French schoolfellow" (23).

10 Albert Memmi's 1957 psychological study of colonization in the Maghreb, *Portrait du colonisé précédé du portrait du colonisateur* (*The Colonizer and the Colonized*), explores the mutual dependence of colonizer and colonized.

11 Western constructions (and constrictions) of the "mother" cause Cardinal to adopt a skeptical stance with respect to this person's "role" in society: "I am a mother and I am very wary of this character" (*Autrement dit* 201).

12 It is equally unsurprising that the daughter's most flagrant act of rebellion takes *physical* form in *Les mots pour le dire:* "And then, suddenly, I had decided on my own to overcome the prejudices of family and class, and the colossus of religion, to have sex with a boy I didn't even love, with whom there couldn't even be the excuse of either passion or reason" (45). The pure physicality of this sexual encounter flies in the face of every system of rules the girl has encountered. In one fell swoop, she defies her class, her family, her mother, and her religion.

13 *Les rêveries de la femme sauvage* describes a fixation with the "motherly" Aïcha— in her tangible, touchable, corporeal reality—as representative of the "motherland," forever removed: "I snuggled up to Aïcha's body and laughing she let me hug her country" (6). This phrase is echoed at various moments in the text: "At the very heart of this Algerian fecundity, which we, I especially, have been dreaming of since the days when I used to walk in order to be within reach at last of the body, the arms, the breasts, the hands" (31); and "From the back of the garden from Aïcha especially, for that is the only Algeria that I was ever able to touch rub

against touch again handle stroke arch my back against her calf clamp my mouth between her breasts crawl around on her spicy slopes. I snuggle up to Aïcha from her knees" (51–52). It is worth noting that among the many aspects of her body enumerated at different points in the text, Aïcha's *skin* is seldom mentioned, with perhaps only this one exception: "Living was my way of thinking and her skin was the book" (53). According to Sara Ahmed's reading of Judith Butler's *Bodies That Matter,* "The skin allows us to consider how boundary-formation, the marking out of the lines of a body, involves an affectivity which already crosses the line. For if the skin is a border, then it is a border that feels" (45). This affective border seems to be sorely missing in the narrator's account of burying her body in that of Aïcha's.

14 It is important to note that in these written accounts of both Cixous and Djebar, the idealized "other" mother is seen through the eyes of a prepubescent girl. In *Les mots pour le dire,* Cardinal describes a fascination with an elderly woman named Daïba, but this figure is not admired for her body, nor even for her pastries, but rather for her stories (101).

15 As Deniz Kandiyoti puts it in a reflection titled "Identity and Its Discontents: Women and the Nation," "The very language of nationalism singles women out as the symbolic repository of group identity" (382).

16 In Stacey Weber-Fève's analysis, Djebar is inspired by Cixous to write women's bodies in(to) the text, and this has the positive outcome of opening to an understanding of "relational identity" (34). According to Weber-Fève, Djebar's depiction of her own mother as possessing "maternal duality—her absent body but present voice" marks a well-articulated departure from early readings of mothers as a metaphor for Africa: "Much first-generation postcolonial theory reads the Mother's body—very much present as illustrated by the appearance of her breasts, stomach, thighs, etc. in many postcolonial primary works—as a metaphor for the African continent, a pre-colonial past or a traditional or indigenous society, the nation, the community, or the family" (34).

17 "I loved math but, in my family, they said that it wasn't feminine. A girl who did math was, apparently, 'unmarriageable,' or only with a math teacher" (*Les mots pour le dire* 43).

18 Maïssa Bey finds similar inspiration in the sea, which figures prominently in the title of her first novel, *Au commencement était la mer* (In the beginning was the sea).

19 According to Josyane Savigneau, "Marie Cardinal, a writer by profession, whom we believed to be at home with success and with the Parisian literary life, has been 'in exile' in Quebec for five years now, because she could no longer stand this *'petit milieu.'*"

20 "Le Ravin de la femme sauvage" is the name of a ravine close to the childhood

home of Cixous, as well as Leïla Sebbar, as this quotation from Sebbar's *Je ne parle pas la langue de mon père* reveals: "Did my father know then who lived in the Arab quarter where the city's poor were at the edge of the Ravin de la femme sauvage, what wild woman? . . . The wild woman of Hélène Cixous, who lived in a house at the Clos-Salembier, as I learned in her *Les rêveries de la femme sauvage?*" (18). This citation of Cixous's publication gives evidence to the mutual influence francophone women writers from Algeria have on each other, and points toward various intertextualities in their work. It is not unlikely that Cixous's work of fiction and its obvious relation to this ravine inspired Sebbar's collection of short stories titled *Le ravin de la femme sauvage*, though the eponymous short story is preoccupied with finding the answer to the question posed above, and not with responding to Cixous's similarly titled text.

21 In order to capture the innovative expressions in the original text, this is my own translation from the French.

22 The reference to the biblical hero Samson is important in this passage not simply because she believes that she is punished like he was, but because of the particular punishment imposed on them both. The blinding Samson suffers following his lover's betrayal finds a parallel in Cixous's severe myopia. This chastisement in her case is representative of a lack of luck at birth, a "natural" fault that blurs the world around her, impeding her from clearly seeing all that is before her.

23 The dreamed locations of this "double" childhood are not limited to the city of Osnabrück. This urban center serves as a symbol for the European continent as well as for the movement that has defined Jewish people throughout history: "My childhood was spent in large part in the landscape of a recounted Europe. It was the legend of Europe told by those who traveled it over. I sense that the French are firmly rooted. The Jews were the travelers of Europe" (*Photos de racines* 183–84).

4. "LA CÉLÉBRATION D'UNE TERRE-MÈRE"

1 This passage stands out in striking contrast to the geographical placement of the young Cixous, as we discovered in the last chapter. Despite the fact that she had not yet left Algeria, the educated and erudite Cixous knew how to place herself on a map, and possessed a firm understanding of the locations and histories of her father, whose family hailed from Spain, and her mother, who had fled Nazi Germany with Cixous's maternal grandmother thanks to a French passport obtained when they lived in Strasbourg. While these places remain imagined for Cixous before her departure from Algeria, she had a complex understanding of her location in North Africa as a child, according to her description in *Photos de racines*.

2 I have translated the final sentence from the original French, in order to remain faithful to its message.

5. ÉCRIRE LES MAUX

1. In this well-known text, as in others from the same time period, men are not excluded from the possibility of composing works that fit the title of *écriture féminine*, but they are less prone to truly abandon themselves to such writing. As Cixous explains in "La venue à l'écriture," men who give themselves over to corporal inspiration must not have a rigid relationship to their sexuality: "Continuity, abundance, drift—are these specifically feminine? I think so. And when a similar wave of writing surges forth from the body of a man, it's because in him femininity is not forbidden. But he doesn't fantasize his sexuality around a faucet" (57).
2. To Cixous's mind, this is what writing the body means: "Women must write through their bodies, they must invent the impregnable language that will wreck partitions, classes and rhetorics, regulations and codes" ("Le rire de la Méduse" 55).
3. Toril Moi states that Cixous's notion of writing as "always in some sense a libidinal object or act" constitutes a "dramatic new departure" for Anglo-American scholars precisely because of its "linking of sexuality and textuality" that "opens up a whole new field of feminist investigation of the articulations of desire in language" (126).
4. In Cixous's explanation, each occupation leads to the next, finally erupting in this moment outside time, at the border of life and death, where the body itself explodes: "While it is the fourth occupation that serves as the goal for the three preceding occupations, each one being the cause of the following, reading brings about reverie that makes one shed tears that are converted into pleasure [*jouissance*] which is the occupation that doesn't have any follow-up effect or consequence but triumph which is not an occupation but the moment in which the finite and the infinite meet.... Death lives, life dies, the soul is caught in the act, the envelop of being is lightning powder and all these states are one the impossible memory of what arrives when thought is no more" (85–86).
5. Cixous's long-standing fidelity to *Des femmes* is marked by no fewer than twenty-six publications, culminating in *Osnabrück* in 1999.
6. Cixous asserts that there is a sort of "history of Eve" in her texts, an *"Èvolution"* in which her "value" and "function" change, and she affirms that "she is also, as the end comes nearer, more and more my mother. I hold to her and hold firm, as time threatens" (*Rencontre terrestre* 63).
7. Nathalie Debrauwere-Miller emphasizes the connection between Cixous's own illness in Algeria and the particular sickness that killed her father; it is not an accident that tuberculosis affects the lungs: "This 'Algerian malady' (6) is an illness of passion for a country and a realization of having been dispossessed of an irreplaceable treasure: the irreparable loss of a father supplanted by the pages of a missing Algeria. The violence of this ill is all the more severe, since it arises

presently in the writing of the body in which the physical symptoms that Cixous evokes resemble the tuberculosis that claimed her father's life" (30).

8 *Les rêveries de la femme sauvage* contains a poignant evocation of the impossibility for the young narrator/protagonist to enter the home of her friend Françoise. See pages 117–33. For more on this period of Algerian history and the plight of Jews whose citizenship was revoked, see Jacques Derrida's *Le monolinguisme de l'autre* and Nancy Wood's "Remembering the Jews of Algeria."

9 When Cixous evokes the body in autobiographical moments in the text, she occasionally describes one of her distinguishing features revealing her "ethnic" origin: her nose. We find the following reference to this unavoidable trait in "La venue à l'écriture," with respect to the early revocation of her French citizenship in Algeria: "I learned to speak French in a garden from which I was on the verge of expulsion for being a Jew. I was of the race of Paradise-losers. Write French? With what right? Show us your credentials! What's the password? Cross yourself! Put out your hands, let's see those paws! What kind of nose is that?" (13). In a more recent essay, "My Algeriance," Cixous reclaims her nose as one of her "prominences," or "excessive traits" that she has chosen to embrace as part of her "destiny" (158).

10 In *Osnabrück,* the father's pet name for the mother is credited with a rejuvenating power: "Totote is a comic-strip heroïne. That explains why she doesn't age" (51).

11 Addressing the body in its relation to death is arguably not a new aspect of Cixous's writing, although it is more present than ever before, particularly in *Le jour où je n'étais pas là,* where the writer expands on earlier allusions to the corpse of her deceased son, who makes a noteworthy appearance in *Souffles:* "The mother covers the body of her little one with flowers, enormous bouquets, and responds to the decomposition that is carrying him off, complicating it horribly by surrounding it with a body that her love organizes. She holds it back and chains it to life through garlands and necklaces of living beings" (123). The premature passing of her father when Cixous was only ten leads her to affirm the following in *Photos de racines:* "My life begins with graves" (191). Early texts like *Tombe* abound with passages referring to the body and death: "At this instant when his body becomes shadow, when I do not yet have mourning clothes, I have the premonition of an unbelievable event" (156).

12 During a lecture at the Center for Jewish Studies at the University of California, Los Angeles, on October 10, 2003, Hélène Cixous claimed that "The Laugh of the Medusa" is a "curse" in the anglophone world, since it is often the only text—and always the foremost—by which she is known. Interestingly enough, this text was very difficult to find in the original, and was re-edited in French and published in 2010 by Galilée. I turn to this new edition in the conclusion.

6. SEXUALITÉS ET SENSUALITÉS

1 It is crucial that Cixous speaks to the question of sexual exchange in "Le rire de la Méduse," arguing that women have been placed in this "market" but that their capacity for giving—and especially for loving—extends beyond this "economy": "She invites life, thought, transformation. This is an 'economy' that cannot be expressed in economical terms. Where she loves, all concepts of the old inventory are surpassed" (68). My translation.

2 The couples in *Les nuits de Strasbourg* by Djebar are of different ages, ethnicities, and nationalities. The most unexpected couple is made up of Eve, a Jewish woman from the Maghreb, and Hans, a German. These two lovers who have immigrated to Strasbourg have to overcome a historical past as well as linguistic differences to create a stable relationship in spite of the "hybrid and unstable" nature of cultures created by the current debate in France, as Mamadou Diouf explains it. In Diouf's analysis, the debate forces actors to accept a compromise "between the French here and the (formerly imperial) elsewhere, between illusion and realities, between memory and assimilation" (29). This negotiation leads to a new definition of "plural identity today."

3 This type of conversation is exemplary of the "performative encounters" described by Mireille Rosello in her book of that subtitle (*France and the Maghreb: Performative Encounters*). Rosello brings out the constructive work that is done during encounters between (representatives of) France and the Maghreb, highlighting the fact that even difficult exchanges lead to better understandings between these two entities.

7. RUPTURES INTIMES

1 In his insightful essay on *Les nuits de Strasbourg,* Ernstpeter Ruhe establishes a connection between the cry of the principal protagonist and the writing project of Assia Djebar, indicating the importance of vocal outbursts to Djebar's written works: "Thelja's cry echoes Assia Djebar's writing and is enriched by it" ("Un cri" 185).

2 The positive potential of revisiting painful wounds and difficult separations in Assia Djebar's "violent" writing is evoked in an article by Katherine Gracki that focuses on the healing that such writing can bring about: "Djebar writes in order to mend the myriad ruptures between self and other" (835).

3 Charles Bonn points out that composing works that belong to specific genres constitutes an act of rupture in the Algerian context because they reveal the intimacy of the person in a society that does not allow for such unveiling: "The novel and the autobiographical narrative are both genres that represent the resurgence of the person who marks a break [*une rupture*] with the unanimous group that conforms to its moral norms" (176).

4 As Djebar reveals in an interview with Mildred Mortimer, French is her *langue paternelle,* since it was a gift from her father (201). Her "mother tongue," then, is arguably composed of the Berber language spoken by her mother's side of the family *and* the dialectical Arabic of Algeria. Mireille Calle-Gruber eloquently explains the particularly complex nature of the mother tongue in Djebar's case: "Nothing clear-cut, nothing simple, however, nothing is less of a dichotomy than the diptych of Assia Djebar: for the mother tongue, itself twofold, is original loss (loss of the origin, loss at the origin). Her mother speaks in an Arabic marked with the Arabo-Andalusian dialectical accent, and thus has no other language than the antiquated, forgotten one of the Andalusian *noubas:* that is to say the language of poetry, passed along from woman to woman over the centuries" (*Assia Djebar ou la résistance de l'écriture* 38). Exposure to multiple tongues from early on in life has had an undeniable impact on the writer's linguistic sensibilities, as Djebar clarified in a 1997 television interview: "All that is alive in Algeria . . . is always in a constant bilingualism, or trilingualism, with a living dialectical Arabic, with Arabic and Berber, with Berber and French" (*Droits d'auteurs*). While she is familiar with spoken Arabic, Djebar is not proficient in classical Arabic and therefore cannot write in this language. Anne Donadey addresses this fact in an essay that contains a detailed study of the use of Arabic words and terms in Djebar's oeuvre: "Because of this diglossia and because they were schooled in French, authors such as Djebar, although they speak regional Arabic, cannot write in classical Arabic and must write in French if they are to write at all" ("The Multilingual Strategies of Postcolonial Literature" 28).

5 Jeanne-Marie Clerc emphasizes the collective nature of this interdict to say "I" among Algerian women in a study of Djebar's depiction of her tradition: "The expression 'I' is completely banished from this collective speech" (55).

6 I have slightly adjusted the English translation to remain faithful to the original.

7 In this telling quotation from *Femmes d'Alger dans leur appartement,* the connection between sunshine and the possibility of Algerian women's liberation in Djebar's thought comes through: "Only in the door open to the full sun, the one Picasso later imposed, do I hope for a concrete and daily liberation of women" (151).

8 For an insightful analysis of Isma's decision to return to her community and take up the veil again, see Anne Donadey, *Recasting Postcolonialism: Women Writing Between Worlds* (Heinemann, 2001), especially 84–86.

8. LOURDS RETOURS

1 It is important to keep in mind the particular stance that Mokeddem adopts in this text, and its potential appeal to a Western readership that has developed a penchant for narratives that depict Muslim women oppressed by men. Anna

Kemp composes a convincing critique of "nativist feminism" in *Voices and Veils,* especially 53–60. However, it is also crucial to remember that Mokeddem, like other women writers from Algeria, has had to leave her homeland because she could not exercise her right to write in the same way there, as Valérie Orlando has argued: "Even the exiled state—extolled in nomadic thought as leading to new paradigms of knowledge fruitful for women's emancipation—is somewhat less appealing when we consider that authors such as Malika Mokeddem, Leïla Marouane, and Assia Djebar are living in exile because of life-threatening sociocultural phenomena and/or economic hardships that cannot be negotiated in positive, nomadic spaces of self-discovery and affirmation in Algeria" ("To Be Singularly Nomadic" 37). In another article, Orlando turns specifically to Mokeddem's *L'Interdite* to assert its importance as a "political testimony" of a particular moment in history: "*L'Interdite* is not only a fictional story but also a political testimony on the internal violence that currently exists in Algeria" ("Écrire d'un autre lieu" 112–13). According to Mokeddem's account of her publishing history, she deliberately sought to avoid labels such as "feminist" when it came to finding a publisher for her first book because of a larger desire not to fall into the trap of "nativist feminism": "I had decided not to 'shut myself up' in a third-world or feminist ghetto" (Chaulet-Achour "Portrait" 27). With respect to *L'Interdite,* she insists that this was a book written with urgency, a work focusing on "the contemporary woman caught up in the dramas of history" ("Portrait" 31).

2 As Pamela Pears points out, "According to Sultana, some *ruptures* are inevitable in order to reach a place in which true liberty exists" (109).

3 We might read this affirmation by the character Sultana as a statement on Malika Mokeddem's writing project in general as "intimately inclusive," so to speak, in accordance with the analysis of Najib Redouane who finds that Mokeddem's autobiographical writing is a "concrete and visible manifestation that allows her to free herself from the burden of the past and legitimize her writing strategy in order to testify to her own condition as a woman but especially to that of those who are deprived of speech, subdued and frustrated in their femininity" (22).

9. FILLE DE HARKI

1 "*Moze* is the contraction of my father's first name and my own. So, what you say is exactly right, it is the contraction of two first names, but it is also meant to communicate to what extent my father's destiny necessarily implicates mine" (Alison Rice, interview with Zahia Rahmani, June 2005, Paris).

2 In his comments on the "historical irony" of the *harkis,* Alec Hargreaves highlights the danger of their remaining in Algeria after the war because of their

status as traitors, all while underscoring the unfriendly welcome they were reserved in France: "Many harkis were massacred by triumphant nationalists when independence came in 1962. Those who were able fled the country, resettling in France. Today, they and their descendants are an embarrassing reminder of the war of independence" (233).

3 Anna Kemp rightly calls attention to the presence of documents embedded in the very text of *Moze* when she analyzes its structure: "The text is structured around a series of interviews, court hearings and interrogations, and is interspersed with copies of official documents and letters, which appear to be genuine, creating a Kafkaesque labyrinth of institutional and judicial power through which Moze and his family are continually processed" (99). It is worth noting that Maïssa Bey takes this textual documentation even further, including photocopied images from the original documents in the appendices at the end of her personal text *Entendez-vous dans les montagnes* (Do you hear in the mountains). These official pieces of evidence that are inserted at the close of the fictional text serve as a curious counterbalance to the inclusion of the only existing photo of Bey's father, an artifact that graces the opening page of the book.

4 Recent scholarship has demonstrated that the labels applied to Algerian-born women in France are inadequate to describe their multiple identities. In *Remnants of Empire in Algeria and Vietnam: Women, Words, and War,* Pamela Pears calls our attention to the way a female character in a recent novel is "pluralized," marked by a "betweenness" that "creates a fragmentation to which no unique name can be attached" (108). Lamia Ben Youssef Zayzafoon also brings to the forefront the plural forces contributing to "the production of the Muslim woman" in her book of that name, a judicious study of the complexity of defining oneself as a woman and a Muslim today.

5 Anna Kemp has elegantly examined the singularity of Rahmani's writing in the following manner: "['*Musulman*' *roman*] distinguishes itself from many other examples of autobiographical or semi-autobiographical work by French women of Muslim origin, in that its dual focus on intimate personal narrative and sweeping critique of the global political and economic order, emphasizes the ways in which the lives of Muslims are increasingly disrupted by the shockwaves of international affairs" (103). Hence, the personal has led—in Rahmani's case— to an opening up to the plural on a worldwide scale, and an autobiographical writing that takes into account the experiences of others from around the globe.

10. FABULATION ET IMAGINATION

1 Ana Soler astutely points out that there are distinct implications for the narrative process when the same affirmation is uttered by the author and narrator, in the paratextual apparatus and within the text respectively: "The sentence

'Maïssa Bey wants to erase [her] childhood, in a single gesture of anger,' is attributed to the real author, when this is a commentary made by the heroine (this passage is found on page 35: 'For I long time I believed I could, in a single gesture of anger, erase my childhood')" (170–71).
2. Suzanne Ruta's interview with Maïssa Bey, from the July 2006 issue of the *Women's Review of Books*, is available online in English translation.
3. Bey pronounced these words at the Bibliothèque Marguerite Durand, Paris, March 7, 2003.
4. Brigitte Weltman-Aron very convincingly makes this point, arguing that Djebar's "fiction, always playing at the border with non-fiction (she was first a historian), displays the evidence of missing links that cannot be recovered. This turn to fiction or a narrative of substitution testifies to a silencing that is itself interrogated. Her task is dual: uncover through fiction, but preserve silence as well in order to reflect on what is at stake in it. She does not attempt to transcribe the contents of a lost memory, but memory loss itself" ("The Pedagogy of Colonial Algeria" 146).
5. Malika was raised by foster parents who were unable to conceive a child before she joined their family; when they surprisingly had offspring of their own later on, Malika became the victim of mistreatment at the hands of her adopted mother and father.
6. It is important to nuance this reading of violent interruptions: bombs left on doorsteps represent real violence, whereas the violence of the abandoned child is rather more symbolic, as it disrupts social and familial norms.
7. The common first name Jeanne evokes the historical figure, "Jeanne d'Arc," who is emblematic of a certain vision of France. Joan of Arc has occupied an important role in Hélène Cixous's work, serving as the central character in a play that reenacts her trial. Despite the imminent threat of death by fire, "Jeanne" boldly defends herself *for writing:* "I learned. They hadn't told me it was a crime" ("Rouen" 63). In another text, Cixous evokes a golden statue of Joan of Arc, indicating that this great woman served as a point of reference when she was young, helping the myopic child find her way (*Voiles* 3). Assia Djebar also makes mention of Joan of Arc in her novel *La femme sans sépulture:* "What all of these Europeans from the city want is to treat me like Joan of Arc" (115). Michael O'Riley argues that "the resistant body of Zoulikha" in this text by Djebar "ultimately conjures the specters of the re-membered body of Joan of Arc, the reference to which signals the figure's appropriation as a counter example of resistance" (67).
8. The 1990s were a decade of remarkable violence in Algeria, characterized by many as a civil war. Mohamed Benrabah describes the climate at this time as follows: "Beginning in 1993, we look on as journalists, physicians, writers, teach-

ers, unionists, and so on, often francophone, republican, and modernist, are physically eliminated. It is a veritable 'cultural civil war' in which those who advocate social and political progress through secularized discourse pay a heavy price. By designating this category of Algerians *hizb frança* and 'traitors of the Nation,' the regime pushed toward a 'final solution': erasing 130 years of French presence from collective memory by eradicating the generation that witnessed the Algerian War and its independence. A generation too young to take up arms between 1954 and 1962 but that benefited from a quality school system in the days following the liberation of the country" (251–52). In light of this scheme to redefine the nation through deliberate suppression of memories and violent repression of forward-looking thinkers, Bey's writing project is bold, brave, and filled with purpose that transcends the individual to implicate an entire country.

9 M'barka bears a resemblance to those who inhabit this country: "Women dressed in grass skirts with the flamboyant colors of Africa watch as this foreigner who looks like them goes by. She is of their race" (130).

10 Since they only have access to M'barka's story through her own words as the narrator relates them, readers of Bey's novel have no clear insights into the character's familial background.

11 It is worth noting that Messaouda in this case is a "false" name, chosen as a cover to hide a true identity, whereas in the case of Cixous's childhood experience, the woman she knew as Aïcha was really named Messaouda, a name with deep significance in Djebar's *Femmes d'Alger dans leur appartement,* as we saw in chapter 3.

12 That the significance of names is a recurring motif in Bey's work is evidenced in passages like the following taken from *Sous le jasmin la nuit* (Under the jasmine at night), in which a female voice speaking in France explains that she is not from "this side of the Mediterranean" and proceeds to illustrate her point by explicating the first names of her parents: "He was named Ali, my father. And my mother, Zahra. *She spells it:* Z, A, H, R, A. The pronunciation of the H is optional, too difficult for you. It means flower. Something like Rose, Violet or Marguerite. All these names mean something where we're from, in my country 'over there,' as people refer to it" (49).

13 Luce Irigaray makes the flat assertion that woman "has no 'proper' name," that the name does not belong to her (365).

14 The narrator ventures to take issue with the expectation that all women should become mothers, suggesting in good humor that those who must devote themselves to this difficult occupation should at least receive courses to prepare them for it.

15 In *Osnabrück,* Hélène Cixous employs the first-person singular to remind her mother that this word is entirely pejorative in its connotations: "You know that the term 'the fatma' is filled with scorn, I say . . . 'The fatma" is a colonialist expression. Europeans in Algeria [*Les colons pieds-noirs*] called all women the

fatma" (112). Cixous's account demonstrates that not only was the singularity of Algerian women effaced when the same first name was applied to all, but they were objectified by the addition of the definite article.

16 This statement recalls Sebbar's own revisiting of her family history on the side of her Arab father and the mixed-race relationships with the French that date back to the early 1800s, as we saw in chapter 6; Malika's suspicion that she was born to an Arab mother and a French father is also reminiscent of Sebbar's own makeup, as the daughter of a French woman and an Arab man.

17 In her autobiographical *L'amour, la fantasia,* Djebar's wedding night is evoked, and the fact that she loses her virginity in Paris, rather than in Algeria, means that the blood shed on this occasion is not exposed for others to see. What is significant in Djebar's personal account in her ongoing autobiographical writings, is that in contrast to the many Algerian women she depicts who have given birth on multiple occasions, she never menstruated and is unable to bear children: "I had a bloodless adolescence, a bloodless coming of age." She brings up this truth about her body in *Vaste est la prison,* and embraces the positive aspects of her sterility: "I gladly accepted the verdict: I would therefore be miraculously sterile, available to be a bosom friend to children, all heart, never any blood!" (321).

18 These comments can be found at the following website: http://www.lesfrancophonies.com/maison-des-auteurs/bey-maisaa.

CONCLUSION

1 In her afterword to the English translation of Maïssa Bey's *Surtout ne te retourne pas,* Mildred Mortimer calls attention to the way her own written expression has inspired Bey to help other women find the courage and means to translate their experiences in written form: "The political engagement she expresses in her writings extends to political action; it led her to establish Paroles et Ecriture, an association founded in 2001 to promote women's writing. Adapting the format of *ateliers d'écriture* (reading and writing workshops), she encourages Algerian women to tell their tales, write their stories, and use writing as a tool for empowerment and social justice" (175).

2 As Lawrence Kritzman notes with respect to Jacques Derrida, "The demanded assimilation of Christian Latin French" in the educational system in Algeria made "any sense of identity ambiguous," particularly that of an atheist Jew ("Intellectuals" 333). While I do not hope to directly evoke religion with this section's subheading, "Music for the Mass(es)," I believe that the textual innovation that occurs in a musically metaphorical sense can possibly have implications of a religious—and linguistic—nature as well, through the destabilization of preconceived ideas and longstanding prejudices, and an opening up of readers' minds to "other" experiences.

BIBLIOGRAPHY

Ahmed, Sara. *Strange Encounters: Embodied Others in Post-Coloniality.* London: Routledge, 2000.
Al-Kassim, Dina. *On Pain of Speech: Fantasies of the First Order and the Literary Rant.* Berkeley: University of California Press, 2010.
Andermatt Conley, Verena. "Pays de rêve: L'Algérie d'Hélène Cixous." *Expressions maghrébines* 2.2 (Winter 2003): 47–54.
Apter, Emily. "Theorizing *Francophonie.*" *Comparative Literature Studies* 42.4 (2005): 297–311.
Aquinas, Thomas. *Selections from the Summa Theologica of Thomas Aquinas.* Translated by A. M. Fairweather. Philadelphia: The Westminster Press, 1954.
Aristotle. *The Poetics.* Translated by W. Hamilton Fyfe. Cambridge, Mass.: Harvard University Press, 1927.
Ashcroft, Bill, Gareth Griffiths, and Helen Tiffin. *The Post-Colonial Studies Reader.* London: Routledge, 2006.
Augustine. *Confessions.* Translated by R. S. Pine-Coffin. London: Penguin Books, 1967.
Barthes, Roland. *Roland Barthes par Roland Barthes.* Paris: Seuil, 1975. Translated by Richard Howard as *Roland Barthes by Roland Barthes.* New York: Farrar, Straus and Giroux, 2010.
Bénayoun-Szmidt, Yvette. "*L'Interdite* de Malika Mokeddem ou Sur-vie d'une écrivaine en marge de sa société." In *Malika Mokeddem,* edited by Najib Redouane, Yvette Bénayoun-Szmidt, and Robert Elbaz, 99–119. Paris: L'Harmattan, 2003.
Benrabah, Mohamed. *Langue et pouvoir en Algérie: Histoire d'un traumatisme linguistique.* Paris: Éditions Séguier, 1999.
Bensmaïa, Réda. *Experimental Nations: Or, the Invention of the Maghreb.* Translated by Alyson Waters. Princeton, N.J.: Princeton University Press, 2003.
Bernhard, Thomas. *Maîtres anciens.* Paris: Gallimard, 1988.
Bey, Maïssa. *À contre-silence.* Grigny: Editions Paroles d'aube, 1998.
———. *Au commencement était la mer.* Paris: Marsa, 1996.
———. *Cette fille-là.* Paris: Éditions de l'Aube, 2001.
———. *Entendez-vous dans les montagnes . . .* Paris: Éditions de l'Aube, 2002.
———. *L'ombre d'un homme qui marche au soleil: Réflexions sur Albert Camus.* Montpellier: Éditions Chèvre-Feuille étoilée, 2004.
———. *Puisque mon coeur est mort.* Paris: Éditions de l'Aube, 2010.

———. *Sous le jasmin la nuit.* Paris: Éditions de l'Aube, 2004.
———. *Surtout ne te retourne pas.* Paris: Éditions de l'Aube, 2005. Translated by Senja L. Djelouah as *Above All, Don't Look Back.* Charlottesville: University of Virginia Press, 2009.
———. *L'une et l'autre.* Paris: Éditions de l'Aube, 2009.
Bhabha, Homi K. "Cultural Diversity and Cultural Differences" In *The Post-Colonial Studies Reader,* edited by Bill Ashcroft, Gareth Griffiths, and Helen Tiffin, 155–57. London: Routledge, 2006.
———. "DissemiNation: time, narrative, and the margins of the modern nation." In *Nation and Narration,* edited by Homi K. Bhabha, 291–322. New York: Routledge, 1990.
Blanchot, Maurice. *L'espace littéraire.* Paris: Gallimard, 1959. Translated by Ann Smock as *The Space of Literature.* Lincoln: University of Nebraska Press, 1989.
———. "L'inconvenance majeure." Preface to *Français, encore un effort si vous voulez être Républicains* by Marquis de Sade. Paris: Editions Jean-Jacques Pauvert, 1965.
———. *L'instant de ma mort.* Paris: Fata Morgana, 1994. Translated by Elizabeth Rottenberg as *The Instant of My Death.* Stanford, Calif.: Stanford University Press, 2000.
———. *Le livre à venir.* Paris: Gallimard, 1959. Translated by Charlotte Mandell as *The Book to Come.* Stanford, Calif.: Stanford University Press, 2002.
Bonn, Charles. *Le roman algérien de langue française—Vers un espace de communication littéraire décolonisé?* Paris: L'Harmattan, 1985.
Bourdieu, Pierre. Preface to *La double absence: Des illusions de l'émigré aux souffrances de l'immigré,* by Abdelmalek Sayad, 9–13. Paris: Seuil, 1999.
———. *Raisons pratiques: Sur la théorie de l'action.* Paris: Seuil, 1994.
Bourget, Carine. *The Star, the Cross, and the Crescent: Religions and Conflicts in Francophone Literature from the Arab World.* Lanham, Md.: Lexington Books, 2010.
Brooks, Peter. *Troubling Confessions: Speaking Guilt in Literature and the Law.* Chicago: University of Chicago Press, 2000.
Butler, Judith. *Bodies That Matter: On the Discursive Limits of "Sex."* London: Routledge, 1993.
Calle-Gruber, Mireille. *Assia Djebar ou la résistance de l'écriture: Regards d'un écrivain d'Algérie.* Paris: Maisonneuve & Larose, 2001.
———. "La servante du texte." In *Assia Djebar: Littérature et transmission,* edited by Wolfgang Asholt, Mireille Calle-Gruber and Dominique Combe, 197–210. Paris: Presses Sorbonne Nouvelle, 2010.
Camus, Albert. *L'envers et l'endroit.* Paris: Gallimard, 1937.

———. *L'étranger.* Paris: Gallimard, 1942. Translated by Stuart Gilbert as *The Stranger.* New York: Alfred A. Knopf, 1946.

———. *Le premier homme.* Paris: Gallimard, 1994. Translated by David Hapgood as *The First Man.* New York: Alfred A. Knopf, 1995.

Camus, Catherine. Preface to *L'ombre d'un homme qui marchait au soleil. Réflexions sur Albert Camus,* by Maïssa Bey, 7–8. Montpellier: Éditions Chèvre-Feuille étoilée, 2004.

Cardinal, Marie. *Au pays de mes racines.* Paris: Grasset, 1980.

———. *Autrement dit.* Paris: Grasset, 1977. Translated by Amy Cooper as *In Other Words.* Bloomington: Indiana University Press, 1995.

———. *Ecoutez la mer.* Paris: Julliard, 1962.

———. *Les mots pour le dire.* Paris: Grasset, 1975. Translated by Bruno Bettelheim as *The Words to Say It.* Cambridge, Mass.: VanVactor & Goodheart, 1983.

Chambers, Iain. *Migrancy, Culture, Identity.* London: Routledge, 1994.

Chaulet-Achour, Christiane. *Albert Camus, Alger: L'Étranger et autres récits.* Paris: Séguier, 1999.

———. "Autobiographie d'Algériennes sur l'autre rive: se définir entre mémoire et rupture." In *Littératures autobiographies de la francophonie,* edited by Martine Mathieu, 291–308. Paris: L'Harmattan, 1996.

———. "Portrait de Malika Mokeddem." In *Malika Mokeddem: Envers et contre tout,* edited by Yolande Aline Helm, 21–34. Paris: L'Harmattan, 2000.

Cherki, Alice. "Confiscation des mémoires et empêchement des identifications plurielles." In *Retours du colonial? Disculpation et réhabilitation de l'histoire coloniale,* edited by Catherine Coquio, 177–85. Nantes: Librairie L'Atalante, 2008.

Chikhi, Beïda. *Assia Djebar: histoires et fantaisies.* Paris: Presses de l'Université Paris-Sorbonne, 2007.

Cixous, Hélène. "L'Affrance." In *C'était leur France: En Algérie, avant l'Indépendance,* edited by Leïla Sebbar, 89–103. Paris: Gallimard, 2007.

———. "The Author in Truth." In *"Coming to Writing" and Other Essays,* edited by Deborah Jenson, 136–81. Cambridge, Mass.: Harvard University Press, 1991.

———. *Benjamin à Montaigne: Il ne faut pas le dire.* Paris: Galilée, 2001.

———. *Ève s'évade.* Paris: Galilée, 2009.

———. *Le livre de Promethea.* Paris: Gallimard, 1983. Translated by Betsy Wing as *The Book of Promethea.* Lincoln: University of Nebraska Press, 1991.

———. "Un effet d'épine rose." In *Le rire de la méduse et autres ironies,* 23–33. Paris: Galilée, 2010.

———. "La Fugitive." In *Algérie à plus d'une langue,* edited by Mireille Calle-Gruber, 75–82. Québec: Presses de l'Université Laval, 2001.

———. *Le jour où je n'étais pas là*. Paris: Galilée, 2000.

———. *Manhattan: Lettres de la préhistoire*. Paris: Galilée, 2002. Translated by Beverley Bie Brahic as *Manhattan: Letters from Prehistory*. New York: Fordham University Press, 2007.

———. "Mon Algériance." *Les inrockuptibles* 115 (20 August–2 September 1997): 71–74. Translated by Eric Prenowitz as "My Algeriance, in other words: to depart, not to arrive from Algeria." In *Stigmata: The Escaping Texts*, 153–72. London: Routledge, 1998.

———. "Obstétriques cruelles." In *AUTODAFE. La Revue du Parlement international des écrivains*, 105–18. Paris: Denoël, 2000.

———. *Or: Les lettres de mon père*. Paris: Des femmes, 1997.

———. *Osnabrück*. Paris: Galilée, 1999.

———. "Pieds nus." In *Une enfance algérienne*, edited by Leïla Sebbar, 53–63. Paris: Gallimard, 1997.

———. "The Place of Crime, The Place of Forgiveness." In *The Hélène Cixous Reader*, edited by Susan Sellers, 151–56. London: Routledge, 1994.

———. *Portrait de Jacques Derrida en jeune saint juif*. Paris: Galilée, 2001. Translated by Beverley Bie Brahic as *Portrait of Jacques Derrida as a Young Jewish Saint*. New York: Columbia University Press, 2004.

———. *Le Prénom de Dieu*. Paris: Grasset, 1967.

———. *Readings: The Poetics of Blanchot, Joyce, Kafka, Kleist, Lispector, and Tsvetayeva*. Translated by Verena Andermatt Conley. Minneapolis: University of Minnesota Press, 1991.

———. *Les rêveries de la femme sauvage: Scènes primitives*. Paris: Galilée, 2000. Translated by Beverley Bie Brahic as *Reveries of the Wild Woman: Primal Scenes*. Evanston, Ill.: Northwestern University Press, 2006.

———. "Le rire de la Méduse." *Le rire de la Méduse et autres ironies* (Paris: Galilée, 2010): 35–68. Originally published in *L'Arc* 61 (1975): 39–54. Translated by Keith Cohen and Paula Cohen as "The Laugh of the Medusa." Originally published in *Signs* 1.4 (1976): 875–94. Reprinted in *The Routledge Language and Cultural Theory Reader*, edited by Lucy Burke, Tony Crowley, and Alan Girvin, 161–66. London: Routledge, 2000.

———. *Le rire de la Méduse et autres ironies*. Paris: Galilée, 2010.

———. *Rouen, la trentième nuit de Mai '31: Théâtre*. Paris: Galilée, 2001.

———. "The School of Roots." *Three Steps on the Ladder of Writing*. Translated by Sarah Cornell and Susan Sellers. New York: Columbia University Press, 1993: 111–56.

———. *Si près*. Paris: Galilée, 2007. Translated by Peggy Kamuf as *So Close*. Cambridge: Polity Press, 2009.

———. *Souffles*. Paris: Des femmes, 1975.

———. *Three Steps on the Ladder of Writing.* Translated by Sarah Cornell and Susan Sellers. New York: Columbia University Press, 1993.

———. *Tombe.* Paris: Seuil, 1973.

———. "La venue à l'écriture." In *Entre l'écriture,* 9–69. Paris: Des femmes, 1986. Translated by Sarah Cornell as "Coming to Writing." In *"Coming to Writing" and Other Essays,* edited by Deborah Jenson, 1–58. Cambridge, Mass.: Harvard University Press, 1991.

———. "Without end, no, State of drawingness, no, rather: The Executioner's taking off." Translated by Catherine A. F. MacGillivray. *Stigmata: Escaping Texts.* London: Routledge, 1998, 2005.

Cixous, Hélène, and Mireille Calle-Gruber. *Photos de racines.* Paris: Des femmes, 1994. Translated by Eric Prenowitz as *Hélène Cixous, Rootprints: Memory and Life Writing.* London: Routledge, 1997.

Cixous, Hélène, and Catherine Clément. *La jeune née.* Paris: Christian Bourgois, 1975. Translated by Betsy Wing as *The Newly Born Woman.* Minneapolis: University of Minnesota Press, 1986.

Cixous, Hélène, and Jacques Derrida. *Voiles.* Paris: Galilée, 1998. Translated by Geoffrey Bennington as *Veils.* Stanford, Calif.: Stanford University Press, 2001.

Cixous, Hélène, and Frédéric-Yves Jeannet. *Rencontre terrestre.* Paris: Galilée, 2005.

Clerc, Jeanne-Marie. *Assia Djebar: Écrire, transgresser, résister.* Paris: L'Harmattan, 1997.

de Clézio, Marguerite. "Mother and Motherland: The Daughter's Quest for Origins." *Stanford French Review* 5 (1981).

Debrauwere-Miller, Nathalie. "Crypts of Hélène Cixous's Past." *Studies in Twentieth and Twenty-First Century Literature* 33.1 (Winter 2009): 28–49.

Derrida, Jacques. *Acts of Literature,* edited by Derek Attridge. New York: Routledge, 1992.

———. "L'animal que donc je suis (à suivre)." In *L'animal autobiographique: Autour de Jacques Derrida,* edited by Marie-Louise Mallet, 11–42. Paris: Galilée, 2003. Translated by David Wills as *The Animal That Therefore I Am.* New York: Fordham University Press, 2008.

———. "Circonfession." In *Jacques Derrida,* by Geoffrey Bennington and Jacques Derrida. Paris: Seuil, 1991. Translated by Geoffrey Bennington as "Circumfession" in *Jacques Derrida.* Chicago: University of Chicago Press, 1993.

———. *Demeure: Maurice Blanchot.* Paris: Galilée, 1998. Translated by Elizabeth Rottenberg as *Demeure: Fiction and Testimony.* Stanford, Calif.: Stanford University Press, 2000.

———. *Genèses, généalogies, genres et le génie: Les Secrets de l'archive.* Paris: Galilée, 2003. Translated by Beverley Bie Brahic as *Geneses, Genealogies, Genres, & Genius: The Secrets of the Archive.* New York: Columbia University Press, 2006.

———. "H. C. pour la vie, c'est à dire." In *Hélène Cixous, croisées d'une oeuvre*, edited by Mireille Calle-Gruber, 13–140. Paris: Galilée, 2000. Translated by Laurent Milesi and Stefan Herbrechter as *H.C. for Life, That is to Say . . .* Stanford, Calif.: Stanford University Press, 2006.

———. *Le monolinguisme de l'autre ou la prothèse d'origine*. Paris: Galilée, 1996. Translated by Patrick Mensah as *Monolingualism of the Other, or the Prosthesis of Origin*. Stanford, Calif.: Stanford University Press, 1998.

———. *Sauf le nom*. Paris: Galilée, 1993. Translated by David Wood as *On the Name*, edited by Thomas Dutoit, 35–85 Stanford, Calif.: Stanford University Press, 1995.

———. *Sur parole: Instantanés philosophiques*. Paris: Éditions de l'aube, 1999.

Djebar, Assia. *L'amour, la fantasia*. Paris: J.-C. Lattès, 1985; Albin Michel, 1995. Translated by Dorothy S. Blair as *Fantasia: An Algerian Cavalcade*. Portsmouth, N.H.: Heinemann, 1993.

———. *Le blanc de l'Algérie*. Paris: Albin Michel, 1996. Translated by David Kelley and Marjolijn de Jager as *Algerian White*. New York: Seven Stories Press, 2003.

———. *Ces voix qui m'assiègent . . . en marge de ma francophonie*. Paris: Albin Michel, 1999.

———. *La disparition de la langue française*. Paris: Albin Michel, 2003.

———. *La femme sans sépulture*. Paris: Albin Michel, 2002.

———. *Femmes d'Alger dans leur appartement*. Paris: Des femmes, 1980. Translated by Marjolijn de Jager as *Women of Algiers in Their Apartment*. Charlottesville: University of Virginia Press, 1992.

———. *Les nuits de Strasbourg*. Arles: Actes Sud, 1997.

———. *Nulle part dans la maison de mon père*. Paris: Fayard, 2007.

———. *Ombre sultane*. Paris: J.-C. Lattès, 1987. Translated by Dorothy S. Blair as *A Sister to Scheherazade*. Portsmouth, N.H.: Heinemann, 1997.

———. *Oran, langue morte*. Arles: Actes Sud, 1997. Translated by Tegan Raleigh as *The Tongue's Blood Does Not Run Dry: Algerian Stories*. New York: Seven Stories Press, 2010.

———. "Le roman maghrébin francophone. Entre les langues, entre les cultures: Quarante ans d'un parcours, Assia Djebar 1957–1997." Ph.D. diss., University Paul-Valéry, Montpellier 3, 1999.

———. "Terres francophones: Leur français dans le texte." *France 3*. Television broadcast, January 21, 1995.

———. *Vaste est la prison*. Paris: Albin Michel, 1991. Translated by Betsy Wing as *So Vast the Prison*. New York: Seven Stories Press, 2001.

Diouf, Mamadou. "Les études postcoloniales à l'épreuve des traditions intellectuelles et des banlieues françaises." *Contretemps* 16 (2006): 17–30.

Donadey, Anne. "African American and Francophone Postcolonial Memory:

Octavia Butler's *Kindred* and Assia Djebar's *La femme sans sépulture.*" *Research in African Literatures* 39.3 (Fall 2008): 65–81.

———. "The Multilingual Strategies of Postcolonial Literature: Assia Djebar's Algerian Palimpsest." *World Literature Today* 74.1 (Winter 2000): 27–36.

———. *Recasting Postcolonialism: Women Writing Between Worlds.* Portsmouth, N.H.: Heinemann, 2001.

Donadey, Anne, and Françoise Lionnet. "Feminisms, Genders, Sexualities." In *Introduction to Scholarship in Modern Languages and Literatures,* edited by David G. Nicholls, 3rd ed., 225–44. New York: The Modern Language Association of America, 2007.

"Droits d'auteurs." *Droits d'auteurs* featuring Assia Djebar. La cinquième. Television interview, March 30, 1997.

Duchen, Claire. "Écriture féminine." In *The New Oxford Companion to Literature in French,* edited by Peter France, 270–71. Oxford: Oxford University Press, 1995.

Dufourmantelle, Anne. *La sauvagerie maternelle.* Paris: Calmann-Lévy, 2001.

Felman, Shoshana, and Dori Laub. *Testimony: Crises of Witnessing in Literature, Psychoanalysis, and History.* New York: Routledge, 1992.

Friedman, Susan Stanford. "Migrations, Diasporas, and Borders." In *Introduction to Scholarship in Modern Languages and Literatures,* 3rd ed., edited by David G. Nicholls, 260–93. New York: The Modern Language Association of America, 2007.

Ghaussy, Sauheila. "A Stepmother Tongue: 'Feminine Writing' in Assia Djebar's *Fantasia: An Algerian Cavalcade.*" *World Literature Today* 68.3 (1994): 457–62.

Gilmore, Leigh. "Endless Autobiography? Jamaica Kincaid and Serial Autobiography." In *Postcolonialism and Autobiography,* edited by Alfred Hornung and Ernstpeter Ruhe, 211–32. Amsterdam: Rodopi, 1998.

———. *The Limits of Autobiography: Trauma and Testimony.* Ithaca, N.Y.: Cornell University Press, 2001.

Gracki, Katherine. "Writing Violence and the Violence of Writing in Assia Djebar's Algerian Quartet." *World Literature Today* 70.4 (Autumn 1996): 835–43.

Hall, Colette. *Marie Cardinal.* Amsterdam: Rodopi, 1994.

Hamil, Mustapha. "Exile and Its Discontents: Malika Mokaddem's *Forbidden Woman*" *Research in African Literatures* 35.1 (Spring 2004): 52–65.

Hargreaves, Alec. "Resistance at the Margins: Writers of Maghrebi Immigrant Origin." In *Post-Colonial Cultures in France,* edited by Alec G. Hargreaves and Mark McKinney, 226–39. London: Routledge, 1997.

Hiddleston, Jane. *Assia Djebar: Out of Algeria.* Liverpool: Liverpool University Press, 2006.

Howard, Richard. Introduction to *Nedjma,* by Kateb Yacine, xiii–xliii. CARAF Book Series. Charlottesville: University of Virginia Press, 1991.

Ireland, Susan. "Facing the Ghosts of the Past in Dalila Kerchouche's *Mon père, ce harki* and Zahia Rahmani's *Moze.*" *Contemporary French and Francophone Studies* 13.3 (June 2009): 303–10.

Irigaray, Luce. *Ce sexe qui n'en est pas un.* Paris: Les Éditions de Minuit, 1977.

Jones, Ann Rosalind. "Writing the Body: toward an understanding of l'écriture féminine." In *Feminisms: An Anthology of Literary Theory and Criticism,* edited by Robyn R. Warhol and Diane Price Herndl, 370–83. New Brunswick, N.J.: Rutgers University Press, 1997.

Kamuf, Peggy. "Seringues, ou les pointes aiguës du hérisson." In *Passions de la littérature: Avec Jacques Derrida,* edited by Michel Lisse, 387–404. Paris: Galilée, 1996.

———. *Signature Pieces: On the Institution of Authorship.* Ithaca, N.Y.: Cornell University Press, 1998.

Kandiyoti, Deniz. "Identity and Its Discontents: Women and the Nation." In *Colonial Discourse and Post-Colonial Theory: A Reader,* edited by Patrick Williams and Laura Chrisman, 276–91. New York: Columbia University Press, 1994.

Kateb, Yacine. *Nedjma.* Paris: Seuil, 1956. Translated by Richard Howard as *Nedjma.* CARAF Book Series. Charlottesville: University of Virginia Press, 1991.

Kelly, Debra. "'An Unfinished Death': The Legacy of Albert Camus and the Work of Textual Memory in Contemporary European and Algerian Literatures." *International Journal of Francophone Studies* 10.1–2 (2007): 217–35.

———. *Autobiography and Independence: Selfhood and Creativity in North African Postcolonial Writing in French.* Liverpool: Liverpool University Press, 2005.

Kemp, Anna. *Voices and Veils: Feminism and Islam in French Women's Writing and Activism.* London: Legenda, 2010.

Khanna, Ranhana. *Algeria Cuts: Women and Representation, 1830 to the Present.* Stanford, Calif.: Stanford University Press, 2007.

Khatibi, Abdelkébir. *Le scribe et son ombre.* Paris: Éditions de la Différence, 2008.

Kofman, Sarah. *Paroles suffoquées.* Paris: Galilée, 1987. Translated by Madeleine Dobie as *Smothered Words.* Evanston, Ill.: Northwestern University Press, 1998.

Kritzman, Lawrence. "Intellectuals Without Borders." In *French Global: A New Approach to Literary History,* edited by Christie McDonald and Susan Robin Suleiman, 320–35. New York: Columbia University Press, 2010.

Lionnet, Françoise. *Autobiographical Voices: Race, Gender, Self-Portraiture.* Ithaca: Cornell University Press, 1989.

Lionnet, Françoise, and Shu-mei Shih. "Introduction: Thinking through the

Minor, Transnationally" In *Minor Transnationalism,* edited by Françoise Lionnet and Shu-mei Shih, 1–23. Durham, N.C.: Duke University Press, 2005.

Loomba, Ania. *Colonialism/Postcolonialism.* London: Routledge, 1998.

Margel, Serge. *De l'imposture: Jean-Jacques Rousseau, Mensonge littéraire et fiction politique.* Paris: Galilée, 2007.

Memmi, Albert. *Portrait du colonisé précédé du portrait du colonisateur.* Paris: Editions Gallimard, 2002.

Miller, Christopher. *Theories of Africans: Francophone Literature and Anthropology in Africa.* Chicago: University of Chicago Press, 1990.

Moi, Toril. *Sexual/Textual Politics: Feminist Literary Theory.* London: Routledge, 1985.

Mokeddem, Malika. *L'Interdite.* Paris: Grasset, 1993. Translated by K. Melissa Marcus as *The Forbidden Woman.* Lincoln: University of Nebraska Press, 1998.

———. *Je dois tout à ton oubli.* Paris: Grasset, 2008.

———. *La transe des insoumis.* Paris: Grasset, 2003.

———. *Mes hommes.* Paris: Grasset, 2005. Translated by Laura Rice and Karim Hamdy as *My Men.* Lincoln: University of Nebraska Press, 2009.

Mongo-Mboussa, Boniface. *Désir d'Afrique.* Paris: Gallimard, 2002.

Mortimer, Mildred. Afterword to *Above All, Don't Look Back,* by Maïssa Bey, 169–90. CARAF Book Series. Charlottesville: University of Virginia Press, 2009.

———. "Entretien avec Assia Djebar, ecrivain algérien." *Research in African Literatures* 19.2 (Summer 1998): 197–205.

The New Oxford Companion to Literature in French. New York: Oxford University Press, 1995.

Noudelmann, François. "Hélène Cixous: La voix étrangère, la plus profonde, la plus antique." *Revue collège international de philosophie* (2002): 111–19.

O'Riley, Michael. *Postcolonial Haunting and Victimization: Assia Djebar's New Novels.* New York: Peter Lang, 2007.

Orlando, Valérie. "Écriture d'un autre lieu: La déterritorialisation des nouveaux rôles féminins dans *L'Interdite*." In *Malika Mokeddem: Envers et contre tout,* edited by Yolande Aline Helm, 105–15. Paris: L'Harmattan, 2000.

———. "To Be Singularly Nomadic or a Territorialized National: At the Crossroads of Francophone Women's Writing of the Maghreb." *Meridians* 6.2 (2006): 33–53.

Pears, Pamela. *Remnants of Empire in Algeria and Vietnam: Women, Words, and War.* Lanham, Md.: Lexington Books, 2004.

Phoca, Sophia. "Hélène Cixous in Conversation." *Wasafiri* 31 (Spring 2000): 9–13.

Rahmani, Zahia. "Figure d'un homme." In *Mon père,* edited by Leïla Sebbar, 245–56. Paris: Chevrefeuille étoilée, 2007.

———. *France, récit d'une enfance.* Paris: Sabine Wespieser, 2006.

———. *Moze.* Paris: Sabine Wespieser, 2003.
———. *"Musulman" roman.* Paris: Sabine Wespieser, 2005.
Redouane, Najib. "À la rencontre de Malika Mokeddem." In *Malika Mokeddem,* edited by Najib Redouane, Yvette Bénayoun-Szmidt, and Robert Elbaz, 17–31. Paris: L'Harmattan, 2003.
Regard, Frédéric. *"AA!"* Preface to *Le rire de la méduse et autres ironies* by Hélène Cixous, 9–22. Paris: Galilée, 2010.
Rice, Alison. Interview with Hélène Cixous, January 2006, Paris.
———. Interview with Zahia Rahmani, June 2005, Paris.
Rieck, Barbara Ann. *Voix ensevelies: Assia Djebar, lieux d'écriture.* Film. ARTE. 1997.
Rosello, Mireille. *France and the Maghreb: Performative Encounters.* Gainesville: University Press of Florida, 2005.
Ross, Kristin. *Fast Cars, Clean Bodies: Decolonization and the Reordering of French Culture.* Cambridge, Mass.: MIT Press, 1995.
Rousseau, Jean-Jacques. *Confessions.* Paris: Hachette, 2002.
———. *Les rêveries du promeneur solitaire.* Paris: Flammarion, 1964. Translated by Charles E. Butterworth as *The Reveries of a Solitary Walker.* Indianapolis: Hackett Publishing, 1992.
Ruhe, Ernstpeter. "'Un cri dans le bleu immergé': Binswanger, Foucault et l'imagination de la chute dans *Les nuits de Strasbourg.*" In *Assia Djebar,* edited by Ernstpeter Ruhe, 169–88. Würzburg: Verlag Königshausen & Neumann, 2001.
———. "Enjambements et envols: Assia Djebar échographe." In *Assia Djebar: littérature et transmission,* edited by Wolfgang Asholt, Mireille Calle-Gruber and Dominique Combe, 37–54. Paris: Presses Sorbonne Nouvelle, 2010.
Ruta, Suzanne. "Algerian Novelist Maïssa Bey: The Rebel's Daughter." *Women's Review of Books* (July 2006), www.wcwonline.org/?option=com_content&task=view&id=1154&Itemid=&Itemid=38, accessed November 10, 2010.
Savigneau, Josyane. "Dévoilements." *Le Monde,* September 11, 1987.
Sayad, Abdelmalek. *La double absence: Des illusions de l'émigré aux souffrances de l'immigré.* Paris: Seuil, 1999.
Scharfman, Ronnie. "Narratives of Internal Exile: Cixous, Derrida, and the Vichy Years in Algeria." In *Postcolonial Theory and Francophone Literary Studies,* edited by H. Adlai Murdoch and Anne Donadey, 87–101. Gainesville: University Press of Florida, 2005.
Sebbar, Leïla. *Je ne parle pas la langue de mon père.* Paris: Julliard, 2003.
———. *Le ravin de la femme sauvage.* Paris: Editions Thierry Magnier, 2007.
———, and Nancy Huston. *Lettres parisiennes: Histoires d'exil.* Paris: Bernard Barrault, 1986.

Soler, Ana. "La parole au féminin: la narratrice de *Cette fille-là* de Maïssa Bey." *Présence Francophone* 70 (2008): 169–83.

Sommer, Doris. "'Not Just a Personal Story': Women's *Testimonios* and the Plural Self." In *Life/Lines: Theorizing Women's Autobiography,* edited by Bella Brodzki and Celeste Schenck, 107–30. Ithaca, N.Y.: Cornell University Press, 1988.

Spivak, Gayatri. "Three Women's Texts and Circumfession." In *Postcolonialism and Autobiography,* edited by Alfred Hornung and Ernstpeter Ruhe, 7–22. Amsterdam: Editions Rodopi, 1998.

Steadman, Jennifer Bernhardt. "A Global Feminist Travels: Assia Djebar and Fantasia." *Meridians: Feminism, Race, Transnationalism* 4.1 (2003): 173–99.

Stora, Benjamin. *La guerre des mémoires: La France face à son passé colonial.* Paris: Éditions de l'Aube, 2007.

Suleiman, Susan Rubin. "Writing Past the Wall: Or the Passion According to H.C." Preface to *"Coming to Writing" and Other Essays,* by Hélène Cixous, edited by Deborah Jenson, vii–xxii. Cambridge, Mass.: Harvard University Press, 1991.

Weber-Fève, Stacey. *Re-hybridizing Transnational Domesticity and Femininity: Women's Contemporary Filmmaking and Lifewriting in France, Algeria, and Tunisia.* Lanham, Md.: Lexington Books, 2010.

Wehrs, Donald R. "The 'Sensible,' the Maternal, and the Ethical Beginnings of Feminist Islamic Discourse in Djebar's *L'amour, la fantasia* and *Loin de Médine.*" *Modern Language Notes* 118 (2003): 841–66.

Weltman-Aron, Brigitte. Review of *Reveries of the Wild Woman: Primal Scenes,* by Hélène Cixous. *Shofar: An Interdisciplinary Journal of Jewish Studies* 27.2 (2009): 197–99.

———. "The Pedagogy of Colonial Algeria: Djebar, Cixous, Derrida." *Yale French Studies* 113 (2008): 132–46.

Wood, Nancy. "Remembering the Jews of Algeria." *Parallax* 7 (April-June 1998): 169–84.

Woodhull, Winifred. *Transfigurations of the Maghreb: Feminism, Decolonization, and Literatures.* Minneapolis: University of Minnesota Press, 1993.

Young, Robert. "The Cultural Politics of Hybridity." In *The Post-Colonial Studies Reader,* edited by Bill Ashcroft, Gareth Griffiths, and Helen Tiffin, 138–62. London: Routledge, 2006.

Zayzafoon, Lamia Ben Youssef. *The Production of the Muslim Woman: Negotiating Text, History, and Ideology.* Lanham, Md.: Lexington Books, 2005.

INDEX

abortion, 79–80, 81
age and aging, 105–8, 203n14, 206n11
Ahmed, Sara, 178, 203n13
Aïcha (women's group), 142
Albert Camus, Alger (Chaulet-Achour), 86–87
"Albert Camus and Falsehood" (colloquium), 86
Algeria: censorship in, 5; children aborted in, 79–80; civil war in (1990s), 157–59, 211–12n8; departure from but not breaking with, 189–92; *métissage* rejected in, 179–80; oppression of women in, 131–35, 145–47, 208–9n1; others' ignorance about, 186; risks of writing in, 46, 48–49, 56, 142; as territory, 73; women's plight in, 52–54, 89, 180–83; women's rights in, 133–34; women's voices excluded in, 165–69; women writers still living in (*see* Bey, Maïssa); writers killed in, 5. *See also* Algerian War of Independence; French-language women writers born in Algeria
Algeria, as homeland: as always unfinished, 95; deterritorialization of, 145; as "incurable sickness," 83; lack of, 151; narrator as foreigner in, 118; returning to, 141–45, 146–48, 175; "un-belonging for/in," 96; writers haunted by, 147–48; writers without a place in, 84–85. *See also* mother and native land, depictions of
Algeria, under French rule: ambiguous status of, 2; designation of domestic help in, 176–77, 212–13n15; divisions of, 35–37, 61; erased in cultural civil war, 211–12n8; French vs. Algerian clothing and, 115–16; homes off-limits in, 104, 202n9, 206n8; in-betweenness in, 104–5, 109–11, 206n9; as key to Bey's life, 49–51; mixed marriages connected to, 120; names and naming under, 172; national fantasies in, 71; nose as evidence of Jewishness in, 206n9; official documents of, 159–60; recovering what was lost in, 171–74; resistance to, 51; sexual hostility and inappropriate touching in, 104–5; "social health" in, 104; state and school linked in, 64–65, 201–2n6; trauma in, 164–65. *See also* citizens and citizenship; colonialism; French culture; French educational system; French language
Algériances, 102–5, 189–90
Algerian War of Independence (1954–62): ambiguities and dilemmas of, 153–56; attempts to repair wrongs on both sides of, 151; disruptions of birth in, 170, 211n6; erasure in cultural civil war, 211–12n8; official documents of, 159–60; reconstituting nation in aftermath of, 170–71, 173; traces of, 17–18; unrecognized in France, 157. *See also harkis*
Al-Kassim, Dina, 18
alterity, concept of, 46. *See also* others and otherness
amour, la fantasia, L' (*Fantasia*)

amour, la fantasia, L' (*cont.*)
(Djebar): father and daughter's walk to school, 113, 169; father figure in, 113–15, 117, 200n3; French homes off-limits in, 202n9; on languages, 111–12, 117–18; multiple women's voices in, 167, 168; other as witness in, 32–33; paratextual apparatus needed in translation, 186–87; *ruptures intimes* in, 129–31, 135–36, 137; space of outdoors in, 138; suicide attempt in, 32, 33–35, 39–40; witnessing one's own life in, 31–32; on writing, 180

Amour Autre, L' (term), 192–93

Antelme, Robert, 6–7

anti-Semitism: homes off-limits due to, 105, 206n8; struggles against, 104, 206n9

Apter, Emily, 184–85

Arabic language: banned, 50, 201n5; *Farkha* (bastard) in, 169; as father's language, 116–17; French attitudes toward names in, 176–77; handwritten, 18; "I" not used in (dialectical), 135–36, 208n5; as mother's language, 52, 208n4; spoken vs. classical, 208n4; voices of women in, 115

Arabization, 51, 52, 182

Arabs: attitudes in France toward, 144; definition of, 51–52; naming traditions of, 171–72; rejecting stereotypes of Arab women, 53–54; U.S. treatment of, 152

Arc, L' (journal), 188

Aristotle, 16, 199n11

Assia Djebar (Hiddleston), 73, 92

Augustine, Saint, 31, 88–89

auto-bio-calligraphy, 18

autobiographical inclusions: approach to, 19, 27; colonialism's effects on, 49–51; confession and testimony in, 27–31; critique of global order linked to, 210n5; in every text, 8, 27, 197n1; experiences of many expressed through, 1–3; as foreigner, 118–19; horrible accident in, 35–37, 198n6; intertextual connections in, 47–49; memory and forgetting in, 140–41; other and all others written in, 55–56; the other as witness in, 32–33; "she" and "I" in, 80–81; solidarity and singularity in, 56–57; suicide attempt in, 32, 33–35, 39–40; visceral effects of, 135–36; writing of everything, despite condemnation, 43–45, 199n13, 199–200n14. *See also* testimony; witnesses

autobiography: constructed from evoked or suppressed memory, 104–5; lovemaking as resembling act of, 28–29, 118; plural type, 166; serial type, 198n7; universal testimonial turn in, 45. *See also* autobiographical inclusions

autographology, 14

barbares, use of term, 50

Barthes, Roland, 107

bearing witness. *See* testimony; witnesses; witnessing

Benameur, Samia. *See* Bey, Maïssa

Bénayoun-Szmidt, Yvette, 140

Beni Ameur tribe, 51

Benjamin à Montaigne (Cixous): on bodily aging, 105–7; "I" as killed without witness in, 39, 42; masturbatory scenes in, 101; on maternal muse, 32

Benrabah, Mohamed, 182, 211–12n8

Bensmaïa, Réda, 164–65, 171

228 Index

Berber language: dislocation from, 157; as mother's language, 194, 208n4; oral tales in, 152; Qur'anic verses in, 156; voices of women in, 115

Bernhard, Thomas, 71, 201–2n6

Bey, Maïssa: birthplace, 85; on Camus, 86, 87, 89–90, 92; colonial context of childhood, 49–51; demythification practice, 165; "double impregnation" of perspective, 54–55; epigraphs used, 48; father's language-legacy, 55; first published writing, 2; on hybridities and identities, 51–52, 123–24; identities, 51–52; influences on, 167; motivation for writing, 183; names and naming motif, 212n12; other and all others incarnated in work of, 55–56; sea as inspiration, 203n18; solidarity and singularity, 56–57; staying in Algeria, 56–57, 182; textual documentation technique, 210n3; translations of, 187; women as focus, 52–54, 89, 180–83; on women's writing, 213n1; work of, as reader making connections, 47–49; on writing as oneself, 46–49. Works: *À contre-silence*, 46, 49, 56; *Au commencement était la mer*, 203n18; *Entendez-vous dans les montagnes . . .*, 55, 123–24, 210n3; *L'ombre d'un homme qui marche au soleil*, 86, 87, 89, 92; *Puisque mon coeur est mort*, 190–92; "Rencontres du nouveau siècle" (lectures), 47; *Sous le jasmin la nuit*, 212n12; *Surtout ne te retourne pas (Above All, Don't Look Back)*, 113–14, 164, 187, 213n1. See also *Cette fille-là*; *une et l'autre, L'*

Bhabha, Homi, 109–10, 120, 122, 184

biblical references, Samson's story, 78, 204n22

Bibliothèque nationale de France, 23

bicycles, 73–76

Blanchot, Maurice, 3, 43, 44, 199–200n14

body: aging and ailing of, 105–8, 203n14, 206n11; double *métissage* of, 119, 121–22; as eluding the colonizer, 118; Jewish stigmata of, 83; language of, 14–15, 111–12; as mother, 61; multiple levels of communication, 13–14, 16; past sexualities written on, 120–21; physical displacement and returns of, 73, 92, 141–45, 146–47; read as sign, 178, 184–85; reading with the, 99–100, 107–8; reclaiming of, 109; sea metaphor and pleasures of, 72–73; truth known through, 15; visibility of culture on, 64–65. See also embodiments; female body

Bonn, Charles, 207n3

borders and boundaries: of dream/reality/fiction, nullified, 78–79; feminist collaboration across, 148–50; sea metaphor and elimination of, 72–73; skin and formation of, 203n13

Boudjedra, Rachid, 143

Bouraoui, Nina, 196

Bourdieu, Pierre, 64, 65, 71

Bourget, Carine, 198n6

Brooks, Peter, 29

Bush, George W., 152

Butler, Judith, 101, 203n13

Calle-Gruber, Mireille, 40, 43–44, 84, 208n4. See also *Photos de racines*

Camus, Albert: Algerian background overlooked, 85; sea, mother, and native land in lexicon of, 93–95; on "solitary and solidarity," 56; women

Index 229

Camus, Albert (*cont.*)
writers' reflections on and connections to, 86, 87–92, 95–96. Works: *L'envers et l'endroit* (*The Wrong Side and the Right Side*), 90; *L'étranger* (*The Stranger*), 87. See also *Le premier homme*
Camus, Catherine, 86
Cardinal, Marie: on abortion, 80; complicated relationship to native land, 69–70, 84–85; divorce of parents, 202n7; as exile and fugitive, 73, 203n19; mother and native land as key subjects, 61–62, 200nn1–2; Prix International du Premier Roman for, 2; sea metaphor, 72–73; translations of, 187; trees motif, 62–63, 201n3; on writing process, 80–81. Works: *Au pays de mes racines*, 200n1; *Autrement dit* (*In Other Words*), 66, 80, 200n1, 202n11; *Ecoutez la mer*, 72–73. See also *Les mots pour le dire*
Casarès, Maria, 94
Ces voix qui m'assiègent (Djebar): on Camus and Algeria, 88, 92; on *écriture féminine*, 114–15; on fugitive person, 73; on loss of the place of origin, 119; on *métissage*, 122; on ripping effects of writing, 129; on writing/love and words/body, 111–12, 117–18
Cette fille-là (Bey): Bey's reflections on, 165; familial connections absent in, 169–70; historical setting of, 173; Kateb's *Nedjma* and, 184–85; multiplicity and otherness in, 178–80; naming and possession in, 174–76; national reconstruction juxtaposed to, 170–71; reading of body as sign in, 178, 184–85; recovering lost names, birthdates, memory in, 171–74; self-naming in, 176–78; self-possession in, 180–83, 185; textual slippage in, 164–65, 210–11n1; time and forgetting in, 183–85; title of, 173–74; women's voices given life in, 53, 165–66, 167–69
Chambers, Iain, 149–50
Chaulet-Achour, Christiane, 86–87, 91, 94, 95, 140
Cherki, Alice, 173
Chikhi, Beïda, 129
Christianity: Catholic prohibitions, 65; French school system linked to, 63–64, 213n2; playful yet precise history of, 156; *rahman* in, 162
citizens and citizenship: difficulties of women's access to, 183; loss of, 82–83, 104; papers of, 161, 162; school system and, 63; subjects vs. citizens, 50–51, 66
Cixous, Hélène: on abortion, 79; on Algériances, 189–90; bicycle and separation from brother, 75–76; birthplace, 198n8; on complacency, 43; complicated relationship to native land, 69–70, 84–85; on confessions, 11, 29, 30, 44, 77–78; connections to women writers of Algeria, 23; dream/reality/fiction in, 78–79, 84; early noteworthy text, 2; ethical stance and critical continuity, 95–96; expiation rejected, 30; father's illness and death, 205–6n7, 206n11; as fugitive, 73, 83; on the francophone, 16, 17; geographical and genealogical parental poles, 81–82, 204n1; handwritten words, 14; on "I," 27–28; in-betweenness of, 104–5, 109, 206n9; Jewish origin, 77, 161; on learning "how not to know,"

8–9; on mother and native land, 61; mother's life and, 103–4; myopia, 204n22; mythic mother in, 67–69, 94, 202–3n13; playfulness encouraged, 192; Prix Médicis for, 1; ravine near childhood home, 203–4n20; on reading the body, 14–15; school experiences in, 63–64; on signatures, 12; taking women's testimony, 32; textural gestures, 75–76, 79, 104; on theater as place to contemplate crime and death, 38–39, 42–43, 199n12; translations of, 187–89; treatment of body (and writing) over time, 99–108; on writing, 1, 43, 44–45, 191, 196, 199n13. Works: "L'Affrance," 63–64; "The Author in Truth," 8–9; "Un effet de'épine rose," 186, 188, 191; *Ève s'évade*, 103; *La Jeune Née (The Newly Born Woman)*, 109, 189; *Le jour où je n'étais pas là*, 206n11; *Manhattan*, 186; "My Algeriance," 140, 189–90, 206n9; "Obstétriques cruelles," 38, 44, 100; *Osnabrück*, 103, 205n5, 206n10, 212–13n15; "Pieds nus," 198n6; *Portrait de Jacques Derrida en jeune saint juif (Portrait of Jacques Derrida as a Young Jewish Saint)*, 14, 83; *Rencontre terrestre*, 27; *Rouen*, 211n7; "The School of Roots," 14; *Souffles*, 102, 206n11; *Three Steps on the Ladder of Writing*, 11, 30; *Tombe*, 206n11; *Voiles* (with Derrida), 211n7; "Writings on the Theater," 38–39. See also *Benjamin à Montaigne; écriture féminine; Photos de racines; rêveries de la femme sauvage, Les;* "Rire de la Méduse, Le"; "venue à l'écriture, La"

Clerc, Jeanne-Marie, 208n5

Clézio, Marguerite de, 200n1

Cocteau, Jean, 48

colonialism: ambiguities and dilemmas of war for independence, 153–56; civilizing mission of, 66, 179–80; interdependence of colonizer/colonized in, 66, 202n10; sexual exchange key to, 111–12; sexual violence inherent in, 105. See also Algeria, under French rule; citizens and citizenship

"Coming to Writing" (Cixous). See "venue à l'écriture, La"

community: created through literature, 47–48; forgiveness and testimony embedded in, 10, 197n2; transnational possibilities of, 175–76; women's writing as constructing, 148–50

confessions: forced, 29; as foreign concept, 44; hierarchy of confessor/confessant in, 29; of imagined crimes, 77–78; model of, 28; as outside true/false, 6; testimony compared with, 30–31; unreadable parts of, 10–11

Confessions (Augustine), 31, 89

Confessions (Rousseau): Cixous's uses of, 28, 77–78; reconsideration of, 10–11; transparency in, 29; on truth and lie, 6, 7; writing everything in, 43

Conley, Verena Andermatt, 67–68

crimes: circular return to scene of, 40–42, 199n10; Cixous's birthplace and, 198n8; confessions of imagined, 77–78; as inspiration, 38–45; serial autobiography and scene of, 198n7

death and dying: attention to aging and, 105–8, 206n11; *ruptures intimes* linked to, 138; theater as place to

Index 231

death and dying (*cont.*)
    contemplate, 38–39, 42–43, 199nn11–12
Debrauwere-Miller, Nathalie, 205–6n7
decolonization, 18, 49–51, 173. *See also* Algeria; colonialism
demythification/demystification, 164–69
Derrida, Jacques: on Cixous's writing, 11, 78–79, 84; on confession, 30–31; on crime as inspiration, 38; education of, 213n2; on fiction, truth, and testimony, 3–6, 7–8, 12–13, 15; forgetfulness of, 40; on forgiveness and testimony, 197n2; on languages, 201n5; on naming, 165; readings of literary fiction, 197n4. Works: "Circonfession," 37, 38, 40; *Le monolinguisme de l'autre*, 165; *Voiles* (with Cixous), 211n7
deterritorialization, 145
Diouf, Mamadou, 207n2
Djaout, Tahar, 141–42
Djebar, Assia: Académie Française election, 23, 135–36; Augustine's influence on, 88–89; on "autobiographical act," 28–29, 118; autobiography in, 27, 211n4; Bey influenced by, 167; birthplace, 85; on Camus, 86, 87–89, 90–92; circularity and echoing, 40, 77, 200n14; childhood restrictions, 73–75; complicated relationship to native land, 69–70, 84–85; on confession, 44, 198n1; connections to women writers of Algeria, 23; early noteworthy text, 2; epigraphs used, 48, 200n1; as exile and fugitive, 73, 92; fabulation, 164–65; father and, 200n3; forgetfulness of, 39–40; French homes off-limits, 202n9; on killing of writers, 5; on *métissage*, 122; on mother and native land, 61, 94; sterility of, 213n17; French language embraced by, 135–36, 208n4; outdoors metaphor, 138–39, 208n7; as rewriting, 167–68; on sexuality and desire, 111; taking (and translating) women's testimony, 31–32; on traces of war, 17–18; on transformation of identities, 122–23; on translating voices into French-language text, 13–14; translations of, 187; on unveiling oneself, 46; vocal outbursts in, 129–31, 207n1; on women's place in Islam, 52; on writing, 1; writing to mend ruptures, 207n2. Works: "Annie and Fatima," 41; *Le blanc de l'Algérie* (*Algerian White*), 5, 88, 90–91, 95; *La disparition de la langue française*, 137, 139; *La femme sans sépulture*, 70, 168, 177, 211n7; *Femmes d'Alger dans leur appartement* (*Women of Algiers in Their Apartment*), 69, 208n7, 212n11; *Ombre Sultane* (*A Sister to Scheherazade*), 139; *Oran, langue morte* (*The Tongue's Blood Does Not Run Dry*), 31, 41; "Regard interdit, son coupé" ("Forbidden Gaze, Severed Sound"), 69; "The Violence of Autobiography," 28–29. See also *amour, la fantasia, L'; Ces voix qui m'assiègent; nuits de Strasbourg, Les; Nulle part dans la maison de mon père; ruptures intimes; Vaste est la prison*
Donadey, Anne, 48, 167–68, 183, 208n4
Dufourmantelle, Anne, 61
Duras, Marguerite, 94

échographie (ultrasound), 40
écriture féminine (feminine writing): algériance (women and bodies) in, 102–5; Cixous's definition of, 205n2; Djebar influenced by, 112; jouissance (pleasure) in, 100–102; potential of, 99–100, 109; preservation of, 114–15; reappropriating language in, 116–17; souffrance (aging and ailing) in, 105–8, 206n11
Éditions Des femmes, 102, 205n5
embodiments: aging and ailing body in, 105–8, 206n11; of ambiguities of twentieth century, 153–56; approach to, 20–21; Cixous's in-betweenness in, 104–5, 109, 206n9; of daughter's revolt, 66, 71–72, 202n12; of displacement and return, 73, 92, 141–45, 146–47; father figure in, 113–18; grafts and hybridities in, 118–22; negotiations and identities in, 122–25; of otherness, 178–80; sexualities and postcolonialities in, 111–12. *See also* body
essentialism, 110, 112
ethnicity, 94, 206n9

fabulation, 164–65, 180
father: ghost of, 150; handwriting of, 155, 156; hybrid status of, 113–15; hybrid text on, 123–24; language of, 55, 116–17, 200nn2–3; restricted movement of women and, 74, 113–14, 169; testimony on war status, 151, 154–56; writing and distancing from, 116–18
Fatma and the fatma, 176–77, 212–13n15
Felman, Shoshana: on language and testimony, 8, 9–10, 45, 197n3; on witnesses, 11–12

female body: Cixous's mythic mother (Aïcha) in relation to, 68, 202–3n13; pleasures and pains of, 72–73, 99–102; as repository of nation, 70–71, 94–95, 179, 203n15; sterility of, 175, 213n17. *See also* body; *écriture féminine*; mother; women
feminine writing. See *écriture féminine*
femininity: bodily revolt against, 66, 71–72, 202n12; country always conjugated in, 95; mobility restrictions on, 73–75, 113–14, 169; of mythic mother, 67–69, 202–3n13
fiction: as cover in constrained context, 5, 49; as lie, 7–8; multiple readings of, 197n4; possibility and responsibility of, 4–5; as testimony, 3–5, 80–81; truths revealed in, 141, 191–92; use of term, 5–6. *See also* literature
forgetfulness, 39–40, 141, 198–99n9. *See also* memory
forgetting, 140–41, 183–85
forgiveness, 10, 30, 38–39, 197n2
France: Algeria known in, 186–87; Algerian War unrecognized in, 157; Arabs and Muslims labeled in, 144, 151–52, 156, 160–63, 210n4; *harkis* and their families not welcomed in, 153–54, 156; Joan of Arc envisioned in, 211n7; "national" values of, 64–65; nostalgia for homeland viewed from, 148; return to, 149; uprisings in (2005 and 2007), 161–62
France, récit d'une enfance (Rahmani): epigraph of, 23–24; lack of homeland, 151; lessons of war, 157–59; religion as source of trouble, 160–61
francophone, 16–17. *See also* French-language women writers born in Algeria

Index   233

French Algeria, 63
French culture: mastery of, 50; sexual violence of, 118; things/actions not done in, 65–66, 202n7, 203n17
French educational system: alienation and humiliation experienced in, 63–64, 213n2; Arabic language banned in, 50, 201n5; benefits of, 135–36; dislocation due to, 156–57; hybridities and, 113–15; Jews barred from, 104; "national" values taught in, 64–65, 201–2n6; streets traversed to get to, 62–63, 201n3
French language: calligraphic text of, 18; children's books in, 152, 157; dialectical Arabic language compared with, 135–36; *fille d'amour* (love child) in, 169–70; lessons for Arab girls in, 113–14; mastery of, 50, 154; translating voices into, 13–14. *See also* French-language women writers born in Algeria
French-language women writers born in Algeria: Algériances, alliances, and dalliances of, 189–92; Camus's connections to, 87, 88, 95–96; commonalities and connections among, 23, 56–57, 115, 204n20; as exiles and fugitives, 73, 92, 203n19; labels applied to, 144, 151–52, 156, 160–63, 210n4; particularities and sensitivities expressed by, 124–25; as putting Algeria on the map, 186–96; risks of writing, 46, 48–49, 56, 142; as without a place in Algeria, 84–85. *See also* Bey, Maïssa; Cardinal, Marie; Cixous, Hélène; Djebar, Assia; Mokeddem, Malika; Sebbar, Leïla
Friedman, Susan Stanford, 145, 148, 149

gender differences: Camus's work and, 90
Ghaussy, Sauheila, 112
ghostly encounters, 150
Gilmore, Leigh, 30, 198n7
Glissant, Édouard, 48, 51, 56
Gracki, Katherine, 207n2
guilt (fault): confessions of crimes and, 77–78; felt by witness of horrible accident, 35–37, 198n6

Hall, Colette, 61, 200n1
Hamil, Mustafa, 147
handwriting, 14, 18, 155, 156
Hargreaves, Alec, 209–10n2
harkis: definition of, 22, 209–10n2; mother's testimony vs. official documents on, 159–60; Rahmani's father as, 153–54; testimony on plight of, 154–56
Hiddleston, Jane, 73, 92, 199n10
hijab. *See* unveiling; veil question
Holocaust, 6–7, 82–83
Howard, Richard, 185
hybridities: concept of, 109–11; cultural politics of, 112; embodiment of, 118–22, 142; flexible, negotiated nature of, 122–25; potential of, 121–22; of young Arab girl's father, 113–15. *See also* identities; *métissage*

"I": in autobiographical inclusions, 80–81; as killed without witness, 39, 42; not used in dialectical Arabic language, 135–36, 208n5; writing as always coming back to, 27–28
identities: absence of ancestral ties in, 174–75, 180; accommodating, flexible nature of, 122–25, 142; biculturalism in, 49–51, 61; of child without family,

169–70; definition of, 207n2; in ethnicity vs. country, 94; labels of, 144, 151–52, 156, 160–63, 210n4; migration as stimulant to expressing, 148–49; mother's body and, 102–3; religion in, 52; self-designation of, 176–78; true name and, 69

Imalayen, Fatima-Zohra. *See* Djebar, Assia

immigrants: Camus as, 91–92; civil war in homeland of, 157–59; dilemma of returning home, 141–45; *harkis* and their families as, 153–54, 156; labels of, 144, 151–52, 156, 160–63, 210n4; languages of, 194–95; migration as choice vs. flight for, 149; nostalgia for homeland, 147–48; visibility of culture on, 64–65

intention, 7

Interdite, L' (*The Forbidden Woman*) (Mokeddem): autobiographical elements in, 140–41; border-crossing collaborations in, 148–50; hauntings of place and memory in, 147–48; hybridity of foreigner and native-born in, 118–20; interracial sexual relations in, 120–22; Mokeddem's reflections on, 209n1; negotiating identities in, 122; physical and metaphysical returns in, 141–45; women's oppressed situation in, 145–47

interpersonal relationships: approach to, 21–22; bicycle's interruption of Cixous and brother's, 75–76; border-crossing collaborations in, 148–50; hauntings of place and memory in, 147–48; identity labels and, 144, 151–52, 156, 160–63, 210n4; physical and metaphysical returns in, 141–45; suffering from sympathy in, 106–7; women's oppressed situation and, 145–47

intertexualities: Cixous and Rousseau, 76–78; evidence of, 204n20; multilingual, 16

Iraq wars, 152, 162

Ireland, Susan, 150, 157

Irigaray, Luce, 112, 212n13

Islam: adopted children's names in, 178; complexities of, 162; divorce and, 131–35; everyday experience of, 52; marriage traditions in, 130; playful yet precise history of, 156; as source of trouble in French village, 160–61. *See also* Muslims; Qur'anic verses

Jeanne d'Arc (Joan of Arc), 171–72, 211n7

Jelloun, Ben, 143

Je ne parle pas la langue de mon père (Sebbar): on banned Arabic language, 201n5; on father and non-belonging, 200n2; father figure in, 115–17; purity questioned in, 120; ravine near childhood home referenced in, 204n20

Jewish identity and people: Cixous's reveries on, 77, 161, 206n9; as travelers of Europe, 204n23; witnessing horrible accident and, 35–36; WWII restrictions and internment of, 82–83, 104. *See also* Holocaust; Judaism

Joan of Arc (Jeanne d'Arc), 171–72, 211n7

Jones, Ann Rosalind, 100

Judaism, 156, 162. *See also* Holocaust; Jewish identity and people

Kamuf, Peggy, 27, 37

Kandiyoti, Deniz, 203n15

Kateb, Yacine (pen name Kateb Yacine), 166, 184–85
Kelly, Debra, 90, 95, 133, 200n1
Kemp, Anna: on French women and nationalism, 70–71; on nativist feminism, 208–9n1; on Rahmani's work, 151, 155, 160, 210n3, 210n5
Khaldoun, Ibn, 48
Khanna, Ranjana, 164, 198–99n9, 199n10
Khatibi, Abdelkébir, 14, 18, 46, 55, 109, 143
Kofman, Sarah, 6–7
Kritzman, Lawrence, 213n2
Kundera, Milan, 48

Labbé, Louise, 28
Lacheraf, Mostefa, 48
Langer, Lawrence, 199n10
languages: availability of multiple, 111–12; definitions of, 12–13; exposure to multiple, 208n4; innovations and mixing of, 194–95; of mother vs. father, 115–17; music as, 192–94; names as incompatible across, 179; politics of, 165; role in testimony, 197n3; transformation through movement, 149–50. *See also* Arabic language; Berber language; French language
Laub, Dori: on language and testimony, 8, 9–10, 45, 197n3; on witnesses, 11–12
lie detector (*détecteur de mensonges*), 6, 13–14, 16. See also *polygraphe*
"life-testimony," 12
Lionnet, Françoise, 61, 176, 183
Lispector, Clarice, 8–9
literature: calligraphic trope of Maghrebian, 18; community created through, 47–48; definition of, 5–6; fictional and autobiographical combined in, 164–65, 210–11n1; forgetfulness linked to narrative form, 40; genre-crossing texts in, 16, 101; open mindset in approaching, 10; playfulness encouraged in, 192; as preceding reality, 191; as testimony, 3–5; unreadable parts of, 10–12. *See also* autobiography; fiction; postcolonial texts; theatrical performance; writing
Loomba, Ania, 71
love: autobiography and making, 28–29, 118; possible happiness in, 117–18; as reunion of hybridities, 121–22; that is other, 192–96; writing linked to, 111–12

maladie algérie, 103–4
Margel, Serge, 6, 7, 10, 189
Marouane, Leïla, 196
Marzloff, Martine, 46
"Mass in A Minor," 192–94
maux, use of term, 104–5
Meddeb, Abdelwahab, 18
media politics, 7
Memmi, Albert, 202n10
memory: conjuring to testify, 9–10; contradictory and complementary, 81–82; end of war and disruptions of, 170–71; evoked or suppressed, 104–5; faulty kinds of, 79; loss of intellectual and corporeal, 113; persistence of ancestral, 175; process of loss, 211n4; recovering what was lost in colonialism, 172–74; returns and hauntings of, 140–41, 147–48; romanticized past in, 183–84; uncertainties and possibilities of, 168–69. *See also* forgetfulness; forgetting

menstruation, 181, 213n17
métissage (hybridity): Arabization as denying, 51, 52, 182; doubling of, 119, 121–22; embodying otherness and, 178–79; homeland's rejection of, 179–80; linguistic innovations as, 195. *See also* hybridities
Michaux, Henri, 48
migration. *See* immigrants
Miller, Christopher, 172
miscegenation, history of, 120
misogyny, Cixous's struggle against, 104–5
Moi, Toril, 205n3
Mokeddem, Malika: first published writing, 2; on hybridity, 118–20; intimately inclusive nature of, 209n3; Prix Littré for, 2; relationships of, 140; on sexuality and desire, 111; translations of, 187. Works: *Je dois tout à ton oubli*, 141; *Mes hommes (My Men)*, 140, 141; *La Transe des insoumis*, 141. *See also* Interdite, L'
Mongo-Mboussa, Boniface, 122, 124
Montaigne, Michel Eyquim de, 27–28
Mortimer, Mildred, 208n4, 213n1
mother: abandoned child's speculations about, 179–80; abortion attempted and abuse by, 79–80; aging of, 105–7; bodily revolt against, 66, 71–72, 202n12; contradictory relationship with, 102–3; daughter's divorce and, 133–34; daughter's secrets known by, 101; desire for reconciliation with, 71–72, 203n16; double childhood landscape due to origins, 81–83; Eve's history and, 205n6; French homophone for, 72; haunting loss of, 147–48; homage to, 159–60, 193–94; language of, 52, 115–17, 194, 202n8, 208n4; as midwife, 67; as muse, 32; native land as, 61, 94–95; "other" knowledge of, passed to daughters, 193–94; from "other world," 70–71; reluctance to become, 181–82, 213n17; as silent and immobile, 89–92; virginity of, 105; western constructions of, 66, 202n11. *See also* mother and native land, depictions of
mother and native land, depictions of: altering relationships to, 73–76; approach to, 19–20; Camus in relation to, 86–96; complicated relationships to, 69–70, 84–85, 87, 91–92; concept of, 200n1; desire to enter birth country, 66–67; double childhood landscape in, 81–83; as dream/reality/fiction, 78–79; failed abortions and metaphorical importance, 79–81; mythic mother in, 67–69, 202–3n13; revolt against mother to reunite with native land, 71–72; sea and eliminating borders in, 72–73; solitary reveries in, 76–85. *See also* Algeria, as homeland; mother
mots pour le dire, Les (The Words to Say It) (Cardinal): bodily revolt in, 66, 71–72, 202n12; on internal (mother) and external (street) worlds, 62–63, 201n3; on mother and native land, 61, 200nn1–2; mother's attempt to abort narrator in, 80; narrator's age in, 203n14; "she" and "I" of, 80–81; on things/actions not done, 65–66, 202n7, 203n17
Moura, Jean-Marc, 122, 123–24
Moze (Rahmani): on father's ghost, 150; on father's status as *harki*, 153–54; mother's stories in, 193–94;

Moze (Rahmani) (*cont.*)
"*Musulman*" *roman* as continuation of, 152, 156; on song, 186; structure, 210n3; testimony of, 151, 154–56; title of, 155, 209n1
multilingual writing, 16
music: alternative melodies and movements in, 192–96; metaphorical sense of, 213n2; possibilities of, 190–92
Muslims: Arabs distinguished from, 51–52; current events and tensions surrounding, 151–52; "indigenous," 50; labels of, 144, 151–52, 156, 160–63, 210n4; mistreated in North Africa, 153; naming traditions of, 171–72; oppression of women, 131–35, 145–47, 208–9n1. *See also* Islam; Qur'anic verses
"*Musulman*" *roman* (Rahmani): dislocated childhood remembered, 156–57; dual focus of, 210n5; father's story continued in, 152, 156; labels in, 160–63; on pain of loss that is irreparable, 150; sources and structure of, 151–52

names and naming: of Cixous's mythic mother, 69; falsification, to avoid possession, 174–75, 212n11; inaccessible to abandoned child, 169–70; incompatibility across languages, 179; recovery of, 171–74; as reminder of past inequities, 165; self-designated, 176–78; women's influence in pen name, 183
nation: creativity required in literary portrait of, 164; cultural civil war and redefinition of, 211–12n8; demythification/demystification of, 164–69; function of time and narrative in, 183–85; mother as, 61, 94–95; reconstituted in aftermath of colonialism, 170–71, 173; women as symbolic repository of, 70–71, 94–95, 179, 203n15. *See also* Algeria
native land. *See* Algeria, as homeland; mother and native land, depictions of
nativist feminism, 208–9n1
Nedjma (Yacine), 184–85
neologisms: Algériances, 102–5, 189–90; Alsagérie, 195; *animâle*, 100, 102; deadsoldier, 155–56; FrenchAlgeria, 63; *rêvexiste* and *rêvexistence*, 78; "un-belonging for/in," 96
nuits de Strasbourg, Les (Djebar): hybrid persons and relationships in, 122, 207n2; linguistic innovations in, 194–95; *ruptures intimes* in, 136–37; space of outdoors in, 138, 139; theatrical metaphor of, 41
Nulle part dans la maison de mon père (Djebar): autobiographical elements in, 27; on bicycles and movement, 73–75; circularity of text, 40–42, 199n10; multiple readings of, 85; secularized confession rejected, 198n1; suicide attempt in, 33–35; as writing everything, 43–44

Oran, in double childhood landscape, 82. *See also* Cette fille-là
Orientalism, 53, 68. *See also* colonialism
O'Riley, Michael, 211n7
Orlando, Valérie, 209n1
Osnabrück: in double childhood landscape, 82–83; symbolism of, 204n23
others and otherness: as always "I," 49; autobiographical encounters with,

46–57; Bey's first and violent encounter with, 55; of Cixous's mythic mother (Aïcha), 69; desire to know and understand, 3; embodiment of, 178–80; feeling for and with, in theater experience, 42–43; fusion with, 35–37; as incarnated in writer, 55–56; love that is, 192–96; openness to, 69–70, 84–85; positioning self with respect to/for, 9–12; self as always already other, 27; space for speaking of, 110

patrie, definition of, 94
Paz, Octavio, 48
Pears, Pamela, 209n2, 210n4
performative encounters, 41, 42, 124, 207n3. *See also* theatrical performance
Phoca, Sophia, 105
Photos de racines (*Rootprints*) (Cixous and Calle-Gruber): on body of the other, 99, 107; on Cixous's father's death, 206n11; on Cixous's place in North Africa, 204n1; on common childhood, 84; on geographical and genealogical parental poles, 81; on WWII restrictions on Jewish people, 82–83
Poetics, The (Aristotle), 199n11
polygraphe, definition of, 15–16. *See also* lie detector
polygraphies: approach to, 19–24; calligraphies invoked by, 18; concept of, 16–17, 125; multiple truths in, 1–3; as reaching out to encourage others' writing, 195–96; strategy underlying, 5–6; trends in translation, 187–89; truths and fiction in, 191–92; as writing for the masses, 192–95

possession/dispossession: approach to, 165; names and naming linked to, 174–75, 177–78, 212n11; self-claimed, 180–83, 185
postcolonial texts: fabulation and testimony in, 164–65; in-betweenness in, 110; multiplicity of voices in, 165–67; of nation born of loss and violence, 184–85; performative encounters in, 124, 207n3; rewriting in, 167–68; sexualities and, 111–12. *See also* hybridities
premier homme, Le (*The First Man*) (Camus): daughter's introduction to, 86; Djebar's reading of, 88; on mother, 89–92; mother and native land depicted in, 93–95
"privileged difference," 36
Proust, Marcel, 28
pseudonyms, 2
purity myth, 119–22

Qur'anic verses, 89, 114, 152, 156

racism: myth of purity and, 119–22; "social health" and, 104
Rahmani, Zahia: attempts to repair wrongs on both sides of war, 151; on duty to live, 158–59; facing ghosts of the past, 150; father's death and, 153, 155–56; first published writing, 2; on the francophone, 17; handwriting, 155, 156; homage to mother, 159–60, 193–94; labels resisted, 151–52, 156, 160–63; on role of women in wars, 158; sources of, 152; textual documentation technique, 155, 210n3; work not yet translated, 187. Works: "Figure d'un homme" ("Figure of a man"), 159–60. *See also France, récit*

Index 239

Rahmani, Zahia (*cont.*)
d'une enfance; Moze; "Musulman" roman
readers: making connections as, 47–49; power to handle book like a syringe, 37; of unreadable parts, 10–12; writers as, 56
reading: with the body, 99–100, 107–8; of body as sign, 178, 184–85; of other's body, 14–15; as testimony, 10–12, 189
Redouane, Najib, 209n3
Regard, Frédéric, 188–89, 192
religion. *See* Christianity; Islam; Judaism
responsibility: in composing literature, 3–4; in testimony, 9–12
rêveries de la femme sauvage, Les (*Reveries of the Wild Woman*) (Cixous): on bicycle and dreams, 75–76, 78–79; confession as criminalization in, 44; desire to enter birth country in, 66–67, 84; ethical stance in, 95–96; horrible accident in, 35–37, 198n6; intertextual reference in title, 76–78; mother figure in, 103, 105; multiple readings of, 83; mythic mother in, 67–69, 202–3n13; narrator as child aborted in Algeria, 79; primal scene in, 29; on school in FrenchAlgeria, 63; Sebbar's citing of, 204n20; on "social health," 104
rêvexiste and *rêvexistence*, 78
rewriting, 167–68
"Rire de la Méduse, Le" ("The Laugh of the Medusa") (Cixous): call for women to "write their bodies," 99, 109, 205n2; Cixous's reflections on, 188, 189, 206n12; ethics of dialogue in, 96; on jouissance (pleasure) in writing, 100–102; on love that is other, 192–93; on sexual exchange, 207n1; translation of, 187–89; on "Truth-Me-I," 192
Roselle, Mireille, 41, 42, 150, 207n3
Ross, Kristin, 201n4
Rousseau, Jean-Jacques: Blanchot's reading of, 43; Cixous influenced by, 28; Cixous's intertexual references to, 76–78; on reading, 10–11, 189. Works: *Les rêveries du promeneur solitaire* (*The Reveries of a Solitary Walker*), 76–78. See also *Confessions*
Ruhe, Ernstpeter, 40, 207n1
ruptures intimes (sentimental splitting): death linked to, 138; farewell to passionate love as, 131–35; inevitability of, 136–37, 209n2; intoxication with poetry and, 132, 137, 138; Mokeddem and, 140; positive nature of, 129, 139, 207n2; scream as signaling, 129–31, 207n1; space of outdoors in, 138–39
Rushdie, Salman, 145
Ruta, Suzanne, 165

Saâda, Lucienne, 48
Sade, Marquis de, 199–200n14
Samson's story (biblical), 78, 204n22
Savigneau, Josyane, 203n19
Sayad, Abdelmalek, 64–65
Scève, Maurice, 28
Scharfman, Ronnie, 36, 44–45, 68, 96
screams and cries: liberation of, 166–69; marriage beginning and ending connected by, 129–31, 207n1; potential as chorus, to make a difference, 190–92
Sebbar, Leïla: on banned Arabic language, 201n5; childhood, education, and family history of, 115–17,

213n16; on failure to intermingle, 56–57; on fiction and memory, 81; first published writing, 2; handwritten words, 14; hybridity of, 115, 120, 200n2; ravine near childhood home of, 203–4n20; translations of, 187. See also *Je ne parle pas la langue de mon père*

self: as always already other, 27; experiences of many expressed through, 1–3; positioning with respect to/for others, 9–12; space for speaking of, 110

sexualities: as catalyst for transformation of identities, 122; colonialism and, 104–5; denunciations for past, 120–21; disrupting categories of, 16, 101–2; postcolonialities and, 111–12; self-possession in response to, 180–81; writing of, 100–101, 110–11, 116–18. See also interpersonal relationships; love

Shih, Shuh-mei, 176

significant other, 136. See also interpersonal relationships

silence: in aftermath of decolonization, 173; about Algerian War, 157; of Camus's mother, 90–92; enforced for women, 168–69; labeling due to, 181; music to overcome, 190–92; of not knowing another's language, 116; writing as ending, 46–47, 159

skin as boundary, 203n13

Soler, Ana, 210–11n1

Sommers, Doris, 11–12

spaces: metaphor of outdoors, 138–39; possibilities for exchanges among women, 175–76; women creating new community and, 148–50; women's absence from visible, 145–47

spectacle. See theatrical performance

speech act, 197n3. See also testimony

Spivak, Gayatri, 45

Steadman, Jennifer Bernhardt, 167

Stendhal (pen name for Marie-Henri Beyle), 28

Stora, Benjamin, 170–71

Suleiman, Susan, 16

"telling all," 4. See also literature; testimony

temporality: circularity and, 40–42; forgetting and construction of modern nation in, 183–85; trauma and justice in context of, 199n10

testimony: approach to, 30–31; definitions of, 5–6, 8, 45, 125; duty of, 6–7; fabulation juxtaposed to, 164–65; fiction as, 3–5, 80–81; forgiveness linked to, 197n2; French terms for, 31–32; function in war crime tribunals, 198–99n9; reading as, 10–12, 189; role of language in, 197n3; testing limits of, 32–37; unconventional means of, 15; on war and father's status, 151, 154–56. See also autobiographical inclusions; fiction; truths

theatrical performance: constructed nature of text scenes and, 101; as place to contemplate crime and death, 38–39, 42–43, 199nn11–12; Rahmani's *"Musulman" roman* and, 152; suicide attempt as, 40–42

third space. See hybridities

translation: alternative pronunciations in, 192–96; difficulty and risk in, 13–14; paratextual apparatus needed in, 186–87; trends in, 187–89

transnationality, 175–76, 184

transparency, 29

trauma: normative speech disrupted by, 167–69; in study of colonialism, 164–65; temporality in justice and, 199n10

truths: communicating unspeakable, 6–7; complexities of, 3–5, 87, 141; definitions of, 12–13; interweaving of false with, 5–6; as key to writing, 43; mother's knowledge of, passed to daughters, 193–94; moving beyond true-false binary, 16; multiplicity of, 1–3, 7; outside of language, 15; reserved and oblique, 8–9; revealed in fiction, 141, 191–92

tuberculosis, 205–6n7

une et l'autre, L' (Bey): on destiny of women, 53–54; on identity, 51–52; intertextual connections in, 47–49; self and others written in, 47, 49, 55–56; on subjects vs. citizens, 50–51; title of, 54–55

United States: ignorance about Algeria in, 186; treatment of Arabs by, 152

University of Paris VIII Vincennes, Centre de Recherches en Études Féminines, 104

unveiling: individuality claimed in, 177; particular genres linked to, 207n3; of voice, 168–69; writing as, 46, 48

Vaste est la prison (*So Vast the Prison*) (Djebar): epigraphs in, 200n1; on fugitive person, 73; "other world" representatives in, 70–71; *ruptures intimes* in, 131–35, 137–38; space of outdoors in, 138–39; on sterility, 213n17; women's intelligence deployed in, 122–23

veil question, 54. *See also* unveiling

"venue à l'écriture, La" ("Coming to Writing") (Cixous): on author's nose, 206n9; on body and writing, 99; confession to crime and, 77–78; on endurance of writing, 17; on geographical and genealogical parental poles, 81; on men's writing, 205n1; mother figure in, 102–3; on pleasure of writing, 100–101

Viau, Théophile de, 28

Villon, François, 28

virginity, 105, 206n10

Voltaire, 16

war crime tribunals, 198–99n9

Weber-Fève, Stacey, 69, 203n16

Wehrs, Donald R., 167

Weltman-Aron, Brigitte, 95, 211n4

whiteness, 63

witnesses: accent of, 34–35; as bystanders, 31; ethical stance and critical continuity of, 95–96; of horrible accident, 35–37, 198n6; lack of, 39–40; the other as, 32–33; readers as, 10–12; theatrical spectators as, 38–39, 42–43, 199nn11–12

witnessing: as active verbal act, 31–32; Camus's importance to, 95; circularity/circulations of, 32–33; fusion with other in, 35–37; productivity of, 44–45

women: as category, 102; Fatma (the fatma) as designating all Algerian, 176–77, 212–13n15; heroic actions of, 146; horizontal interaction and community of, 148–50, 175–76; importance of Arab-Muslim-Algerian, 54; labels applied to, 144, 151–52, 156, 160–63, 210n4; mobility

242 Index

restrictions on, 73–75, 113–14, 169; Muslim oppression of, 52, 131–35, 145–47, 208–9n1; names of, as not their own, 175, 212n13; nation and temporality linked to, 183–85; plight of, 52–54, 89, 180–83; reluctance to become, 181–82; rights of, 133–34, 158, 183; role in wars, 158; as symbolic repository of nationalism, 70–71, 94–95, 179, 203n15; voices of, brought to written history, 165–69; women's separation from other, 134–35, 147–48. See also *écriture féminine;* female body; French-language women writers born in Algeria; mother

Woodhull, Winifred, 143

World War I, Muslims forced to participate in, 153

World War II, restrictions and internment of Jewish people during, 82–83, 104

writing: call for women's, 99, 109, 195–96, 205n2, 213n1; community constructed in, 148–50; differently, 84; ending silence by, 46–47, 159; endurance of, 17–18; of everything, 43–45, 199n13, 199–200n14; as giving birth, 55–56; by hand, 14–15; inventing multiple forms of, 16; love linked to, 111–12; for the masses, 192–96; multiple levels of body in, 13–14; pleasure in, 100–102; risks of, 46, 48–49, 56, 142; selectivity in, 7–8; as territory, 73; women's voices given life in, 165–69, 180; of world into the body, 107–8. *See also* autobiography; fiction; literature; multilingual writing

Young, Robert, 110, 111, 112

Zayzafoon, Lamia Ben Youssef, 210n4